CONTENTS

ACKNOWLEDGEMENTS

First and foremost I must thank my publishers Mercier Press for allowing this project to realise its full potential and become my first printed work. Without their original interest my research may very well have remained an undisclosed assortment of files collected over the years.

There have been many organisations that have helped while I have been writing this book. I would especially like to thank the Shipwrecked Mariners' Society, The Royal National Lifeboat Institute and the Irish Red Cross, who all assisted with offers of archival material where it was available. I am also greatly appreciative of the assistance provided by Commandant Victor Laing, Captain S. MacEoin and the archivists at the Military Archives in Dublin and to the archivists at the Deutsches U-Boot Museum, Cuxhaven. The information provided by these institutions, along with the larger repositories of the National Archives in Dublin and London, was invaluable in putting together the most detailed story possible. I must also thank the National Maritime Institute of Ireland for access to their collection of archival material and exhibits held at the National Maritime Museum of Ireland.

It has been my pleasure to correspond and meet with some of the actual survivors who are mentioned in this book. I have had the honour to meet several times with Sam Williams, who survived the sinking of the *Isolda*, and I have corresponded over the years with John Lester, who was on board the *Richmond Castle* when it was sunk in 1942. The first-hand accounts and personal insights that both men provided were immensely valuable.

Many people have helped with the research of this book and I am particularly grateful to Captain Jerry Mason, USN (ret.), Rainer Kolbicz and Klaus-Peter Pohland, who all provided invaluable assistance with the U-boat perspective of this story. I would also like to thank Siri Lawson for her kind permission to use invaluable information relating to Norwergian ships and seafarers contained on her website warsailors.com. I have also been fortunate to correspond with Martin Gleeson and Tony Kearns, who not only provided information on the aeronautical background to the story, but also assisted with guidance when it came to researching at the Military Archives in Dublin and for this I am truly grateful. Finally I would like to thank all the supporters of MercantileMarine.org who have given so much help over the years with regard to researching the Merchant Navy.

PREFACE

The Battle of the Atlantic, the longest uninterrupted campaign of the Second World War, was of such enormous proportions that it is difficult to comprehend the complexity of how the opposing sides were able to continue such a bitter struggle for the duration of the war. From September 1939 until the surrender of Germany in May 1945, the Allied navies of Britain and later the USA were involved in a desperate fight with the navies of Germany and, to a lesser extent, Italy, which were attempting to halt the flow of imported materials vital to the British war effort. This period in history has so many facets that a detailed history of every event has still to be told. Many stories of the great convoy battles, with detailed insights into the fighting men from the opposing navies and accounts of the hardships endured by the British Merchant Navy, have already been told. However, the forgotten ships and unsung heroes of the Atlantic are just as fascinating and also merit recording.

For many seafarers who found themselves adrift after their ship had become another casualty of the war, safety was found on the shores of that small country that looked out across the great expanse of the Atlantic. While the survivors' time in Ireland may have been relatively short, the circumstances that brought them to Ireland give a great insight into the ordeals these men faced making it safely to shore and their stories make up an important part of Ireland's maritime heritage.

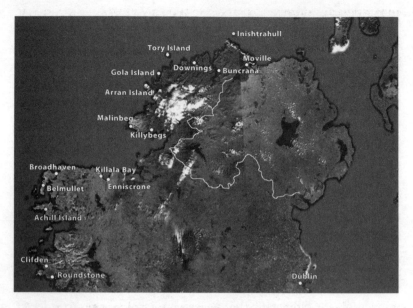

Landing sites in the north and west of Ireland where survivors came ashore

The arrival of a lifeboat with its weary occupants off the coast is merely the end to a saga with its beginnings in locations around the globe, all connected by the great commercial shipping routes. This book only covers the survivors who landed in neutral Ireland and not those who arrived in Northern Ireland, where many men were disembarked from rescue ships at ports such as Belfast and Londonderry. These British naval bases played an important role that steadily increased as the war progressed, and their story deserves to be told in greater detail.

Only the survivors of those ships sunk through belligerent action are covered here, not non-combat losses. The numbers of ships lost through mechanical breakdown and winter storms is quite substantial, particularly in the winter of 1940 when large numbers of ships were wrecked off the Donegal coast. I also omitted those men who landed

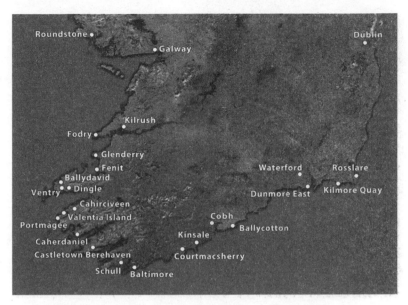

Landing sites in the south of Ireland where survivors came ashore

wounded in Ireland after an enemy attack but whose ships remained seaworthy. There were many cases of injured fishermen landing in Ireland after their boats had been subjected to air attack off the Irish coast. These two sub-categories account for many extra ships and men, but as the list of survivors found during the research steadily grew I was obliged to limit the extent of my work.

The final list of ships given in Appendix I is as complete and detailed as was possible to compile given the archival material available. Throughout my research, ships were identified that were considered to have had survivors who landed in Ireland, but where an actual reference in the Dublin or London archives was not found, I omitted these possibles. The final list therefore may not be definitive, and additions may need to be made later to those already identified.

One of the most enjoyable aspects of conducting the research for this book has been the many surprising facts that were uncovered regarding the history of the ships and the people and places involved. Although the small correction of when and where a few foreign seamen came ashore on some remote beach may not be a startling revelation, it remains an important footnote of history that should be faithful to the greater chronicle. The stories told in this book are just a small selection from many others that are equally as important. When telling the survivors' stories we must also remember those who were not as fortunate and who never made it ashore. Their final moments cannot be told, but their legacy is not forgotten.

INTRODUCTION

At the beginning of September 1939 there was an unexpected influx in the numbers of passengers disembarking at Dublin and Dun Laoghaire. Over the course of that first turbulent weekend in September, when mainland Europe was on the precipice of another war, an estimated 10,000 people, desperate to return home, landed at the busy east-coast ports. The numbers heading for Dublin on the crowded Irish Sea ferries were so great that many passengers were forced to stand outside in heavy rain for the duration of the crossing.

At Rosslare the numbers of arrivals were such that trains were delayed as the masses of women and children boarded with heavy loads of baggage. When the trains finally departed there was little room left for passengers intending to board at Waterford station. The recently arrived refugees were apparently all travelling towards Limerick and Cork. Although the vast majority were Irish, the fear of the impending war and sudden gas attacks on British cities compelled some worried British parents to send their children over to stay with relations in neutral Ireland.

Although this initial surge in passenger traffic was significant, over the coming weeks the numbers remained inflated as a steady stream of returning Irish citizens sought refuge from a war that had yet to claim any casualties on mainland Britain.

As the influx of refugees continued on the east coast there were similar scenes at Ireland's two transatlantic liner ports. At Cobh,

Co. Cork, and Galway, the arrival of two Cunard White Star liners en route to America was shrouded in rumour. Disembarking passengers described how destroyers had accompanied the large passenger liner *Mauretania* during the night before it passed Roches Point and entered Cork Harbour on 1 September. *Mauretania* arrived in total darkness and only turned on its external lights once inside the harbour entrance, to allow the tender to come alongside for the 163 passengers disembarking at Cobh. There were similar reports when the liner *Samaria* called at Galway before continuing across the Atlantic to New York. Many American citizens were following the advice of the American consulate offices and returning home at the earliest opportunity. Cunard liner calls were cancelled after 3 September.[1]

With the departure of the Cunard liners, it was left to neutral American passenger ships to continue the transatlantic trade, which consisted primarily of the evacuation of US citizens from Britain. Throughout September and October they called regularly to Cobh. The last American liner to call at Cobh was on 17 November 1939, while in Galway there were two specially arranged visits by ships in May and July 1940.

As with other smaller European nations, Ireland exercised its sovereign right to remain neutral in the impending conflict and set itself outside the sphere of influence of the belligerent nations. The fledgling Irish state was on the periphery of European politics where the great Continental powers dominated affairs. From the perspective of the Irish government, neutrality was the only realistic option. Ireland was powerless to influence the will of the warring factions and therefore took the decision to remain outside the conflict. However, this small island nation, with its conspicuous geographical location jutting out into the eastern Atlantic, formed a large salient around which the busiest shipping lanes in the world flowed. This unique position meant that Ireland would not be immune from the impending war, and this was highlighted by Taoiseach Éamon de Valera when he addressed the Dáil in September 1939. Stressing the seriousness of the situation, de Valera noted, 'Although we are not immediately in the operation of the land conflict, we are in the centre of the sea conflict.'[2]

From the outset the German Kriegsmarine was at a disadvantage and in no position to contest the supremacy of the Royal Navy. However, as the First World War had shown, Britain was entirely dependent on its sea trade, and it would be the task of the Kriegsmarine to interdict British mercantile trade on the high seas.

The small German U-boat force in service at the beginning of the war lacked the necessary numbers to conduct an effective blockade. Nevertheless, by 3 September it had taken up positions covering the strategic shipping routes passing through the Western Approaches. The volume of traffic was greatest in the South-West Approaches, with shipping from West Africa, the Mediterranean and the South Atlantic merging as it crossed the Bay of Biscay to enter the English Channel or proceed through St George's Channel. This narrow seaway between Wales and Ireland was dominated by the industrial ports of the Bristol Channel and the great city port of Liverpool. These two shipping hubs generated vast commercial wealth, which the British Merchant Navy conveyed around the world. Along Ireland's northern coast the Atlantic and North Sea routes passed through the North Channel to Glasgow and the extensive shipyards and docklands bordering the River

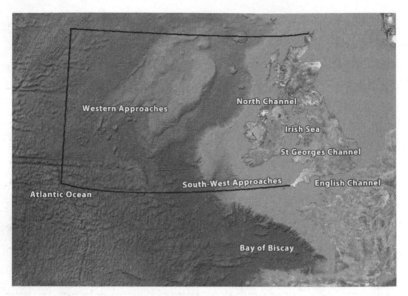

Area of the Western Approaches

Clyde, while across the Irish Sea the port of Belfast was the most influential mercantile trading outpost in Northern Ireland. As a consequence, Ireland found itself enveloped by the war at sea and liable to the same blockade that was meant to restrict Britain. While this was to have a profound effect on the Irish economy, more significantly it placed Ireland on the front line of a bitterly contested campaign that would last six years.

The war fought around the Irish coast developed into several key stages influenced by the changing geopolitical map of Europe and by important technological developments. Each stage marked a shift in the patterns of the numbers of survivors reaching the Irish coast and where they landed. From September 1939 until June 1940, U-boat operations were divided between the approaches to the North Channel, the English Channel and the Irish Sea.

During this period the numbers of operational U-boats and the poor north Atlantic winter weather kept shipping losses down. The dispersal of the landing sites of the survivors of these losses between Cork and Donegal reflects the fact that the battle was still fluid throughout the Western Approaches.

In July 1940 there was a change in the dynamics of the campaign as German U-boats and aircraft moved into newly acquired bases in western France. Reacting to this strategic shift in German forces, the South-West Approaches were abandoned by British merchant shipping and the approaches to the North Channel became the main focus of operations. There was now the added danger posed by German aircraft. In particular, the near coastal areas of Ireland and the Irish Sea would see a dramatic increase in the number of shipping losses. The surge in survivor landings as a result of the U-boat activity off the coast of Donegal soon dissipated as attacks gradually moved further out into the Atlantic. However, the aerial threat lingered, and up to the end of November 1941 the full fury of the anti-shipping campaign waged by the Luftwaffe was endured by the crews who served on board the trawlers and small coasters trading between Britain and Ireland.

Improved British air protection for convoys forced the U-boats to operate further out into the Atlantic, and 1942 and 1943 would see a dramatic decline in the numbers of survivors reaching Ireland. This was due in part to the distances involved – the ships were sunk nearer to Newfoundland than to Ireland. It is also significant that of the four merchant-navy crews who landed in Ireland during this two-year period, only one had to sail the full distance to reach safety, whereas the other three crews were picked up by Irish ships returning home.

The defeat of the U-boats in the Atlantic and the reduction of merchant-shipping losses due to superior Allied convoy protection and technological advances meant that 1944 was the only year in which no survivors from merchant shipping landed in Ireland. There was, however, a group of arrivals at Cobh on 1 January 1944 who were unique in the lengthy story of survivors finding refuge from the sea. When the Irish coaster *Kerlogue* picked up 168 German sailors from the Bay of Biscay, it was the first time that naval personnel from any of the belligerent nations had landed in Ireland. This contingent was the second largest group of survivors to reach the country, next to those from the ill-fated *Athenia*.

The rapid advances made in technology by both sides stimulated a resurgent U-boat campaign around the British Isles from October 1944 until the end of the war. The development of the schnorchel device for U-boats, which allowed them to remain submerged for much longer periods and thus stay out of view of Allied aircraft and ships, combined with new tactics for operating in shallow coastal waters, meant that the Irish coast was once again on the fringes of the battle. To counter this threat the British laid defensive minefields, and in March 1945 U-260 fell foul of one off the southern Irish coast. The entire crew reached the safety of the shore at Cork and were later transferred to the Curragh to join the survivors from the Biscay action.

Even at this late stage, with the inevitability of German defeat apparent, the U-boat inshore campaign continued. Just two weeks before the end of the war in Europe, the British coaster *Monmouth Coast* became one of the last U-boat victims when it was sunk off the Donegal coast. The sole survivor was found by local fishermen and brought ashore, bringing an end to Ireland's involvement in the longest campaign of the Second World War. During this period a total of 2,330 survivors landed along the Irish coast from ships lost through hostile action.

At the beginning of the war there was no formal procedure for documenting and recording the status of the landed crews. Many survivors from ships sunk in the early period of 1939 went unrecorded by any government department. It was not until 1940, when better lines of communication were defined and reports of landings from the Coast Watching Service and the police were sent to the G2 intelligence branch of Army Headquarters that more thorough records were kept. By September 1940 the basic principles to be followed when survivors arrived along the Irish coast were issued to the relevant government departments. The initial report of landing, when received by G2, was passed on to the Department of Local Government, which would notify the nearest Board of Health and Red Cross branch. Other notifications were passed on to the Department of Transport and Marine and the Department of Industry and Commerce. Then, depending on the nationality of the ship and crew, the appropriate consulate offices would be informed, with details of survivors passed on as they became available. What was particularly important was to ascertain from the survivors if there were any members of the crew unaccounted for and still at sea. Search and rescue operations could then be undertaken by the RNLI (Royal National Lifeboat Institution) and the Irish Air Corps. Information about the landing of survivors, irrespective of nationality, was also passed on to the British government representative's office in Dublin. The process worked well, and merchant-navy survivors were generally in the country for a relatively short period of time. For members of the armed forces from any belligerent nation the circumstances were different and, as some cases would later show, somewhat more problematical for the Irish government to manage.

The rights of a shipwrecked sailor were defined under international maritime law and the landed men were free to return to their country of residence as soon as it could be arranged. There is a distinction here with the use of the word 'sailor', which is given to mean men serving in the armed forces and not in the civilian merchant navy. However, the Irish government took a different view of the situation from the outset of the war and decided not to adopt this international doctrine. Instead, members of the armed forces belonging to any of the belligerent nations who landed in Ireland would be interned for the duration of the war. At first this policy only applied to air crews from the Luftwaffe and RAF, as no naval personnel had landed in Ireland. However, there was one branch of the armed forces serving on board British merchant ships that blurred the distinction between civilian and military and provided an embarrassing example of Ireland's biased neutrality. From the outset of the war, defensive guns were fitted on board an increasing number of British and Allied merchant ships. As a way of ensuring the guns were properly manned, Royal Navy DEMS gunners were placed on board the merchant ships and signed on the ships' articles as merchant seamen.[3] In 1940, there were two occasions when survivors landed from British ships carrying DEMS gunners. The first was when a gunner from *Langleeford* landed wearing his naval uniform, and the second was when two gunners from *Clan MacPhee*, also wearing naval insignia, arrived at Galway in August 1940. Technically, under the Irish internment policy, these men should not have been allowed to leave Ireland. Yet, when both cases were reviewed, the government felt that:

> It would be ridiculous if we were to intern an unfortunate naval rating because when picked out of the sea he was wearing the tattered remnants of a uniform, when every day British naval ratings are allowed to disembark from merchantmen in our ports provided they change their clothes beforehand.[4]

Allowing DEMS gunners ashore in civilian clothes while their ships were in Irish ports made a mockery of any suggestion that DEMS gunners landing on the Irish coast by lifeboat should be unfairly punished. Yet it would be another year before a final judgement was made on this thorny issue and it would take another gunner landing to bring the matter to a conclusion.

Thomas Wood had served on board the British steamer *Lapwing* when he was torpedoed. Along with eighteen other survivors from the great battle around convoy HG-73, he managed to land near Clifden in October 1941. Wearing naval clothing and also identifying himself as a gunner, the case of Wood once again raised the uncomfortable question of what action should be taken by the government in such circumstances. At this time it was the view of the Department of External Affairs that 'we should try to avoid the question being raised whether such people should be interned.'[5] The solution epitomised Ireland's philosophy towards neutrality and internment during the Second World War. Gunner Wood was allowed to leave the country, but to prevent any further ambiguity should there be another occurrence of DEMS gunners landing in Ireland, a Department of Defence Internment Order was drafted stating that all members of the armed forces from any of the belligerent nations who landed in Ireland wearing a uniform or part of a uniform would be interned. This should have put the matter to rest, but a final twist saw the Irish government subvert its own authority by issuing contradictory orders. It was decided that, through the Department of Justice, the police would be advised that any DEMS gunners who landed in Ireland wearing a uniform should be changed into civilian clothing as soon as possible.

In the end, the issue of DEMS gunners was quietly forgotten as the war at sea moved further away from the Irish coast and the number of survivors coming ashore reduced. Despite its discrepant guidelines, the repatriation of the occasional gunner was a political expediency for an Irish government that wanted to handle these cases 'discreetly and humanely' at a time when they were being harangued by foreign governments still smarting over Ireland's determination to remain neutral.

In the Department of Defence Internment Order generated by this episode there was one final stipulation that would affect landings later in the war. This was not to do with single naval ratings on merchant ships but was specific to large boatloads of naval personnel landing in Ireland. The consensus within the government was that it would not be possible to facilitate the return of such a large number of naval personnel to their former units. This important proviso would keep the German sailors rescued from the battle of Biscay in December 1943 in Ireland without the possibility of repatriation.

* * *

The care of the survivors once they were ashore was primarily handled by two volunteer agencies, whose invaluable work has been much under-rated and seldom publicised. The Shipwrecked Fishermen and Mariners' Benevolent Society (henceforth Shipwrecked Mariners' Society) was founded in 1839 to help cater for the welfare of shipwrecked mariners.[6] Wholly reliant on charitable donations, this society operated throughout Britain and Ireland with its cadre of volunteer honorary agents located around the coastal regions of both countries. The network was extensive and there was not a part of the coast that did not have an agent nearby to render assistance should it be required. In Ireland, away from the larger ports such as Dublin and Cork, agents could be found in coastal towns such as Clifden, Burtonport and Ballyglass. The role of the Shipwrecked Mariners' Society cannot be underestimated, especially in the remote western and north-western regions where so many survivors landed during the war. In addition to looking after the welfare of the distressed seamen, the agents acted as intermediaries with government officials, passing on information about the seamen and liaising with the shipowners.

Invariably, survivors landing in Ireland after their ship had been sunk arrived with only the clothes they were wearing. Without any personal possessions and no money, the survivors relied on donations supplied by agencies such as the Shipwrecked Mariners' Society and the Red Cross. There was a clear protocol in these societies' mandates as to how funds could be used to assist survivors. In general, the ultimate financial responsibility for helping crew members from a merchant-navy vessel lay with the owners of the ship.

The Shipwrecked Mariners' Society provided dry clothing for the seamen and, as the war continued, donations of clothing became as important as financial contributions. This need for clothing was considered to be of such importance that the British government worked closely with the society to distribute consignments of new clothes to overseas locations for use by survivors. As part of his obligations, the honorary agent would identify a place where survivors could be provided with overnight accommodation and food. The survivors would be taken to this accommodation to wait for onwards repatriation. As the war progressed certain hotels became closely linked to the plight of the survivors. In particular, the Railway Hotel in Clifden hosted crews from five different ships throughout the war, accommodating seventy survivors, and it was mentioned several times in letters of thanks written by appreciative merchant seamen.

It would have been unfeasible to wait for the shipowners to transfer funds to the survivors on remote parts of the coast, so it was more practical for the honorary agent to settle all outstanding bills for accommodation provided during the survivors' stay. An account of expenditure was then sent to the shipowner who would reimburse the Shipwrecked Mariners' Society. This system was both practical and functional: there was never any delay in looking after the immediate needs of the survivors, and the society's noble work could continue with the cooperation of the local community and the shipowners. The same procedure was used when it came to arranging repatriation for the survivors. This invariably involved travel to one of the ferry ports on the east coast. Again, the society's honorary agent would provide rail warrants and ferry tickets, all of which would be refunded by the shipowner.

As the war progressed, the work of the Shipwrecked Mariners' Society was in ever greater demand. The number of survivors coming ashore and the inevitable expenditure of resources put an enormous strain on the society. At the very beginning of the war, it was involved in assisting the survivors from *Athenia*. On 5 September, when *Knute Nelson* arrived with 449 survivors from the sinking of the passenger liner, it was through the work of Mr E. McQuillan, the honorary agent for Galway, that the entire crew was accommodated, clothed and returned to their homes in Glasgow with such efficiency.[7] This was the largest single contingent of survivors from one ship to be landed in Ireland throughout the war. By the end of September, another 135 survivors landed along the Cork coast, and they were treated with similar efficiency by Mr J. C. Rohan of Cork city. Most of the uninjured seamen stayed less than twenty-four hours in the country before being repatriated. This high level of organisation and the commitment to care for the survivors was always appreciated by the 'seamen who withal do their duty with the fearlessness which characterises the hardy mariners of these islands'.[8]

From the annual reports of the Shipwrecked Mariners' Society, the lists of assistance rendered shows the true extent of the work carried out during the Second World War. It is touching to note that the example shown in the report from 1940 of letters of gratitude sent by survivors is from a crew that landed in Ireland. On 14 February 1940 the British steamer *Langleeford* was sunk off the west coast of Ireland. Over the next three days, two lifeboats, each with fifteen survivors, landed at Fodry, Co. Clare, and at Glenderry, Co. Kerry. When the crew returned home after their ordeal, two officers wrote to the society. The sentiment portrayed in both letters is a good example of the high esteem in which merchant seamen held the society's work. Captain Percival Hewison wrote:

I would also like to mention the good work the local agent for your esteemed Society here has done for us; firstly in trying to find us in exceptionally heavy weather with the local lifeboat, and afterwards in seeing to our comfort and fitting of us with requisite clothing and railway warrants, etc. Everyone here has been so kind that I can speak for all of us and say that we couldn't have been treated better anywhere.[9]

Third Officer Daniel Buckley had been in the same lifeboat as the captain and wrote, 'I now wish to record my thanks for the great kindness and consideration shown me by your Mr Barrett, honorary member of the Fenit branch, Eire. He was kindness itself, and I hope to meet again, although under different circumstances.'[10]

The work of the Shipwrecked Mariners' Society continued right up to the end of the war, and it was available to give assistance to the last merchant-navy seaman to come ashore in Ireland in April 1945.

Assistance provided by the society extended beyond caring for survivors from shipwrecks. With the war came the inescapable list of dead merchant seamen who left behind wives and children unable to support themselves. The society was pivotal in providing care and support to many widows and orphans, the unseen victims of the war at sea.

Although the Shipwrecked Mariners' Society was an organisation dedicated to helping merchant navy and fishermen survivors, it was not the only charitable organisation willing to assist. Cooperation between the society and the local community was best demonstrated by the involvement of the Irish Red Cross Society. From the 1920s there had been Red Cross branches throughout Ireland, but it was not until August 1939 that the Irish Red Cross Society was established by an Act of the Oireachtas. The coming into being of the organisation was timely, as within a month of its inception it would be at the forefront of providing care to the many victims of the Battle of the Atlantic. Volunteers of the Red Cross came from the local community and were some of the first on the scene when survivors were coming ashore. The Red Cross afforded succour not just to merchant seamen and fishermen but also to passengers stranded in Ireland and military personnel who were landed later in the war. Care was administered without distinction of political ties or nationality, which meant that aid would be provided to every seaman landing in Ireland regardless of his allegiances. This was an important distinction from the Shipwrecked Mariners' Society, although in reality the difference never became apparent, as no merchant seamen from an Axis nation ever landed in Ireland.

As the effects of the war became all too apparent, there was huge expansion in the membership of the Red Cross Society. Around the coast there was a surge in the growth of local branches. In Cork alone in early 1940, Ballycotton, Kinsale, Cobh, Courtmacsherry, Bantry and Berehaven Red Cross branches were all brought into existence through the need to have established, shore-based organisations who could look after survivors once they came ashore. The formation of the Kinsale branch is typical of the effect the war at sea had on convincing people to participate in the Red Cross. The early months of the war had seen several survivors landing along the south coast. The local residents were 'inspired by the knowledge that the town centred around a very important port'.[11] Within weeks of the branch forming, it was involved in assisting the survivors from the Norwegian cargo ship *Songa*.

In July 1940, just as the northern shores of Ireland were about to witness harrowing times for unprotected convoys, new Red Cross branches were formed in Donegal town and in Rathmullen, Co. Donegal. Noting the obvious similarities in the work carried out by both organisations, members of the Shipwrecked Mariners'

Society were encouraged to join the newly formed Red Cross branches. The systematic approach that the honorary agents brought with them from their dealings with previous survivor landings would be of tremendous value in the coming months. Over the course of the remaining months of 1940 these new Red Cross branches would provide comfort and aid to 181 survivors coming ashore along the Donegal coast.

In order to properly manage emergency supplies, a central supplies depot for the Irish Red Cross was opened in April 1940. Located in Dublin, the lengthily named Irish Red Cross Society's Emergency Hospital Supplies Depot ensured that satellite depots in maritime counties were sufficiently stocked with clothes for survivors. The demands placed on local depots were so high in the summer of 1940 that by September the central depot was desperately short of both clothing and funds to replace the clothing already handed out to shipwrecked seamen. Volunteers were requested not only to work at the busy depot but also to knit garments for the survivors. The knitting initiative had already been taken up elsewhere, and the Irish Girl Guides of Cobh had bestowed the first hand-knit garments to the survivors of *Arlington Court* in November 1939. Further along the coast, the call went out in Kinsale: 'Appealing to the girls and women of the town to join the classes which were being conducted twice weekly in the local depot for sewing and making up garments and converting old garments.'[12] Apart from clothing, there was also a great demand for other everyday personal items, such as shaving sets, combs and toiletries in general. Outfitted with these simple items, seamen were able to take the first steps back into society after the life-threatening ordeal which had deprived many of all their worldly possessions.

The growth of the Red Cross across the country during the lean war years was only made possible by the generous and charitable disposition of the people of Ireland. The level of involvement of Red Cross volunteers was easily quantified when looking at direct aid and charity donations. However, when the private transportation that members of the Red Cross provided is taken into account, their involvement becomes even more impressive. It must be borne in mind that, especially in rural areas of west and north-west Ireland, the transport infrastructure would not have been as robust as in the larger towns and cities. With the restrictions imposed by fuel rationing, the system rapidly deteriorated, with services restricted and finally cancelled as the scarcity of petrol became more common. Volunteers would meet survivors at train and bus stations and take them to their hotel, the seaman's mission or wherever they were heading to. In the end transport problems would become such an issue that, from 1943, direct government intervention was required to guarantee survivors could travel across the country. This was particularly the case when the crew of *Empire Breeze* arrived at Waterford in September 1943. The rail service had been cancelled as there was not enough coal to keep the train running. It was left to the Minister for Supplies, Seán Lemass, to authorise the use of special coaches to be sent from Dublin to collect the British seamen. But it was this level of personal investment from members of the Red Cross that made such a difference to the lives of the survivors. Each one was asked to 'live an active membership' and 'give not only monetary but their personal help in carrying out the necessary and obvious duties during this time of great hardship'.[13]

This was especially true when considering the large numbers

of seamen stranded in Dublin from 1940 onwards. With Europe under German occupation, many seamen were unable to return to their country of residence and remained in Dublin while consulate offices arranged for travel to Britain. During their stay in Dublin, merchant navy officers were accommodated in hotels while ratings lived in the Seaman's Institute on Eden Quay. In many cases, the stranded seamen had no access to wages and relied on the generosity of the Red Cross to help them live while waiting for their next employment. For Swedish nationals, the wait could be particularly long as, unlike other Europeans, the Swedes only manned Swedish-registered ships. As a result of this policy the Swedes would remain in Ireland until such time as a berth on a suitable ship became available. For the crews of the Swedish ships *Canton* and *Siljan*, sunk in August and September 1940 respectively, their stay in Ireland was one of the longest recorded for any crew. After seven months enjoying the hospitality of the Irish capital, the last members from both crews took the ferry to Liverpool at the end of March 1941 to join the Swedish ship *Mansuria*.

With so many Allied and neutral foreign seamen staying in Dublin, the British authorities were concerned that subversive elements inside Ireland could undermine their morale. There was even the possibility that some seamen could be persuaded to divulge information to Axis spies and jeopardise the safety of merchant ships at sea. As a result of these concerns, the Mission to Seafarers, a British charity similar to the Seaman's Institute already established in Dublin, was set up in the capital with a view to providing care for the stranded seamen and ensuring they did not become swayed by subversive ideals. British fears of Dublin exerting a demoralising effect over the stranded seamen, or German spies trying to glean information from them, were unfounded, but the addition of another charity to care for seafarers was welcome.

* * *

Many thousands of seamen endured unimaginable hardships in a bitter struggle for survival at sea. Yet it is worth noting that of the 2,330 men who landed safely in Ireland, only six died as a result of injuries sustained during the attacks on their ships or while making the arduous lifeboat journey to safety. This remarkably low mortality rate is testament to the care and good treatment that was afforded to the survivors while they were in Ireland.

There are few reminders of the events of the Battle of the Atlantic that unfolded so dramatically off the Irish coast. At Ventry, Co. Kerry, there is a memorial to commemorate the landing of the crew from the Greek ship *Diamantis* in October 1939, while at Kilmore Quay, Co. Wexford, a monument lists the names of the crew from *Isolda* who were killed when their ship was attacked on 19 December 1940.

Some artefacts from ships sunk around the coast have been recovered, including the bell from the British steamer *Hazelside*, which is on display in the Cape Clear Museum, Cape Clear Island, Co. Cork. Crockery recovered from the wreck of *Cumberland*, sunk off the Donegal coast, is on display at the Inishowen Maritime Museum, Greencastle, Co. Donegal. Some of the best-preserved artefacts relating to survivors landed in Ireland are at the National Maritime Museum, Dun Laoghaire, Co. Dublin. Featured in its collection are items from *Kerlogue* and the dramatic rescue of 168 German sailors from the battle of Biscay in December 1943.

1

ATHENIA

An uninterrupted swell moving across the vast open space of the north Atlantic Ocean caused the crowded passenger ship to roll through the seaway. There was a calm serenity to the Sunday morning as both passengers and crew slowly stirred to the beginning of another day. Many of the passengers remained confined to their beds as the effects of the ship's movement curbed any desire for the breakfast that was being served in the dining rooms. Stewards calling on cabins were met with sickly responses to be left alone as the occupants suffered the dizzying effects of seasickness. Those passengers who were unaffected found the corridors and stairways devoid of the crowds they had become used to and the dining rooms were mainly empty. The promenade decks were similarly desolate; the solitary few out walking contemplated the cloudy view of the Atlantic.

Elsewhere, the crew continued their daily routines unperturbed by the sea conditions. Captain Cook was awake earlier than usual and visited the bridge where Chief Officer Copland and Third Officer Porteus shared the morning watch. It had been a quiet morning, and, with nothing special of interest to discuss, Cook returned to his cabin for breakfast.

Gradually the rest of the ship stirred as passengers broke free from their early morning malaise and ventured out onto the open decks. As the sun rose steadily, the early morning cloud cover soon dissipated and the refreshing glow of the sun's rays warmed the faces of the revived passengers. Those feeling well enough attended the Sunday church service, although many preferred the fresh air, and growing numbers of passengers sat out on the hatches and embraced the brisk sea breeze.

Second Radio Officer McRae was on watch in the radio room where he listened to the routine radio traffic filling the airwaves. There had been a steady flow of telegrams from passengers to coast stations, and the morning passed quickly. Just after 1100 hrs, McRae jotted down a message broadcast from Valentia radio informing all ships that Britain had declared war on Germany. The message was quickly passed on to Captain Cook who went to his cabin, where he opened a sealed envelope containing instructions from the Admiralty for this eventuality. Shortly after, Chief Officer Copland and Chief Purser Wotherspoon were called. After informing both men that war had been declared, Chief Officer Copland was directed to provision and prepare the lifeboats. There were twenty-six lifeboats on board with each davit holding two boats in an upper and lower arrangement. Additional safety equipment, such as for fighting fires and the ship's watertight doors, was also to be checked. Captain Cook stressed the importance of not alarming the passengers, and if anyone should ask they were to be told that the readying of the lifeboats was merely a precautionary measure.

After the meeting was concluded Copland and Wotherspoon went to the purser's office where they composed a short notice

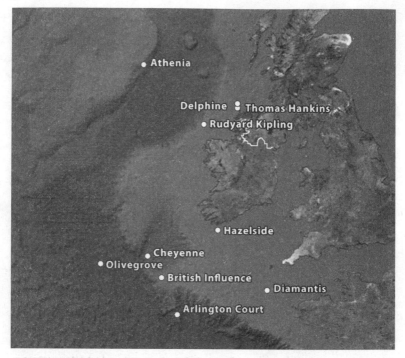

Position of ships sunk in 1939 whose survivors landed in Ireland

informing the passengers that war had been declared. The single sheet of typed paper was posted on the noticeboard where crowds of passengers soon congregated. News of the declaration swept through the ship. While some people openly wept, others withdrew into contemplative silence. Only the night before the ship had buzzed with relieved excitement as those on board the Atlantic liner fled from a continent on the brink of war. The reversal in the outlook of the passengers was unmistakable as they grew sombre, feeling trepidation regarding the possibility of an attack.

Since departing Glasgow on the morning of 1 September, Captain Cook had pressed hard to save as much time as possible.

As the last crowds boarded *Athenia*, the ship was soon readied for sea and the mooring lines cast off. The passage down the River Clyde seemed faster than normal for the crew, who watched familiar landmarks streak past windows and portholes. Although no formal declaration of war had yet been announced, Captain Cook had calculated that should hostilities at sea commence he would have until Sunday afternoon to clear any threat that German U-boats would pose. Later in the evening there was a brief stop when *Athenia* anchored at the entrance to Belfast Lough and waited while passengers were brought out from Belfast. Then it was on to Liverpool, but in his haste to depart as early as possible Captain Cook decided against berthing alongside the passenger terminal and instead anchored midstream in the River Mersey on the morning of 2 September. It was 1630 hrs when the river pilot boarded to take *Athenia* back out to sea. The ship carried 1,102 passengers and cargo which included such diverse items as schoolbooks, building bricks and curling stones. One American passenger had managed to get his car on board, which he was particularly pleased with as he did not want to leave it behind.

Below decks the accommodation spaces were jammed full of luggage and people busily adjusting to the crowded environment. At Glasgow workers had hurriedly prepared additional berths in many spaces not normally used by passengers. Empty storerooms, public areas, such as smoking rooms, and baggage-storage areas were given over as temporary sleeping quarters, while almost every cabin and stateroom was shared by several occupants. In the corridors luggage littered the walkways as there was simply no room to store it anywhere else. Nevertheless, despite the cramped conditions there was a universal feeling of relief about being on board and spirits were generally high among the passengers. Almost three-quarters were Canadian and American citizens eager to return home before war plunged Europe into turmoil. There were also over 150 European refugees fleeing a continent that was fractured by oppressive regimes, where intolerance and economic hardship had compelled them to seek a better life across the Atlantic. The remainder of the passengers were made up of British and Irish nationals travelling to Montreal on either holidays or business trips.

That night *Athenia* travelled north through the Irish Sea at its best speed. Since leaving Liverpool a blackout had been enforced and all doors except the emergency exits leading to the open decks were locked. Windows and doors in public spaces were covered to prevent the slightest sliver of light escaping. The portholes of the lower decks had already been boarded up by workers in Glasgow. Whatever might happen in the coming days, it was considered prudent to take immediate appropriate measures to safeguard the ship. As a matter of safety and to prevent collision with other ships, *Athenia* continued to display its navigation lights, although they were partially dimmed, limiting the range of visibility.

When time came for Sunday lunch to be served, the initial shock of the news had subsided. Many remained in their beds as their seasickness persisted and the dining rooms were once again only half full. This did not seem to bother those passengers who sat surrounded by the unoccupied seats. In the afternoon, the sun's heat enticed those passengers who were sufficiently well out on deck. Only a slight breeze disrupted the surface of the swell, and the sea appeared serene. Deckchairs were unfolded and the neat lines arranged along the open decks. The large number of children on board became particularly evident as they entertained themselves by running through the myriad of prams parked near their mothers' deckchairs. For the adults there was deck tennis and quoits, while others simply preferred to enjoy the sun. The afternoon was a welcome distraction for the passengers still concerned about the news of war.

As the sun began to sink below the horizon the crowds slowly dispersed as passengers returned to their cabins to prepare for dinner. With so many people on board there were three dinner sittings arranged, and each passenger was allotted a specific time. After completing a walk around the ship, Chief Officer Copland took his seat in the dining room. Later, Captain Cook, who had remained conspicuously absent since the morning, entered the dining room and took his seat. The presence of the captain, who appeared in good spirits, was reassuring to the passengers. The dining room settled into a relaxed atmosphere and people sharing tables talked openly as conversation turned to topics other than war.

Just after 1920 hrs, the bosun finished checking all the portholes and windows for the blackout. With twilight lingering on the western horizon, Third Officer Porteus delayed switching on the dimmed navigation lights. Since *Athenia* had made good speed throughout the day and the supposed danger zone was well astern, the remainder of the evening promised to pass off unhindered by imagined threats to the ship.

On deck, the quiet was broken by a shout from the lookout posted in the crow's nest. From his vantage point high above the forecastle deck, Seaman McKinnon spotted a disturbance on the sea surface: a white streak of foam marked by an unidentified object. Passengers who heard the lookout's shout turned instinctively towards the sea – as the torpedo powered towards the ship some thought they saw a fish, while others could only make out a trail of ripples on the sea surface. On the port side tourist deck, passengers who had finished their dinner and were enjoying the quiet evening were suddenly confronted with a rising spout of water reaching high above the ship's rails. Immediately after this, a massive concussive force knocked most people off their feet or out of their chairs. The collapsing water spout then drenched the decks and the bewildered passengers.

The torpedo explosion occurred in way of No. 5 cargo hold, and deadly wood and metal splinters were sent flying through the air, cutting a swathe through the passengers on deck, killing several and badly lacerating many more. Below decks, the corridors and cabin spaces adjacent to the torpedo impact area disintegrated into a crumpled mess of twisted metal. There was flooding in the engine and boiler-room spaces, which created a massive updraught of escaping air that swept through the engine room and was strong enough to pin men against bulkheads. Secondary damage buckled the plates of the propeller shaft tunnels, which led to uncontrolled flooding of adjacent compartments.

In the dining room, both Captain Cook and Chief Officer Copland were on their feet immediately after the first unmistakable crash was heard. The entire ship was plunged into total darkness, and it was only both men's familiarity with the ship's layout that allowed them to swiftly vacate the dining room. Unsure of what exactly had happened, the passengers were told to proceed calmly to their cabins where they should collect their life jackets and wait for further instructions. The ringing of alarm bells was followed by emergency signals bellowing out on the ship's whistle as Third

Officer Porteus sprinted from the bridge wing and closed the ship's watertight doors.[1] As the young officer stood by the engine telegraph and rang down for the engines to be stopped, the ship reeled under the force of the torpedo explosion and listed heavily to starboard before returning slowly past the upright mark and settling with a slight port list. The opening shot of the war at sea had been fired and an ill-judged decision on the part of the U-boat commander had resulted in *Athenia* being the unlucky victim.

It did not take long for Captain Cook to reach the bridge where he joined Third Officer Porteus. Cook checked that the watertight doors had been closed, then called the radio room and instructed the operators to send out a distress message in naval code. The problem with this was that the coded message could only be received by a shore station. Radio Officer McRae waited for Valentia Island radio station, which was busy transmitting traffic, and it was almost fifteen minutes before the SOS message got through. A second distress message was sent in plain language, which was almost immediately acknowledged by the Norwegian cargo ship *Knute Nelson*.

Chief Officer Copland had managed to get on deck quickly and was soon joined by the mustering crew, which set about preparing the lifeboats for lowering. The list had increased slightly and was estimated by the preliminary enquiry into the boat's sinking to be about 6 degrees to port. Many of the passengers went straight out on deck without attempting to navigate through the pitch-black corridors back to their cabins to collect life jackets. Below deck there was less order as panic-stricken passengers groped about in the dark for the stairways that would lead them out on deck. In the crazed shoving for a place on the stairs, mothers became separated from children and soon the shrill cries of desperate people filled the air.

Not long after the first explosion, another sharp crack followed by flying debris led many passengers and crew to believe that the ship was still under attack, but it was the build-up of air pressure in the flooded No. 5 cargo hold that had forced the covered hatch boards to burst violently open in a hail of heavy wooden planks and torn canvas.

Emergency power was soon connected, and the lighting around the lifeboat embarkation points revealed fearful waiting crowds. Captain Cook dismissed Third Officer Porteus and the helmsman, and they reported to their respective lifeboat stations. Cook watched as the first lifeboats were lowered with the passengers sitting tightly packed together. From the bridge the whole operation appeared to be running smoothly. Despite the initial confusion when most of the passengers had found themselves trapped in the dark, the situation was soon alleviated by the restored lighting. As the lifeboats were lowered to embarkation deck level they were quickly filled. The whole operation went surprisingly well, although the increased port list did cause some problems when it came to launching the upper lifeboats on the starboard side. One of the reasons for the slower launching and lowering of the lifeboats was the fact that so many of the passengers were women. With many of them caring for children, they were unwilling to try and take charge of the situation themselves and were probably waiting for instructions from the crew. In contrast, some of the male passengers did try to disregard the orders of officers in charge of lowering lifeboats, only to be curtly stopped by the attending crew.

With only a few lifeboats under his charge remaining to be

lowered, Chief Officer Copland took the opportunity to survey the damage and to check for any passengers left on board. The task of checking all public and cabin spaces for passengers had already been carried out by the chief and second stewards, but while below decks Copland thought that an additional search would be wise. The damage and flooding encountered by the chief officer were primarily confined to the area surrounding No. 5 cargo hold, with no signs of any damage or flooding in the forward sections. Unseen by Copland were the flooded engine-room spaces, which, when considered in conjunction with the flooded No. 5 hold, meant there was no hope of *Athenia* remaining afloat. It was just a matter of time before the ship succumbed and slipped beneath the waves. On his inspection, Copland discovered several dead bodies, apparently killed in the explosion, but the ship was otherwise empty, and he returned to the deck to assist with the launching of the last lifeboat from the starboard side. This done, Copland went to report to the captain on the bridge. It had taken just over an hour to successfully launch all lifeboats, and by 2100 hrs there remained only several officers and ratings on board, along with four male passengers. The ship was surrounded by scattered lifeboats. Some rowed clear of the sinking ship and set the sea anchor while others remained nearby. Captain Cook hailed Lifeboat 5 from the bridge wing and instructed the boat to come alongside and take off the last four passengers; it was then to wait close by, ready to take the crew when the time came to abandon *Athenia*.

While they waited for the lifeboat to come and collect the four passengers, the radio room reported to Captain Cook that *Knute Nelson* was proceeding at its best speed towards *Athenia* and was expected to arrive at about midnight. There were also messages from the Swedish yacht *Southern Cross* and the American steamer *City of Flint*, which were also en route but would take much longer to arrive. Unsure how much longer they could safely remain on board *Athenia*, Captain Cook ordered all officers and ratings to abandon ship just after 2300 hrs.

Before leaving the radio room, Radio Officer McRae sent a message to *Knute Nelson* informing the Norwegians that they were abandoning ship but that he would leave his Morse key screwed down so the rescue ship could home in on its transmissions. The last to leave, Captain Cook could see the lights of the approaching Norwegian ship on the darkened horizon as he stepped off *Athenia* onto the waiting lifeboat. The doomed ship was well down by the stern with a pronounced port list. The emergency lighting was still working on the open decks and exaggerated the contorted attitude of the ship when viewed from the furthest lifeboats.

As *Knute Nelson* approached the scene and was spotted by the closest lifeboats, the incandescent light from distress flares dazzled through the darkness. Some of the occupants cheered at the sight of the large ship getting closer. Just as the Norwegian ship loomed large, acting as a beacon for the scattered lifeboats, so the lights on *Athenia* blinked momentarily before being doused for the last time.

Captain Anderssen and the crew of *Knute Nelson* were unsure of what to expect as they approached *Athenia*. As the ship slowed, Anderssen knew that the retrieval of survivors from the lifeboats was not going to be an easy task. The Norwegian ship was in ballast, and a large freeboard would make boarding the ship difficult for many of the passengers. In addition, the moderate swell meant that lifeboats would find it difficult to stay alongside the ship for long enough to disembark the survivors. A quickly rising and falling lifeboat would make transferring onto the ship's accommodation ladder a risky affair. Assuming that many of the survivors would not be able to contend with such an obstacle, Captain Anderssen instructed his crew to prepare a bosun's chair. Once a lifeboat was alongside, the chair would be lowered down and passengers heaved aboard. In any event, both methods of boarding the ship had their dangers, and Captain Anderssen would need to constantly manoeuvre *Knute Nelson* to keep the lifeboats positioned near to the ladder and to the bosun's chair rigging.

The first lifeboat alongside was 8A, which was carrying mainly European refugees who were initially reluctant to go alongside. When *Knute Nelson* was first sighted, one of the female passengers in the lifeboat suggested that it was the German passenger ship *Bremen*. Unwilling to board a ship that might take them back to Germany, the Europeans refused to row over, and it took some time to convince everyone that the ship was not German. The transfer went well considering the conditions. The men jumped for the accommodation ladder where Norwegian seamen waited on the lower platform to catch them. At the same time, the women and children were hauled on board using the bosun's chair.

The next alongside was lifeboat 5, containing Captain Cook and Third Officer Porteus. The transfer of personnel was once again completed without much difficulty, and Captain Cook later remarked that the use of the bosun's chair was safer and just as quick as the accommodation ladder. The two captains conferred with each other on the bridge – James Cook was naturally extremely grateful for the timely arrival of his Norwegian colleague.

Around the same time that Captain Cook and lifeboat 5 were

boarding *Knute Nelson*, the Swedish yacht *Southern Cross* arrived on the scene from the south and was soon picking up survivors.

By 0300 hrs, First Officer Emmery in lifeboat 12 was alongside *Knute Nelson* watching the transfer of his mainly women and children passengers proceed in good order. Other lifeboats were waiting their turn, and lifeboat 5A, with just over ninety people on board, approached astern of Emmery's lifeboat and made fast a line lowered by the Norwegian seamen. In charge of 5A was Quartermaster Dillon, who had acquiesced to the demands of the majority of those in the lifeboat insisting that they go alongside the rescue ship. Under the circumstances, it was not the most prudent action to take as the lifeboat found itself dangerously close to the stern. On the bridge Captain Anderssen was busy concentrating on keeping his ship in the best possible position as the transfer of survivors continued. The engines were ordered ahead to help keep the heading steady. Below, in lifeboat 12, First Officer Emmery watched as the line holding 5A alongside became taut and then parted under the strain of the ship moving ahead. In a matter of seconds, the lifeboat drifted astern towards the threshing propeller blades. Drawn in by the flow of water, lifeboat 5A was struck by the turning propeller, forcing people to jump into the water. The lifeboat was dissected by the large bronze blades of the propeller while all around stunned survivors struggled in the cold water – many not wearing life jackets. Others were seen floating in the water, knocked unconscious or fatally wounded by the terrifying accident. Those who survived clung onto the upturned keel of the shattered lifeboat. They were rescued several hours later when only a handful from the original complement of lifeboat 5A was picked up by HMS *Escort*.

Despite the terrible accident, the rescue effort continued, and, as dawn approached, *Knute Nelson* was still searching for survivors. With the much anticipated arrival of daylight, the true extent of the damage to *Athenia* was revealed. By now the ship was listing almost 30 degrees to port and was well down by the stern with the lowermost decks already awash. The surrounding sea was strewn with lifeboats from the passenger ship, but they had been vacated during the night, and the discarded boats drifted aimlessly across the Atlantic. Several other rescue ships had arrived, including three British destroyers, and Captain Anderssen decided that with his ship full to capacity he would depart the scene and make for the nearest convenient port.[2] From the bridge of *Knute Nelson* Captain Cook observed *Athenia* through binoculars. The stricken liner remained afloat for another two hours before finally sinking and becoming the first casualty of the Battle of the Atlantic.

It was a miserable bedraggled collection of souls that was on board *Knute Nelson*. Family members separated from each other searched frantically for familiar faces. There were emotional reunions as mothers were reunited with lost children and husbands found wives safe in some quiet corner of the ship. Elsewhere, survivors deeply affected by the ordeal roamed the ship inconsolable or simply sat immobile with fearful expressions. Many were in varying states of undress as they had come straight from their cabins. Others found that they had lost their shoes in the scramble and plodded around the decks in their bare feet. Blankets and whatever spare clothing the Norwegian crew could provide went some way to helping, but they were understandably unable to provide ladies' shoes, and temporary moccasins were made out of sackcloth. For many of the survivors there was an overwhelming need to sleep given that they had missed a night's rest and had spent several hours in a cold lifeboat; others, unable to relax, roamed the ship.

Captain Anderssen decided to land the survivors at Galway, from where he could continue his Atlantic crossing once they had disembarked. A message sent via Malin Head radio station informed Galway harbour authorities of the expected arrival of *Knute Nelson* with 449 survivors on board.

Once the news of the survivors' expected arrival in Ireland was known, the city of Galway became the first place in neutral Ireland to mobilise as a result of the war in Europe. The call for assistance was a humanitarian appeal that would involve every public service the city could muster. The two driving personalities behind the preparations were Mayor Joseph Costello and the Revd Dr Browne, the Bishop of Galway. On the evening of 4 September, a meeting was convened that included the Irish army and police, the hospital staff of Galway Central Hospital and the Irish Red Cross. In preparation for the large numbers of survivors, the hospital discharged as many patients as possible in order to free up beds. Additional places were provided by the army at Renmore Barracks, while more beds went to the classrooms of the Sisters of Mercy convent, which was converted into temporary accommodation. Ambulances were called in from neighbouring towns such as Loughrea and, as a novel temporary measure, a local furniture retailer provided several removal lorries stocked with mattresses to help carry the expected casualties. To transport those survivors not needing medical attention there were plenty of local citizens who provided the use of their cars. At Galway Harbour a nearby warehouse was turned into a reception facility. There, hot food and drinks would be provided while the Red Cross tended to the injured waiting for transport to hospital. In another sign of the extraordinary outpouring of generosity from the people of the city, the bakery provided an entire day's supply of bread.

Back at sea, the survivors on board *Knute Nelson* entered an uneasy sleep. The darkness brought back memories of the previous night and fears of another attack spread through the panicky crowds. During the night a large wave broke against the ship's bow, causing it to shudder under the force of the impact. The jolt was enough to awaken the jittery survivors and to provoke screams of terror before they were finally reassured that there was no cause for concern.

In Galway, in the early morning darkness of 5 September, an advance party of doctors and nurses boarded the tender *Cathair na Gaillimhe* lying at anchor outside Galway docks. Also on board was a detachment of soldiers from Renmore Barracks and a select few members of the press. *Cathair na Gaillimhe* proceeded out into the bay where *Knute Nelson* waited at anchor. The morning was perfectly described by one of the correspondents on board who said, 'The morning was in harmony with the situation. It was grim weather with white cloudlets scudding across the horizon and white capped waves thudding against the sides of the tender.'[3] On board *Knute Nelson* the survivors lined the railings watching for the arrival of the tender. When it was sighted breaking through the morning mist, a resounding cheer from the men and women of *Athenia* echoed around Galway Bay, an expression of their relief that their ordeal, unimaginable to them three days before, was finally coming to an end. The emotion of this joyous moment overcame many passengers, who fell to the decks and wept openly.

The transfer of personnel that had been carefully planned by the harbour authorities the previous night went according to plan. The doctors boarded first to tend to the immediate needs of the injured. There were several with serious burns, while broken limbs and shock were the two other most common complaints. The soldiers were then charged with the difficult task of moving the stretcher cases from *Knute Nelson*, down the steep angled accommodation ladder, to the heaving deck of the tender waiting below. Inside *Cathair na Gaillimhe* the nurses received the survivors with all the care and compassion of their profession. There was no rush, and Captain Cook had plenty of time to thank Captain Anderssen and the crew of *Knute Nelson* for their tireless efforts in rescuing so many from *Athenia*.[4]

It was late afternoon before the tender was ready to return to Galway docks. Over Galway Bay, the weather had cleared up, and crowds of onlookers lined the shore approaches to the docks to cheer the safe arrival of the survivors. So many people had turned out that the police cordoned off the docks and restricted access to only those directly involved in humanitarian work. The carefully choreographed mission continued as soon as the tender berthed. The survivors were taken to the temporary reception facility where transport was arranged according to their status. Among the prominent figures there to meet the survivors were Mayor Costello and Dr Browne. Both wore the regalia appropriate to their positions, which may have seemed disproportionately extravagant given the state of their guests. Another important figure waiting to meet the survivors was John Cudahy, the American Ambassador to Ireland. With so many American citizens on board, the Ambassador was keen to gather as much information about the sinking and whether any American casualties had been sustained.

Throughout the remainder of the day hospitals and hotels accepted the influx of survivors coming from the bustling docks. As they had left all their possessions behind on the sinking ship and many were lacking suitable attire, the Red Cross was busy distributing donated clothing. For many the single overriding task in their minds was to let anxious relatives know that they were safe. It was not long before a backlog of telegrams at Galway General Post Office had built up to such a degree that messages were taken by car to the town of Tuam for transmission. Lists of the survivors landed in Galway were hurriedly prepared and forwarded to the Donaldson Shipping Offices in Glasgow. In the confusion of the rescue operation, the exact details regarding the disposition of passengers and crew picked up by the various rescue ships was still unknown. With so many families separated it was also imperative to establish a definitive list of survivors landed at Galway and at Greenock in Scotland. It would be several days before a list of survivors on board *City of Flint*, which had continued on its original course for America after picking up survivors, could be compiled and sent by radio.

Another significant statistic that required confirmation was the final number of casualties. From the eyewitness accounts of the dead seen on board after the torpedo explosion and the horrible accident with lifeboat 5A, deaths were known to have occurred, and initial estimates placed the total at approximately 200 passengers and crew. The final assessment was that 112 passengers and crew were killed in the explosion and subsequent events.[5] It was a shocking loss of life and the first of a conflict that would claim far greater numbers as it inexorably dragged on over the next six years.

Outside Galway, at a small improvised airfield, an aircraft

landed carrying two naval officers from London. Captain Alan
Kirk, US Naval Attaché, and Commander Norman Hitchcock,
Assistant Naval Attaché, had flown to Galway to conduct a
preliminary investigation into the events surrounding the loss of
Athenia. In the city they met Captain Cook and several of his
officers and ratings, where they talked openly about the sinking.
From the witness statements it was accepted that a submarine
was responsible for the attack and that a single torpedo caused
the only explosion. The identity of the submarine was unknown,
although several crewmen stated that they saw it on the surface
briefly before it submerged. Some crew reported that they had
seen a flash from what they thought was a gun coming from the
submarine. However, this claim could not be verified as nobody
had heard a projectile in the air or had seen splashes from falling
shot. Captain Cook did state that he thought the submarine may
have fired on them in an attempt to destroy the ship's radio, but
he later admitted that this was an erroneous claim on his behalf as
there was no evidence to this effect.

The interviews between the US naval officers and the crew from
Athenia gave the first unambiguous picture of what had happened
on the evening of 3 September. Based on the crew's statements
it was evident that a submarine was responsible for the attack on
Athenia. The reported sightings of a submarine nearby could not be
verified, and any intimation that the stricken passenger liner had
come under direct gunfire was discounted.

At the conclusion of the interviews with the naval attachés,
Captain Cook and his crew retired to the hotel accommodation
organised for them. It had been an exhausting forty-eight hours
and travel arrangements were already in place to bring Captain

Cook back to Glasgow. In the quiet solitude of his hotel room he would have been able to reflect on recent events.

Far from Galway, Oberleutnant zur See Fritz-Julius Lemp was also in a contemplative mood after the terrible blunder he had committed. On that fateful evening of 3 September, Lemp had observed a large ship from the conning tower of his command, U-30. The unidentified steamer was travelling at high speed and appeared to be steering a zigzag course.[6] The ship was in darkness with no lights displayed. It was imperative that a decision on whether to attack was reached as the ever-increasing outline of the ship drew nearer. Caught up in those emotional preliminary stages of the war, Lemp reached the conclusion that he was observing a British Armed Merchant Cruiser (AMC), and, based on this judgement, the order was given to clear the conning tower and prepare for a submerged attack.[7] The successful torpedo impact against the suspected AMC was temporarily tempered by a scare on board the U-boat when a second torpedo failed to launch from the tube. There was a real danger that the running torpedo could explode if it was not ejected. Fortunately, the crew managed to clear the blocked tube, and the faulty torpedo later exploded safely ahead of the U-boat.[8] There was nervous elation throughout the U-boat as the distant din of the torpedo explosion was heard by the crew.

Their first attack of the war appeared to be a success. In the commander's control room, Lemp watched through the periscope as the target ship came to a stop. After waiting about thirty minutes for the shroud of darkness to obscure them from view, the U-boat surfaced, and Lemp was joined by First Officer Hinsch in the conning tower. Despite nightfall's restrictions, both officers were confronted with a scenario that was immediately and alarmingly clear. In stunned silence Lemp and Hinsch watched as lifeboats crowded with passengers were launched from the stricken ship. Later, an intercepted distress message from the torpedoed ship identified it as the passenger liner *Athenia*. Acutely aware of his grievous mistake, Lemp slipped away from the scene, knowing that the area would soon be teeming with rescue ships responding to the distress call. U-30 remained silent after the attack and would only make contact with Befehlshaber der Unterseeboote (BdU)[9] on 12 September after a request was made for a situation report.[10]

* * *

On the morning of 6 September, Captain Cook and his crew began the journey back to Glasgow. The controversy surrounding the sinking and its serious international implications meant that there were many more questions to be asked of the captain.

Around Galway, many of the survivors who remained behind would enjoy the hospitality of the city for several more days. Without travel documentation, personal belongings or money, it was mainly the American and Canadian passengers who found themselves stranded without the means to leave. Also, many of the injured were in no fit state to travel and some would remain patients at Galway Central Hospital for six weeks. While in Galway, each stranded survivor was treated as a guest of the city. It was not uncommon for them to be lavished with gifts of meals and drinks. Their different accents and ad-hoc dress style differentiated them from the local populace. (Later donations to the Red Cross appeal would provide more up-to-date fashions.) For the hospital patients, life was equally amiable, with frequent visits by the Red Cross with bouquets of flowers to cheer up their bedsides.

Eventually the numbers of survivors in Galway decreased. Their routes home were varied, depending on whether they could get a berth on another passenger ship. Some who had left relatives in Scotland returned there to wait for another ship leaving Glasgow. Others waited in Ireland and departed on one of the transatlantic liners that left from Galway and Cobh in the coming weeks. On their return home the survivors would write letters expressing heartfelt thanks to the people of Galway. The western city had responded to the call for help. The carefully organised reception plan to accommodate and care for so many survivors was a tribute to the leading public figures who were its driving force. Although never repeated on the same scale as the *Athenia* incident, the compassion of many unnamed civilians would be repeated throughout the country over the next six years.

2

A Tale of Two Tankers

From the beginning of hostilities, Admiral Dönitz, commander of the German submarine fleet, had positioned his available U-boats to cover the approaches to the North Channel, St George's Channel and the English Channel. All British trade coming from the Atlantic and the Mediterranean would have to pass through these sea approaches, which presented the greatest concentration of shipping that the screening U-boat force could attack. During the period before the commencement of this defensive measure, the small numbers of U-boats available were expected to inflict significant losses on British merchant shipping. The British were expected to adopt the convoy system as a defensive measure against the U-boat threat, but it was also expected that it would take weeks before the system could be fully implemented.[1] At the beginning of hostilities many ships were already at sea and could not therefore be included in a convoy. These ships would be obliged to complete their voyages independently following routing instructions provided by the Admiralty. It was among these ships that the U-boats were to find the majority of their targets during this initial phase of the war.

The U-boats were expected to wage the war at sea in accordance with the London Naval Treaty, which defined how a submarine should conduct operations against merchant ships.[2] At the outbreak of hostilities with Britain, Dönitz instructed his U-boat commanders at sea that they should conduct operations in accordance with the German Prize Regulations.[3] If, however, the merchant ship was armed, resisted being stopped or transmitted radio signals that identified the presence of a U-boat, then the commander was released from the requirements of the Prize Regulations and could take appropriate measures. It was a cumbersome arrangement but worthy of merit, as its goal was to save lives at sea. However, the Prize Regulations were an unfavourable set of restrictive rules that negated the advantages of the U-boat and placed it in real danger while it carried out its duty. Throughout the early months of the war both sides would take steps that would slowly erode the sanctity of the London Naval Treaty and jeopardise the lives of countless merchant seamen.

During the first weeks of the war the majority of ships sunk were attempting to reach the UK through the South-West Approaches. The steady flow of shipping off southern Ireland provided a rich hunting ground for the U-boats that patrolled this area. On 8 September, Kapitänleutnant Otto Schuhart, in command of U-29, stopped and sank the fully laden British tanker *Regent Tiger* 280 miles south-west of the Fastnet lighthouse. *Regent Tiger* was a large modern tanker that had only been completed the year before, and its loss, along with the cargo of oil that the ship carried, was sorely felt. Sailing alone and unescorted the unarmed tanker had little option but to stop once challenged by Schuhart. Over the coming weeks other tankers would attempt to break through the screen of U-boats that watched over the world's busiest sea lanes.

In May 1939 Captain Hugh McMichael took command of the tanker *British Influence*. The ship was a large modern motor tanker which was one of several new builds that the British Tanker Company had launched that year. For its second voyage, Captain McMichael was ordered to sail to the Persian Gulf for a cargo destined for UK ports. The passage presented few difficulties and was the same as the ship's maiden voyage. The ship was scheduled to load at Abadan and to make the short voyage to discharge at Karachi before returning to load again at Abadan and then begin the journey back to England. There was relief on board *British Influence* when the ship departed Abadan on 15 August after loading a full cargo of fuel oil. The interminable heat of the Persian Gulf in the summer had taken its toll and had tested each man's endurance. The cool winds of the south-west monsoon that prevailed across the Arabian Sea brought a welcome respite to the men working inside the sweltering confines of the tanker.

There were several more days of intense glaring sun once the ship entered the Red Sea. It came to a stop south of Suez, where McMichael and his men waited for a northbound convoy to transit the canal. Meanwhile, the news from Europe became increasingly dire, and war seemed inevitable.

On 30 August the captain performed a particularly sobering duty, when he assembled his officers together and informed them of their responsibilities as described in the Admiralty War Instructions. The crew were in a contemplative mood as the ship transited the canal. The threat of war seemed to have been thrust abruptly upon each man on board, with the captain feeling the additional burden of command as *British Influence* entered the Mediterranean. Before they reached Gibraltar, the news came that war had been declared. Captain McMichael would have known that the illusion of peace would be quickly dispelled once they passed Gibraltar, with U-boats stalking the Atlantic trade routes to Britain.

The final part of the journey would be the most perilous for *British Influence* as the threat of meeting the enemy was very real. The convoys departing from Gibraltar bound for Britain had not yet started, which left only the option of sailing unescorted through the South-West Approaches.[4] At Gibraltar, Captain McMichael received detailed routing instructions for the homeward journey. Instead of taking the normal route which followed the west coasts of Portugal and Spain before crossing the Bay of Biscay, *British Influence* was ordered to take the precaution of heading out west until past 15 degrees west of longitude before turning north. Then, as the ship reached a position where it was possible to steer an easterly course for the English Channel, McMichael should order his ship to head east and make the final run through.

On 13 September *British Influence* was approaching the designated waypoint marking the beginning of the easterly course that terminated in the English Channel. Less than 200 miles north, the salvage tug *Neptunia* was en route to rendezvous with the broken-down destroyer HMS *Walker* when its journey was abruptly brought to an end by Otto Schuhart and U-29.[5] Once the crew had abandoned ship, the tug was duly sunk. Schuhart was most apologetic to the crew that he was unable to help secure their rescue, giving as his reason that there were destroyers in the vicinity. After providing provisions to the two lifeboats, U-29 departed on the surface while both crews wished each other well. Schuhart headed east, and as the night drew down the sea was once again devoid of targets. Further west *British Influence* altered its course and started the final dash across the danger zone. McMichael hoped that with an uninterrupted twenty-four hours steaming they could reach the safety of the English coast.

The morning of 14 September started off overcast, with a gentle breeze forming small wavelets that caressed a moderate north Atlantic swell. The gentle rolling of *British Influence* induced an unconscious counter-rocking movement in the lookouts who swayed in perfect symmetry with the ship. Captain McMichael remained on the bridge with the third officer throughout the morning as he was acutely aware of the probability of danger being close by. Shortly before midday the sky began to brighten as the thick cloud cover dissipated and allowed the sunshine through. There was a general stirring of personnel on board as the duty watches changed and the crew prepared for lunch. The sudden arrival of a silhouette on the horizon soon dispelled any belief that the day would continue in an upbeat spirit, when the bridge lookout spotted a U-boat surfacing astern of the tanker. Schuhart had sighted the tanker earlier that morning and had made his final approach submerged before disclosing his position. While McMichael and his bridge team were transfixed by the sudden appearance of the U-boat, Schuhart ordered a warning shot that splashed harmlessly ahead of the tanker. McMichael wasted no time and ordered a distress message to be sent immediately. A second warning shot was enough to convince the practical tanker captain that any chance of escape was unlikely. Without any unnecessary commotion the engine telegraph was put to stop while the emergency signal calling the crew to lifeboat stations echoed harshly throughout the ship.

Chief Officer Alfred Laddle directed the crew to prepare both lifeboats, and their launching was carried out in an orderly manner. Within fifteen minutes both lifeboats had pulled away from the stopped tanker. The entire crew were accounted for, and there had been no casualties except a few slight sprains and sore backs for excited men jumping from the main deck into the lifeboats. U-29 had stopped a short distance off the port beam of the drifting tanker and waited patiently while the lifeboats rowed over. When they had made it to within 20 yards Schuhart came down from the conning tower to talk with them. After a civil round of questions and answers Schuhart advised both boats to stand clear while he sank their ship.

While both lifeboats rowed clear, Schuhart steered around the tanker and considered placing a prize crew on board. The capture of a new tanker with a full cargo of fuel oil would have been a remarkable coup had Schuhart been able to execute the plan. However, the moderate swell prevented the U-boat crew launching their flimsy inflatable dinghies and so the idea was abandoned.[6] A single torpedo struck the ship in the engine room aft. The heavy, pungent smell of black fuel oil hung in the air as the emulsified cocktail of seawater and fuel cascaded over the damaged tanker. The torpedo explosion had completely blown the aft section of the ship away, allowing the inrush of water to drag the wreckage beneath the waves. As the bow rose slowly out of the water, the ship seemed to stop momentarily as the buoyancy of the remaining intact forward cargo tanks kept the ship afloat. After waiting twenty minutes, Schuhart gave the order to fire several rounds from the deck gun to expedite the tanker's demise. Half a dozen well-placed shots into the hull and the tanker resumed its slide into the Atlantic.

The survivors of *British Influence* remained in the vicinity with the sea anchors streamed. Schuhart had given them a compass course to steer, telling them they would either reach land or be picked up by another ship. However, the assiduous German commander remained close by and kept a lookout for any potential rescue ships. A U-boat manoeuvring slowly on the surface would have been susceptible to an attack by RAF aircraft or by destroyers on patrol, and Schuhart was taking a considerable risk – and risking the safety of his own crew – so that the men of *British Influence* could be saved. Regardless of the dangers, Schuhart remained in the vicinity of the two lifeboats for over five hours. Finally, an approaching merchant ship was sighted on the horizon, and U-29 fired off three distress rockets to attract its attention. The unidentified merchant ship was very suspicious about the situation and initially steered away from the unusual sight. Seeing that the ship was not responding to his distress rockets, Schuhart abandoned his duties as chaperon and headed off in pursuit of the fleeing merchant ship. When the U-boat caught up, it signalled by Morse light and finally convinced Captain Anton Zakariassen, in command of the Norwegian ship *Ida Bakke*, to return and pick up the survivors in the lifeboats.

With everyone safely on board *Ida Bakke*, the men of *British Influence* turned to the watching U-boat and gave three cheers to its commander and crew, who in turn gave three cheers back. Schuhart then waved goodbye and went below as those on the deck of the Norwegian ship watched the conning tower disappear under the water. The gratitude expressed by the crew of *British Influence* towards Otto Schuhart was summed up perfectly by Patrick Walsh who said, 'That commander was a proper good fellow and a perfect gentleman.'[7]

With the forty-two men from *British Influence* on board, Captain Zakariassen decided to land the survivors in neutral Ireland which was just over 180 miles away. A wireless message was sent to Valentia Island requesting that a rendezvous with a lifeboat should be arranged off the Old Head of Kinsale for the following morning. Through the Coastal Life-Saving Service (Coastguard), the Courtmacsherry lifeboat was contacted and delegated the task of meeting the Norwegian ship and landing the survivors. The following morning, under the conspicuous promontory of the Old Head, the transfer of survivors took place. The lifeboats from *British Influence*, which *Ida Bakke* had taken on board, were lowered into the water, and some of the men got into these while the remainder boarded the RNLI lifeboat. The two rescued lifeboats were taken in tow, and the trio set off on the short journey across the bay to Courtmacsherry.

On arrival at the village it seemed that every resident had turned out to meet the survivors. The rescued men were organised into small groups by Mr F. Ruddock, Honorary Secretary of the local RNLI, and taken to the homes of the locals where they were given hot food and drinks. The warm hospitality of the Irish families that accompanied the refreshments revived the flagging spirits of the men. Second Engineer Norman Ray was especially thankful for the care he received and later said, 'The people of Courtmacsherry nearly killed us with kindness.'[8] In these most heartening surroundings the men could relax and reflect on the events of the past twenty-four hours.

In the afternoon a chartered bus arrived to transport the crew to Cork city, where they were accommodated at the Metropole Hotel while onward travel arrangements were made. The following day they were on their way to Rosslare, from where a ferry would bring them home across the Irish Sea. The whole episode of the loss of *British Influence* and the subsequent rescue of the crew had been remarkably well executed. The men had been well looked after and returned home in a very short space of time. The actions of Otto Schuhart were instrumental in this and doubtless prevented any unnecessary hardship being forced upon the survivors.

The steady flow of largely unprotected shipping destined for the UK continued throughout September. The losses in men and material incurred were regrettable and perhaps even avoidable, but they never outweighed the numbers of ships that successfully evaded the U-boats. There were simply too few U-boats on patrol to effectively blockade the Atlantic Approaches. However, as losses were bound to happen, it was fortuitous for those seamen involved when their experience resembled the loss of *British Influence*.

* * *

Captain Hugh Kerr, in command of the motor tanker *Cheyenne*, had loaded a cargo of aviation spirit at Aruba at the end of August. War was imminent and, before he was allowed to proceed back to the UK, Captain Kerr was ordered to Port of Spain where the Royal Navy authorities provided routing instructions for the Atlantic crossing. Although war had not yet been declared, the subject of defensive armament was raised by the captain. However, there was none available at the port and none would be fitted until the ship's arrival in the UK. The derisory consolation defensive measure provided by the authorities was an application of grey paint on the funnel and ship's upper works. The laden tanker was also instructed on a new method that was to be used to prevent an explosion occurring in the cargo tanks should the ship come under attack. The procedure involved introducing steam into the top of each cargo tank, which would act as a blanket to suppress the flammable vapours of the cargo. This was all theoretical, and the procedure had yet to be tried. Captain Kerr and his chief engineer George Armstrong were cautiously sceptical and naturally not too keen on having to test the theory.

The reality of war became apparent to Kerr as *Cheyenne* approached the UK and distress messages from *Regent Tiger* and *British Influence* were received. Kerr's success in evading the enemy would be entirely dependent on his route through the South-West Approaches and the proximity of a watchful U-boat. *Cheyenne* was only a day behind *British Influence* on 14 September, and their routes were very similar, but Captain Kerr would follow a course that was 50 miles further north of where the latter had been sunk.

Otto Schuhart remained in his designated patrol area but moved further west to avoid any British patrols sent to out reconnoitre the area after the attack on *British Influence*. However, he was not alone in watching the approaches, and Kapitänleutnant Ernst-Günter Heinicke, in command of U-53, was stationed north of U-29. These two U-boats represented the most westerly patrols in the South-West Approaches. Schuhart had already claimed one ship that had entered from the Atlantic while Heinicke waited patiently for a target to appear.

Just before dawn on 15 September, the lookouts on the conning tower of U-53 sighted the navigation lights of an unidentified merchant ship. Heinicke concluded that any ship sailing through these waters that continued to display lights at night might possibly be from a neutral country. It was a tempting target, worthy of further investigation, but there was a possible cause for concern. Sighted close to the unknown merchant ship was a darkened silhouette that the wary commander assessed to be that of a Royal Navy destroyer. It was not to be the last sighting of the day, and later in the afternoon Heinicke was called to the conning tower for another merchant ship that had been sighted heading east. With the vessels closing fast on each other, U-53 altered course so that it lay on a parallel to that of the merchant ship. But the distance between the vessels was enough for the lookouts on *Cheyenne* to spot the prowling U-boat. A mismatched contest between the vessels commenced and, although the result may have been a foregone conclusion, the determined merchant captain from Belfast was intent on frustrating the enemy's ambition to sink his ship.

When *Cheyenne* spotted U-53, it was off the port bow, about 5 miles distant. Kerr immediately ordered a turn to starboard and for maximum revolutions from the engine room. Calculating that it would take the U-boat some time to close the gap sufficiently for *Cheyenne* to come under effective artillery fire, Kerr ordered a distress message be transmitted in the hope that any nearby warships would arrive in time to save his ship. As he watched the merchant ship flee, Heinicke ordered a warning shot be fired at the tanker. It fell short, and the tanker gave no indication of responding to the hostile action. The unwillingness of Kerr to capitulate under such circumstances was a trait that would be shared among many Merchant Navy captains during the war, and, although his act of defiance was commendable, it did expose his crew to considerable danger. After ignoring further warning shots and with the constant transmission of distress messages from *Cheyenne*, Heinicke ordered his gun crew to take the tanker under direct fire. The frightened merchant seamen took cover wherever they could find it, and although no hits were registered on *Cheyenne*, the fall of shot gradually crept closer as the distance between the adversaries steadily reduced.

Captain Kerr monitored the U-boat's position relative to his own, and after about thirty minutes into the chase he had to admit that there could be no outrunning the Germans. As Kerr doggedly hung on to the hope that a friendly warship would come to his assistance, a final volley of well-placed shots that landed close to the tanker ended the chase. Mindful of the volatile nature of the cargo and dutifully looking out for the safety of his crew, Kerr finally capitulated and grudgingly brought the engine telegraph to stop. The order to abandon ship was passed down from the bridge, and the crew who had remained under cover during the dramatic chase quickly proceeded aft, where both lifeboats had already been swung out. It did not take long for them to be lowered and clear away from the tanker. Some of the crew were able to retrieve personal possessions. The chief steward had used the time during the chase to prepare a small suitcase of belongings that included a typewriter, while the bosun boarded his lifeboat with his pet canaries in a cage. Shortly after they had launched the limitations of the wooden lifeboats, the standard survival craft for the period, became all too apparent. The loose clinker-built boards started to leak as neither lifeboat had been in the water for some time and the boards had not been given a chance to tighten. Those men not manning the oars were set to bailing out the steady trickle of seawater that seeped through.

Meanwhile, Heinicke drew closer and fired a torpedo at

Cheyenne that hit No. 4 starboard cargo tank located just forward of the bridge. There seemed to be little obvious effect from the torpedo's impact, and Heinicke noted that a single large crack in the side plating was the only visible sign of damage. The crew in the lifeboats, however, could see that although the explosion seemed small and muffled, the impact on the starboard side had caused the side plating on the port side to rupture, which left a large gaping hole. But with no indication that the tanker was going to sink imminently a second torpedo was fired. The second explosion hit the same place, but the effects were much more dramatic and the tanker was almost cut in two. As the engineering compartment flooded and dragged the larger stern section deeper into the sea, the smaller bow section slowly rose out of the water until it had folded back into an unnatural vertical position. Finally, the last girders of steel that held the right-angled hulk together sheared and the stern section broke off, leaving the bow section to fall back into the sea. As the two buoyant sections slowly floated away from each other, the surrounding sea was stained with petroleum. There had been no fire or explosion during the torpedo attacks, which could possibly be attributed to the injection of steam into the tanks during the chase.

Satisfied that *Cheyenne* was sinking, Heinicke steered U-53 towards the lifeboats. As they drew close to each other, the German commander asked to see the ship's official papers, but Kerr responded by saying that he had not had time to gather all his documents together and that they remained on board.[9] When Heinicke asked why the tanker captain had tried to escape, Kerr replied succinctly 'self preservation'.[10] A similarly matter-of-fact Heinicke said, 'You made me lose 25 rounds of ammunition' – perhaps making the point that the hour-long chase and the unnecessary expenditure of ammunition could have been avoided if Kerr had stopped after the first warning shot.[11] The awkward dialogue between the two men ended when Heinicke told the lifeboats to follow the U-boat south-west. During the chase, U-53 had sighted another merchant ship heading south that it would attempt to contact to secure a speedy rescue for the crew of *Cheyenne*. U-53 departed in search of the other merchant ship while the lifeboats followed behind. They prepared sails so that they could follow the U-boat at a better speed than the tiring rowing permitted. It was not without some difficulty that the sails were finally hoisted and the lifeboats continued in the direction of their unconventional custodian.

Heinicke finally spotted the ship he hoped would rescue the crew of *Cheyenne*. The ship fleeing to the south was the Union Castle refrigerated cargo ship *Rothesay Castle*, which was naturally alarmed when a U-boat began to chase it on the surface and started to transmit warning messages.[12] Despite chasing *Rothesay Castle* for over an hour and firing several distress flares and two warning shots from the deck gun, the prospective rescue ship refused to stop. Heinicke finally accepted the situation and, mindful of the crew he had left behind in the lifeboats, he headed back to the wreck of *Cheyenne* while there was still some remaining daylight. As the sleek outline of *Rothesay Castle* gradually grew smaller on the southern horizon, the lookouts on the conning tower also noted a thin vertical pall of smoke in the distance.[13] The unseen ship remained out of sight, however, and U-53 hurried back on its increasingly protracted rescue mission.

On his return Heinicke observed that the obstinate fore and aft sections of *Cheyenne* remained afloat and would have to be sunk by gunfire. Both lifeboats were informed that the U-boat would tow them towards the Irish coast once this had been done. Conscious that the survivors had already been several hours in the open lifeboats, Heinicke advised Kerr and his men that hot tea would be provided when they returned. Regardless of the belligerent nature of the scenario, the outlook for Kerr and his crew was remarkably positive. They were to be towed to safety, and even shortly to be served hot tea. Heinicke stated one condition: that neither lifeboat show any lights while being towed in the darkness. This was a fair request of goodwill in return for rescue.

U-53 approached the floating fore part of *Cheyenne*, which stood vertical in the water with only 5 metres of the forecastle deck visible above the waterline. The stern section was upright and trimmed so that the propeller was visibly clear of the water. In addition to the deck gun crew, who were ready to fire, a large group of German seamen had assembled on the U-boat deck to witness the sinking of their first merchant ship. The narrow pressure hull of the U-boat edged closer towards the drifting wreck until it had closed in to a sufficiently short distance, whereupon the gun crew opened fire on the stern section and scored two direct hits near the waterline. The casual celebratory atmosphere was abruptly halted when two shots were directed against the unsuspecting U-boat, falling dangerously close. HMS *Mackay* had been searching for *Cheyenne* since the early afternoon when its radio distress messages were received. *Mackay* had been searching too far south for the tanker and failed to intervene in time to save it. Later, when *Rothesay Castle* began to transmit its warning message, *Mackay* altered course and eventually sighted the floating remains of *Cheyenne*. U-53 had been temporarily obscured behind the larger floating stern section, but once it was sighted the destroyer opened fire at near maximum range. With the destroyer fast approaching, Heinicke gave the order to dive, but with so many of the crew unnecessarily on deck, U-53 delayed precious seconds on the surface while everyone scrambled below deck. Finally, after some initial confusion, the U-boat managed to submerge with enough time in hand to take avoiding action before the expected depth-charge attack. *Mackay* carried out a search around the immediate locality of the wreck but could not find U-53, which successfully evaded the destroyer.

With the arrival of *Mackay* on the scene there was an immediate change to the dynamics of the situation for the crew of *Cheyenne*. The recently arrived destroyer would doubtless have picked them up, but a Norwegian merchant ship already familiar with the duties of a rescue ship was en route after receiving the distress messages. *Ida Bakke*, which had disembarked the crew of *British Influence* that very morning, had resumed its interrupted passage across the Atlantic. Captain Zakariassen manoeuvred close to the lifeboats and the relieved men from *Cheyenne* climbed the Jacobs' ladders lowered from the main deck. In their haste to reach safety some men jumped for the ladder while the lifeboat was in a trough, which resulted in some minor bruising to the unfortunate seamen's legs as the lifeboat was lifted on the crests of the following wave. The rescued seamen watched in the diminishing evening light as *Mackay* fired several rounds into the still floating remains of *Cheyenne* and finally ignited the leaking inflammable cargo. The area surrounding the wreck was covered in aviation spirit which erupted into a spectacular wall of flame and produced a powerful shockwave that surged through the crowds of onlookers lined up at the rails. It was a dramatic ending to the day.

Ida Bakke headed back to the Irish coast for the second time in consecutive days and requested a rendezvous with a lifeboat off Mizen Head the following morning. Mizen Head was further west than the Old Head of Kinsale, and Captain Zakariassen did not want to waste any more time by retracing his route any further than necessary. Once again the Courtmacsherry lifeboat answered the call and the volunteer crew set off early along the west Cork coastline. The transfer of personnel and lifeboats was a well-practised procedure for both parties and one they completed just before sunrise on 16 September. *Ida Bakke* once again resumed its voyage to the USA, while the RNLI crew decided to land the survivors at Baltimore, Co. Cork.

The hospitality and friendliness of the west Cork people was again demonstrated when the Courtmacsherry lifeboat towing the two lifeboats from the *Cheyenne* came into Baltimore Harbour. To the British seamen watching the congregation, it seemed that the whole village had turned out. Prior arrangements had been made by the people of the village, and each cottage hosted a couple of the strangers from *Cheyenne* and provided each man with a well-deserved breakfast. The homely surroundings and satisfying meal demonstrated the unreserved generosity of their hosts to the survivors. With their bellies full and feeling comfortable, the hospitality turned towards a more traditional Irish welcome in the form of large quantities of whiskey. While the crew waited for the bus to come and collect them, many of the men became hopelessly drunk as stories abounded about life at sea and family left at home.

When the time came for Captain Kerr and his men to depart Baltimore, there was much hand-shaking and cordial waves goodbye between the crew and the local people who had befriended them.

The journey from Baltimore to Cork was considerably slower than expected, due to repeated stops for calls of nature induced by the excessive liquid refreshment at Baltimore. From Cork the majority of the crew travelled onwards to Rosslare for the ferry home, while several others made their way to Dublin and Belfast. Captain Kerr travelled to London to deliver the ship's official papers to the Mercantile Marine Office before returning to Belfast on leave.

On two consecutive days, two U-boat commanders personally intervened to ensure that the men they had forced into lifeboats on the open sea would be rescued. Their actions were in accordance with the London Naval Treaty and, while there is no denying that their intention was the destruction of the enemy ship, the considerate nature with which they treated the merchant seamen is unquestionable.

Sadly, the war would ultimately exact its price on the survivors of both ships. Chief Officer Alfred Laddle who survived the sinking of *British Influence* was promoted to captain but was killed when his ship, *Oltenia II*, was sunk in 1943 when sailing in convoy TM-1. Several others from the crew also became casualties at sea. For the men of *Cheyenne* there were also casualties. Second Officer Alexander Allison was later promoted to chief officer but was killed when his ship *Rosewood* was torpedoed. A minor coincidence in the fate of *Cheyenne* and *Rosewood* is that both ships broke in two after being torpedoed and had to be sunk by gunfire from Allied warships. Another loss was that of Storekeeper Richard Curtis, who was lost along with the entire crew of *Victor Ross* on 2 December 1940.

There was one crew member of *Cheyenne* who had the most extraordinary wartime experience, one that eclipsed the relatively minor affair off Ireland in September 1939. Alexander Hurst started his career at sea on large sailing vessels trading worldwide. Before returning to college to study for his certificate of competency, Hurst decided to gain some experience on power-driven vessels. His first appointment was on board *Cheyenne*, which ended as described. After serving on several other ships and passing his mate's certificate of competency, Hurst joined the cargo ship *Dalhousie* which was stopped and sunk by the German auxiliary cruiser *Stier*. The crew of *Dalhousie* were taken prisoner on board the German surface raider and later transferred to the supply ship *Charlotte Schliemann*. *Charlotte Schliemann* did not return to Europe but rather steamed for Tokyo Bay where the prisoners were handed over to the Japanese authorities. For the remainder of the war, Hurst and his fellow captives were detained and made to work at what amounted to nothing short of slave labour. The brief moments spent in Baltimore must have seemed like a distant dream when compared to what Hurst later endured.

3

DESTINATION VENTRY

In the early hours of 4 September, the British steamer *Blairbeg* was fired upon by a U-boat. The assailant had fired a shot from the deck gun, which Captain Sinclair of *Blairbeg* understood to be a warning, and he ordered the ship to be stopped and his crew to abandon it. Both lifeboats got away safely and maintained their distance from the stationary vessel, which they fully expected to erupt in a shattering explosion. However, after the U-boat submerged there followed a period of unexpected inactivity. *Blairbeg* remained afloat with no attack forthcoming, and after four hours waiting in the lifeboats Captain Sinclair took his crew back on board to resume the homeward passage. Once they were under way, destroyers, which had come from the scene of the *Athenia* rescue, arrived and searched the area. The presence of the warships convinced the U-boat commander that any further attacks were an unnecessary risk and so he retired from the area. This was the first attack of the war for Oberleutnant zur See Johannes Franz and the crew of U-27. Their wartime career was to be short and, despite the great expectations of the crew, they would meet with only minor success during the first weeks of the war.

U-27 had departed Wilhelmshaven on 23 August and had

taken up position in its allotted operational area prior to the commencement of hostilities against Britain. The young crew were naturally excited at the thought of going into action and finally getting to test their mettle. Their first combat initiation, against *Blairbeg*, was a disaster. After firing the warning shot, Franz had submerged for a torpedo attack. However, the torpedo missed, and while Franz vacillated about what to do next, the arrival of Royal Navy destroyers ruled out further offensive action. For the next week a combination of bad weather and sightings of only neutral shipping prevented U-27 from engaging with the enemy. Its only success was on 13 September when the British trawler *Davara* was stopped and sunk by gunfire. By this time both fuel and fresh provisions were in short supply. While inspecting the paperwork of a stopped neutral Danish ship on the evening of 14 September, the boarding party took the opportunity to requisition some fresh meat. The following day there was further disappointment with another neutral ship stopped and a distant sighting that remained too far away to pursue given their limited remaining fuel.

The crew were called to action stations on 16 September after a destroyer was sighted. U-27 managed to dive and evade the destroyer, although some anxious moments passed before Franz considered it safe to resurface. It wasn't long after surfacing that the lookouts on the conning tower sighted another vessel. It was a trawler and, however benign the fishing vessel may have appeared, Franz nevertheless took the precaution of approaching submerged before surfacing close by and firing a warning shot. He ordered the crew of the trawler to abandon ship by using flag signals, while at the same time a German boarding party readied themselves. The trawler was the *Rudyard Kipling* from Fleetwood, and the skipper, along with the twelve other crew, were soon rowing towards the waiting Germans. While the majority of the British fishermen were taken onto the deck of the U-boat, two crew remained in the lifeboat and helped row the five-strong boarding party over to the trawler. Demolition charges were placed, while other sailors foraged for provisions. Among the stores liberated from *Rudyard Kipling* were tea, bread and butter, while two boxes of fresh fish were taken from the hold. One forgotten member of the British crew was also retrieved by a considerate sailor: the trawler's cat had been forgotten in the scramble for the boat.

Rudyard Kipling was obliterated as the demolition charges tore the small wooden-hulled boat apart. With the crew of thirteen still on deck, Franz had the lifeboat taken in tow and steered east towards the Donegal coast. It was less than 100 miles to the coast and Franz took the decision to alight the British fishermen sufficiently near to land in their own boat. The only stipulation was that they would have to remain on the exposed open deck for the short journey. The Germans provided coats for their hitchhiking guests and, when Franz saw that they were short one coat, he surrendered his own for use by the fishermen. Later, hot soup, tea and a tot of rum came up from the galley, which helped warm the men standing on deck. It must surely have been a strange and perplexing experience for the men from Fleetwood, who found themselves enjoying the late evening twilight while standing on the deck of an enemy submarine. A second tot of rum, issued two hours after the first, was graciously accepted and further buoyed their spirits with a sense of cordiality being shared between the two crews. Early the following morning Franz stopped just 5 miles west of Rathlin O'Birne lighthouse. The towed lifeboat was hauled in and bailed out, then the thankful fishermen handed back their loaned coats and said farewell to the considerate Germans.

Franz and his crew were to enjoy no further successes and their luck was slowly running out. On 17 September a torpedo which had been fired at a steamer exploded prematurely, causing damage to the U-boat. Finally Franz was forced to return to Germany as fuel was running low.

In the early hours of 20 September, a large enemy force of warships was sighted, and the eager German commander sought to capitalise on the poor return he had thus far accrued. He was thwarted yet again by torpedo failures and registered no hits on any of the warships targeted. In the counter-attack that ensued the escorting destroyers seriously damaged the U-boat and Franz was forced to surface, where his crew abandoned ship.[1]

After the lifeboat from *Rudyard Kipling* had left U-27, the crew steered towards the lighthouse on Rathlin O'Birne Island. It was a comfortable enough journey and, as daylight revealed the mainland, they adjusted their course to approach the nearest headland. A narrow isthmus of rock covered with a rich green felt of Donegal pasture hid from view the secluded Silver Strand of Malinbeg. It was an ideal site to beach their lifeboat and just after nine in the morning thirteen fishermen and a lucky cat came ashore on the strand. So it was that while the crew from *Cheyenne* enjoyed the hospitality of the people of Baltimore, the crew of *Rudyard Kipling* were being welcomed into the homes of the villagers of Malinbeg. The fishermen were later transported to Killybegs and on to Londonderry.

The previous three days had seen some remarkable incidents at sea. In the South-West Approaches there were the rescue efforts of the U-boat commanders who sank *British Influence* and *Cheyenne*. It could be said that these efforts were surpassed by the actions of Johannes Franz on behalf of the crew of *Rudyard Kipling*. However, as the first month of the war concluded and the days grew shorter, another extraordinary arrival along Ireland's coast would eclipse even those memorable events.

Two days after *Rudyard Kipling* was sunk, trawlers from Fleetwood were busy along the edge of the continental shelf. West of the Outer Hebrides a group of trawlers were caught by U-35, which was en route to its designated patrol zone. In command was Kapitänleutnant Werner Lott, who had already completed a very brief war patrol in the Baltic Sea. Lott was recalled and U-35 was prepared for operations in the Atlantic. The encounter with the Fleetwood trawlers began when the trawler *St Alvis* was encountered just after midday on 18 September. Lott's intention had been to sink the trawler once the British crew had boarded their lifeboat. However, he observed that the lifeboat was too small to hold the entire crew. His resolve was also swayed when he saw that some of the British fishermen were only young boys. Wary of their chances of safely reaching land once adrift in the tiny survival craft, Lott decided against sinking *St Alvis* on the condition that they throw their radio set overboard. The fishermen acquiesced and Lott left them to continue their work. Just over five hours later, a group of three trawlers was encountered, which presented Lott with yet another dilemma. He had initially thought of towing the lifeboats towards land with the crews on board his U-boat, but discounted the idea as the total number of fishermen was almost forty. Finally a novel solution was found: Lott would sink two of the trawlers and the third could act as a rescue ship. *Arlita* and *Lord*

Minto were sunk, which left *Nancy Hague* to take the two other crews home. The approach taken by Lott in both circumstances indicated the high moral and ethical importance he placed on adhering to the German Prize Regulations.

The patrol area assigned to U-35 covered the western entrance to the English Channel. Lott reached his assigned search area on 21 September and found that it was a busy sea lane, with heavy coastal traffic, both military and commercial. RAF activity forced Lott to stay submerged for most of the daylight hours. The high concentration of British air and sea activity precluded any action in accordance with the Prize Regulations. Having conducted his reconnaissance of the area and reported back to BdU, U-35 moved to a new patrol line further west at the beginning of October.

Free from the constraints imposed by the English Channel, Lott found success when he encountered the Belgian steamer *Suzon* on the afternoon of his arrival west of Ushant. After examining the ship's paperwork, it was found that the neutral ship was carrying a contraband cargo from Bordeaux to Cardiff. After their ship sank, the crew were left to make their way towards the French coast, just 40 miles to the south.

On 2 October the U-boat was continually hampered by both the presence of British aircraft and a steadily increasing wind. The weather continued to deteriorate, and at midnight on 3 October U-35 was heading west while running ahead of a north-easterly gale. The narrow seas heaped up to produce high unsettled waves that threw about the cylindrical hull of the U-boat. Visibility, however, remained good and as dawn broke the lookouts had an unobstructed view of the horizon. The seascape that surrounded them was a torrent of towering waves shrouded in sea foam and blinding salt spray. It was a tiring experience for the men as they were tossed violently about. But despite the weather conditions Lott continued on the surface, hopeful that his lookouts would sight a prospective target.

His confidence in the lookouts was rewarded when a steamer was sighted off the port bow and, despite the adverse conditions, Lott decided to proceed with an attack. U-35 submerged and plotted an intercept course for the approaching steamer. As Lott neared, he could see that it wore Greek neutral markings (Greece didn't enter the war until October 1940), which prompted a change in procedure. As the weather prevented the use of small boats to transfer persons for the inspection of paperwork, Lott decided to escort the steamer towards the south-west coast of Ireland. From a sheltered location along the coast, the Germans could then conduct their inspection as per the Prize Regulations. It was an admirable plan that respected the rights of the ship under the terms of the Prize Regulations, provided the Greek crew were willing to comply with such a request.

U-35 surfaced close to the surprised steamer and immediately signalled the Greek ship to stop and not to use its radio. The steamer quickly complied and identified itself via international call signs as *Diamantis*. With the first phase of the procedure accomplished, Lott then ordered *Diamantis* to follow. It was at this juncture that doubts about the underlying intentions of the German commander must have crept into the mind of the Greek captain. Lott himself was suspicious of *Diamantis* as the neutral cargo ship was clearly heavily laden and was heading north from a position that could only indicate a destination in either the Bristol Channel or the Irish Sea. Unwilling to relent and let the stubborn steamer go on account of the weather, the U-boat circled the ship, repeating the signal to follow. However, *Diamantis* remained immobile. The lack of compliance began to test Lott's patience. In an attempt to coerce the Greek captain, the deck gun for U-35 was called to action stations. On board *Diamantis* this overt sign of impending aggression resulted in panic spreading through the crew, who were soon lowering the lifeboats. Lott's attempt to convince the Greek crew to follow him had been misconstrued, with potentially serious consequences for the abandoning crew. Signals from the conning tower instructing the Greek crew not to abandon ship went unheeded and Lott watched as lifeboats were lowered away from both sides.

Events soon escalated as Lott's carefully conceived plan completely unravelled. Lookouts reported that one lifeboat from *Diamantis* had capsized and thrown its occupants into the sea. Then a shouted report came up the conning tower confirming that a distress message originating from *Diamantis* was being transmitted. The rules of the scenario had completely changed with the Greeks' use of their radio. In doing so they had forfeited their non-combat status regardless of whatever neutral markings were displayed, and Lott was therefore no longer obliged to render any assistance or to give prior warning of any possible aggressive action.

The German commander was incensed by the actions of the Greek crew, who had not only endangered themselves but also the Germans, who could now expect the arrival of a Coastal Command aircraft at any moment. Yet Lott was not prepared to leave the stranded Greek seamen in the water. With the gun crew still tethered by their safety harnesses on deck, Lott manoeuvred the boat through the difficult seas towards the men in the water. The fearless deck crew ran through the waves that swept the exposed deck, unhooking their harnesses to reach out and grab the exhausted seamen. Then it was the turn of the men in the lifeboat to be hauled on board. It was a difficult and dangerous rescue effort, but it was successfully completed in good time and without anyone left behind. As the last of the Greek seamen was being directed down through the conning tower, a sighting report was shouted out and the expected RAF aircraft was seen lumbering across the sky. The German sailors were soon below and U-35 gradually slipped beneath the waves. In addition to the forty-three Germans on board, Lott found himself in the company of twenty-eight very wet and frightened Greek merchant seamen.

The extra weight displaced throughout the U-boat made it difficult to control the depth, but Chief Engineer Stamer was able to quickly correct the trim and maintain the boat at periscope depth. Meanwhile, Lott, who was still irked by the hasty evacuation of the steamer, confronted Captain Pateras of *Diamantis*, seeking an explanation. The apologetic Greek captain told Lott that his crew had panicked and, without listening to his calls to remain on board, had lowered the lifeboats and abandoned ship. The matter was dropped, and Lott turned to examining the ship's paperwork, which Captain Pateras had brought with him. As suspected, the ship was carrying a contraband cargo, 7,700 tons of manganese ore which was to be discharged at the Irish Sea port of Barrow. Orders echoed through the control room as preparations were made to torpedo *Diamantis*. The difficult sea conditions doubtless interfered with the torpedo depth control and mechanisms and the first two torpedoes detonated prematurely. Lott watched as the third torpedo broke the surface but managed to run straight and strike the target. *Diamantis* sank slowly by the stern, its former crew comparatively safe inside the U-boat.

In the overcrowded living quarters the Greek guests were invited to dry their clothes and to avail of their hosts' bunks. Although initially unsure as to what they could expect while on board the U-boat, the Greeks soon warmed to the hospitality. Having taken responsibility for the safety of the Greek seamen, Lott had to decide where he could land the survivors without endangering their lives and those of his own crew.

Given that it was still daylight and there was a Coastal Command aircraft in the vicinity, U-35 remained submerged until the cover of darkness allowed it to surface and its diesel engines grumbled back into life. Seeking a quiet stretch of coast where the British enemy was unlikely to surprise his boat, Lott ordered a course set towards the south-west coast of Ireland. His initial intention was to proceed towards the Dingle Bay region, there to find a safe landing spot. However, if a suitable merchant ship or fishing boat was encountered, then the Greek seamen would be transferred into their custody.

They had not been long on the surface when radio messages about the loss of *Diamantis* were broadcast. A Hungarian steamer had found the capsized lifeboat and, with no crew sighted in the water, the airwaves were buzzing with lively chatter. Concerned about false information spreading about his conduct, Lott sent a radio message to BdU informing them of his actions. Whatever happened over the next twenty-four hours, the prudent commander had at the very least ensured that the conduct of his crew would not become blemished by accusations of any wrong-doing.

Throughout the night the gale-force winds continued unabated. The violent movements of the U-boat in the stormy seaway came as a surprise to the Greeks, but by morning there was some respite as the wind decreased and the boat gradually came under the shelter of the Irish coast. Lott had decided that he would land the Greek crew at a secluded inlet on the southern shores of the Dingle Peninsula. Ventry Harbour was well protected on three sides, and the depth of water allowed the U-boat to approach very close inshore. U-35 sailed past the majestic stony outcrops of the Skelligs, unseen by the majority of the men who were wedged in tight to each other. The jagged prehistoric landmarks guided the Germans across the entrance of Dingle Bay. The U-boat slowed as it neared the entrance to Ventry Harbour and rounded the rocks of Parkmore Point into the sheltered haven. Kapitänleutnant Lott and his crew had arrived in Ireland.

It was going to take some time to land all twenty-eight rescued seamen. The large lifeboats from *Diamantis* had been left behind, and all that was available to ferry the men ashore was a small rubber dinghy from the U-boat. The departing Greeks were mustered on deck while the dinghy was prepared. Lott steered the boat as close to the shore as possible, then, with one German sailor and two Greek passengers, the dinghy headed towards the shoreline. It would take another thirteen journeys back and forth before the transfer was complete. As the Greeks came up through the conning tower to wait their turn on deck, they thanked the German commander who had saved their lives. The sincerity of their gratitude and the heartfelt farewell overwhelmed Lott, who did not seek the high regard the rescued men had for him.

The number of Greek sailors standing on the empty beach

steadily grew. While they surveyed the area as if marooned on some remote desert island beach, bewildered locals lined the cliffs above and watched in amazement. As the last pair prepared to leave, Captain Pateras said his farewell to Werner Lott. Both men were deeply respectful of the other's position. Pateras took with him all the ship's paperwork from *Diamantis*. While some commanders preferred to keep these documents as proof of what ship they had sunk or as personal mementos, Lott did not care for such things. With all the Greeks safely ashore, U-35 slowly manoeuvred astern before turning and heading back out into Dingle Bay. The Greek sailors and the Irish onlookers exchanged waves with the German sailors. Lott observed from the conning tower as the local residents went down to greet the strangers standing on the shore. U-35 left the Irish coast and started on the journey back to Germany, leaving behind not just a wholly thankful crew but also the possibility of an embarrassing diplomatic exchange between Ireland and Britain.

Captain Pateras and his crew were soon joined by several Irish locals. While none of the Greek seamen spoke much English, some basic words and plenty of articulate gesturing sufficed for both nationalities to understand each other. Initially all twenty-eight were taken to the houses of the residents at Ballymore. Later, transport and accommodation in Dingle were arranged, where they stayed the night. Five men were held at the hospital for observation overnight. On the morning of 5 October, as the rested survivors prepared to make the journey from Dingle to Tralee, where they would catch the train for Dublin, the national newspapers in Ireland and England were describing the dramatic events that had occurred over the previous forty-eight hours. The stories were all based on the facts as released by the Irish authorities the previous night and on later interviews given by the Greek crew and eyewitnesses at Ventry. The story would also be published in American newspapers. For many civilians it was the rescue on that desperate night and the kind treatment the Greeks enjoyed while on board U-35 that captured their imaginations. Here was a shining example of humanity at a time when the world was ready to descend into crisis. The story was so appealing that the American magazine *Life* would run it with a picture of U-35 on the front page of its 16 October edition.

While accolades may have been bestowed upon Lott by the international media for his noble deed, behind the scenes the political fallout put the Irish government under increasing pressure. This breach of Irish territorial waters came just weeks after the announcement by the British authorities that a German sailor captured from a U-boat had in his possession cigarettes made in Ireland.[2] Naturally the Irish government was quick to refute any suggestions that German U-boats were landing in Ireland or using Irish harbours as bases. However, the incident planted the first seeds of suspicion for the British. The arrival of U-35 in Ventry on 4 October and subsequent rumours of the German commander's alleged acquaintances ashore did not help an already strained diplomatic relationship.[3] From the British viewpoint this incident further challenged Ireland's impartial neutrality and increased doubts as to the true extent of U-boat activity around Ireland's west coast.

Regardless of what the political institutions had to say, the episode was unique in the story of survivors landing in Ireland during the war. It was the only time that a belligerent warship landed seamen on the shores of this neutral state and it was all the more exceptional given the relationship between the rescued crew and U-35. Of the landings that occurred throughout the war, few are remembered so fondly and with such great reverence.

4

ARLINGTON COURT

After the loss of *Diamantis* in early October there was a temporary lull in U-boat activity in the South-West Approaches. The small number of U-boats operational at the start of the war meant that it was always going to be difficult for Admiral Dönitz to maintain a sufficient presence at sea. However, a wave of new U-boats would be ready to sail by mid-October. They were to operate together against the British convoys that were giving an added measure of defence to merchant shipping.

While there remained plenty of independently routed shipping in the Approaches, Dönitz knew that dispersing the U-boats to locate and then sink these lone ships was not an efficient use of limited resources. A concentrated pack of coordinated U-boats would improve their chances of destroying whole convoys. By mid-October, U-boats were once again departing Germany for the South-West Approaches, although a failure to locate enemy convoys and the inability to concentrate sufficient forces on sighting reports hindered any real chance of large-scale successes for this first pack operation.

The Royal Navy provided escorts to defend the fledgling convoys and allocated a level of protection commensurate with

the convoy route and the anticipated threat. At the beginning
of the war, outbound convoys from Liverpool and the Thames
were escorted as far as their dispersal point, which was selected
on the basis of how far west into the Atlantic the U-boat threat
extended. The shorter convoy route between Britain and Gibraltar
was considered especially at risk due to the continuing presence
of enemy submarine activity, so outward and homeward convoys
were allotted an escort for the duration of the voyage. For the long
ocean-passage convoys that departed from Halifax, Nova Scotia,
and Freetown, West Africa, an AMC was the usual ocean escort.
The SL series of convoys that departed from Freetown had the
furthest to travel of all the commercial Atlantic convoys. The
remote location of the assembly port and the limited range of
the early U-boat campaigns precluded any significant attacks on
these homeward convoys. However, poor conditions at Freetown
and the long voyage north took their toll on many ships which
could not then keep up with the main convoy.[1] Those unable to
maintain contact ended up falling astern and were left without
protection. Many of these stragglers would fall foul of U-boats or,
later, prowling FW200 aircraft, which cast a long shadow from
the skies around the Irish coast. Over thirty such strays from SL
convoys were sunk over the course of the war at sea. Survivors
from ten of these ships landed along the Irish coast.

On 14 September 1939, the first SL-series convoy sailed from
Freetown for the UK. When the route was announced, merchant
ships which had recently loaded at ports in the south Atlantic and
in the Indian Ocean were directed towards the West African port
of Freetown to wait for the next convoy sailing north. Many of the
ships were involved in the vital work of bringing South American

grain back to Britain – an important cargo and one that was to become progressively more so as the war continued.

Captain Charles Hurst had left the Bristol Channel in July when war was still not a certainty. Over the next two months the redefined political landscape of Europe had altered mercantile trade across the globe. After loading a full cargo of maize along the river ports of the Río de la Plata, *Arlington Court* proceeded to Freetown to await a convoy bound for home. Once through the boom defences Captain Hurst anchored among the growing number of ships that arrived daily at the tiny West African port.

The rudimentary facilities at Freetown had been overwhelmed and naval personnel drafted to the developing port found that there was very little infrastructure to service the increasing merchant and naval traffic. Fresh water, a basic necessity, had to be provided from limited onshore supplies while the local authorities waited for ships with fresh-water distilling facilities to arrive and ease the shortage. Similarly, stockpiles of coal dwindled as the ever-increasing demand emptied the coal wharves, leaving some ships having to wait for the next collier to arrive before they could start the journey home. Harbour facilities were equally unfit for the surge in traffic that followed the declaration of war, and limited numbers of small boats, lighters and tugs meant that the naval authority had to requisition local boats to help with daily harbour duties.[2]

The time spent waiting at anchor at Freetown was not an enjoyable one for the crew of *Arlington Court*. They were unfortunate to catch the end of the Sierra Leone rainy season. Heavy showers and hot humid days and nights created an uncomfortable atmosphere on board. Mosquitoes were prevalent, spreading dreaded malaria when they fed on the unsuspecting sailors. Conditions must have been hellish for those who worked in the engine room. Finally, Captain Hurst was called ashore for the captains' conference about the forthcoming convoy. The merchant captains were briefed and the importance of maintaining the designated speed of 9 knots was impressed upon them.[3]

At sunrise on the morning of 31 October 1939, the ships of convoy SL-7A weighed anchor and steamed out of the inhospitable Freetown. Shepherding the twenty-seven ships on the voyage was the AMC HMS *Montclare*. If the departure from Freetown marked an upturn in the mood of *Arlington Court*'s crew, it was only a temporary reprieve. Symptoms of the fever synonymous with the coastal region of Sierra Leone had begun to strike down the crew before the ship had left port. Affected crew members became delirious as malaria ravaged their bodies and rendered them incapable of performing their duties. This included a disproportionate number of firemen and trimmers who were now incapable of working below. That first morning at sea was a confused scramble: the convoy was badly spread out and ships found it difficult to achieve the required speed. As an emergency measure, several deck ratings on board *Arlington Court* were charged with stoking the boilers. However, with so many men immobile the boilers were not properly tended and the ship began to lose speed. Soon the horizon became an empty void where the convoy had been.

Less than a week into the voyage Captain Hurst had to confront an unwanted reality: his ship was not going to catch up with the convoy and he would be on his own for the rest of the journey to Britain. He read through the confidential Admiralty instructions received at Freetown, which detailed courses and rendezvous positions that applied in this particular set of circumstances, and *Arlington Court* began to steer its own independent zigzag course while the radio officers maintained a listening watch for any further instructions.

By the beginning of November Admiral Dönitz was ready to attempt another pack operation, and several U-boats departed Wilhelmshaven for the South-West Approaches. For Kapitän-leutnant Wilhelm Ambrosius, in command of the large type-IX U-boat U-43, this was to be his first wartime patrol. Ambrosius entered the North Sea on 6 November and headed for the Shet-lands. Two more U-boats followed him on his route around the British Isles, their commanders having been ordered to assemble south of Ireland for pack operations.[4] The weather was poor for the transit across the North Sea. However, this was to the advantage of the U-boat commanders who could run for longer on the surface while the poor visibility and tempestuous waves kept their boats hidden from the British.

On 10 November Ambrosius sighted a lone merchant ship west of the Orkney Islands and decided to attack. After three unsuccessful attempts with torpedoes, he broke off and, unwilling to expend any more torpedoes, let the unidentified ship steam away. It was a frustrating start to his first patrol.

Late in the evening of 13 November, U-43 reached its intended operational area, but the weather soon deteriorated and strong gale-force winds with intermittent poor visibility restricted the U-boat's effectiveness. There was more disappointment the following morning when another attack on a sighted steamer missed its target. It was doubtless the high seas that affected the running of the torpedoes. Concerned that the continuing winter gales might hinder the proposed pack operations, BdU ordered U-43 to proceed to a position closer to Cape Finisterre. Ambrosius headed south, where it was hoped that more favourable conditions would finally bring the crew their first successful attack. They did not have to wait too long before a lone merchant ship presented itself.

The early onset of an Atlantic winter brought the first storms to the South-West Approaches. The weather had deteriorated over the previous twenty-four hours, and a stubborn south-westerly wind churned over the sea in near gale conditions. The rough seas afforded some protection, reducing the horizontal visibility and obscuring the lonely *Arlington Court* from any unwanted attention. Captain Hurst had succeeded in getting his ship to within two days' steaming from the south coast of England, and he held some hope that they might escape the attentions of the patrolling U-boats. On the afternoon of 16 November, Hurst was handed a radio message by Radio Officer Hatfield for decoding. He went to his cabin with the message while Hatfield remained on the bridge to talk to Second Officer Claude Boothby. No sooner had they finished their conversation than there was a terrific explosion as a torpedo slammed into the port side of the ship. The force smashed the hatch covers on No. 2 hold, transforming the wood into a deadly shower of splinters. The covered end of the port bridge wing, which extended out to the ship's side, was completely torn away, and Boothby and Hatfield were lucky to escape serious injury. The radio room, which was located behind the bridge on the port side, was wrecked and the equipment completely destroyed. Captain Hurst had been sitting in his cabin ready to decode the message when the explosion threw him against a bulkhead. As he lay semi-conscious and incapable of making sense of what had happened, the remainder of the crew scrambled towards the lifeboats.

Thomas Rice had been working by the coal bunkers when he was knocked off his feet by the impact and plunged into total darkness. Choking coal dust filled the air. With some difficulty, Rice, along with two Maltese firemen, made it to the upper deck and went to their lifeboat stations.

From the poop deck Thomas Cahill saw the explosion and watched in amazement as the cargo of grain came streaming out of the hole in No. 2 hold. Startled into action, Cahill ran forward to alert the off-duty crew in the forecastle, only to be stopped in his tracks by the same crew running aft as they came back to prepare the lifeboats. Both deck boys, Malcolm Morrison and Kirian Corcoran, were asleep at the time of the attack. The young cadets quickly dressed and escaped their quarters. Second Engineer John McKissock ran down to the engine room to ensure that the main engines had stopped before any attempt was made to launch the lifeboats. Then he mustered the engine-room staff and led them on deck.

When Captain Hurst regained his senses, he made his way on deck, where the majority of the crew was already congregated, and ordered them to lower the lifeboats. By now the ship had taken a heavy list to starboard and was rolling heavily. Large waves breaking against the exposed weather side made the launching of the lifeboats a dangerous business. Twenty-three men, including Captain Hurst and Second Officer Boothby, made ready the starboard lifeboat. This was the lee side, and it should have been comparatively easy to lower this one. However, it crashed against the ship's side several times, damaging not only it but also injuring Captain Hurst in the chest. Once waterborne, its crew tried to pull away from the foundering ship. This proved to be extremely difficult as, being on the lee side, the ship was bearing down on them. It was only through the greatest of efforts that Hurst and his men managed to push far enough off to be able to start rowing and to get clear of the ship.

Preparing the port lifeboat was an especially onerous task as this was the weather side. The lifeboat was lowered unevenly, and the aft section became waterborne prematurely. It was immediately enveloped by a hostile incoming wave that swamped it, leaving it hanging limp on the forward falls and full of seawater up to the level of the thwarts. The lifeboat crew feared they might lose the craft, and in desperation they jumped in. There was a struggle to release the forward falls and to clear the half-submerged lifeboat away from the ship. *Arlington Court* was soon drifting away at a faster rate than the lumbering lifeboat. The soaked men inside found themselves standing up to waist height in water and began to bail out.

Ambrosius kept U-43 submerged as he watched the crew of the stricken steamer abandon ship through his periscope. Although the ship had appeared to settle deeper in the water, there were no obvious signs that it was about to sink. He had sighted the steamer in the morning and had carefully observed as it approached that it displayed neither a ship's name, a national flag nor any painted markings that would identify it as belonging to a neutral country. Satisfied that the sighted ship was a legitimate target, Ambrosius had manoeuvred U-43 into an optimum firing position. Once submerged, he had surveyed his target through the periscope and had then methodically proceeded through the firing sequence. The U-boat crew listened as the single torpedo was sent hurtling through the water. Every head was cocked slightly upwards in anticipation of the detonation that had failed to materialise on the previous two occasions. Then an unmistakable eruption reverberated throughout U-43, heralding their first success.

Now Ambrosius decided to hasten the fate of the cargo ship, and, about ten minutes after both lifeboats had been launched, a *coup de grâce* hit *Arlington Court* forward. Within minutes the ship had disappeared from view. U-43 remained submerged and departed the scene without surfacing to question the survivors.

The port and starboard lifeboats drifted apart quickly as each contended with its own difficulties.[5] In the starboard lifeboat Captain Hurst and his men had to bail continuously. Every time a wave surged past, it broke against the lifeboat's gunwales, drenching those inside and filling the boat. Those not bailing tried to minimise the effects of the high seas by keeping the lifeboat's head to wind. During the afternoon the sea anchor was streamed and the lifeboat performed better as it contended with the waves head on. There were some glimpses of the port lifeboat, but, as darkness fell, it disappeared from sight and contact with this boat was never regained.[6]

That first night seemed endless as sea spray and freezing rain swept through the lifeboat. In an effort to retain some warmth, the group huddled together and sheltered under a canvas boat cover. Despite being soaked through, the lifeboat's blankets brought some comfort to the shivering seamen. The following day, after a cold sleepless night, Hurst ordered his men to haul in the sea anchor. As the wind remained too strong to allow the sail to be hoisted safely, the men began rowing. Although physically demanding, this did have the effect of warming them up. The bailing out continued – because of the damage which had been sustained and the sea spray there was always some water to be removed. Later on the wind eased and Hurst decided to hoist the sail and steer a course for Land's End.

There was no escape from the incessant sea spray blowing off the high waves onto the men, some of whom had only the most basic clothing on and who were therefore too sparsely dressed for the conditions in which they found themselves. Hurst had one of the thwarts broken up and, by tearing up the canvas boat cover, they managed to jury-rig a dodger which was fixed to the weather side and that helped to deflect the wind. Food and water were issued and, although the lifeboat was amply stocked, they limited themselves to one dipper of water, one biscuit, some condensed milk and a little tinned meat, to be issued three times a day.

During the second night they streamed the sea anchor and covered themselves with the large canvas boat cover again, although sleep was difficult as they had to continue with the bailing. The weather improved considerably on the third day, which made sailing the lifeboat much easier. However, the terrible conditions they had endured over the previous days had taken their toll. Chief Engineer Pearson, who had been in a poor state since that first night in the lifeboat, had deteriorated considerably over the past twenty-four hours. On Sunday morning, 19 November, Pearson died and was buried at sea. Several others among the survivors looked like they might also succumb to exposure and Hurst feared that unless they were rescued soon he would be burying more of his men in the coming days.

Early on the morning of 20 November, the men in the lifeboat sighted the unmistakable outline of a ship on their starboard beam. A distress flare was lit but there was no response. A second flare also failed to get a reaction from the unknown steamer. Finally, on the third try, the flare was sighted and the ship altered its course. Rescue was at last within reach of the twenty-two survivors.

When the Dutch steamer *Algenib* drew alongside, lifelines were lowered. After being hauled on board by the Dutch seamen, the survivors found it difficult to walk as their legs and feet were swollen from being immersed in icy seawater. The hospitality of the Dutch crew was unsurpassed as they provided hot soup, hot coffee, sandwiches and a change of clothing for every man. They provided each survivor with a bunk, but most found it difficult to sleep. They ached all over from their ordeal and the pain prevented them from taking the rest they deserved. Captain Hurst had managed to sail the lifeboat 170 miles before being picked up by *Algenib*. It was a tribute to his navigating skills and to each man's endurance that they had sailed so far under such difficult conditions.

The Dutch captain decided that it would be prudent to land the rescued men at the nearest convenient port, which was neutral Cork. At Cobh, preparations to receive the survivors began shortly after a radio message from *Algenib* was received, advising that it was en route to Cork Harbour. The local shipping agent secured the full services of the army's medical ambulances and medical staff from Collins Barracks were ready to meet the survivors. In addition, the steam launch *Wyndham*, which was used by the military at Cobh, was made available to transfer the survivors from *Algenib* to dry land. Meanwhile, the South Infirmary readied two wards. The hospital was practically full on the Monday morning, but when news came that they would have an additional twenty-two charges later that evening, they did some quick rearranging. Patients were moved to other parts of the hospital, and those convalescents who were fit to return home were discharged. Once some additional beds had been installed in the wards the hospital was ready.

That night a large crowd gathered in Cobh to await the arrival of the survivors. *Wyndham* proceeded out to the Dutch ship, which was anchored off Roches Point, with a medical team. It wasn't long before the first survivor was making his way down the ladder, still wearing the clothes that his Dutch rescuers had given him. Once on shore, the men were helped to the waiting fleet of ambulances and motor cars. The majority were transferred to the South Infirmary, although Captain Hurst, Second Officer Boothby and Second Engineer McKissock all spent the night at the European Hotel in Cobh. The recovery of the men went very well and by the end of the week almost half the survivors were ready to start the final leg of their journey. On Thursday 23 November, Captain Hurst, accompanied by ten others, left Cork by train for Rosslare. Thomas Cahill was also discharged from the South Infirmary on the Thursday, but he would stay on in Cork with his sisters until Saturday and then make his way back to his home town of Cardiff. The remaining ten men were kept under observation in hospital until the Saturday and then followed the same route home.

The landing and subsequent treatment of the men from *Arlington Court* was testament to the quick response and organisational proficiency of everyone involved. The staff of the South Infirmary was able to secure the required bed spaces for the expected survivors and to ensure that the full medical staff was available to treat the men. The Irish Red Cross provided them with such comforts as clothing, toiletries and tobacco, and the Shipwrecked Mariners' Society provided railway warrants for the journey home to Cardiff. It was a tribute to all of them that every man who landed at Cork made a full recovery and was safely repatriated.

5

A Bad Winter for Neutrals

The beginning of 1940 was relatively quiet in the Atlantic. Another unintentional lull in U-boat activity had been forced upon the Germans, due to returning boats needing lengthy refits to repair defective machinery. In addition, the unusually cold winter and the ice conditions that prevailed around the waters of the Baltic and North Sea ports delayed the sailing of those U-boats that were ready to depart. As a result, there were only a few operational at sea. Of these, one would return with engine problems and the other two were involved in mine-laying operations at UK ports.[1]

As the first weeks of January passed there was a steady departure of U-boats for their intended operational areas in the Western Approaches and off the north-west coast of Spain and Portugal. Shipping losses inevitably escalated as the U-boats made their presence felt. Among the losses for the month of January there was a high percentage of neutral shipping. Sailing independently, these ships were particularly vulnerable when they approached or transited the UK's coastal waters.[2] The German response to the British Contraband Control, which allowed all ships to be taken to designated ports to be searched and cargo deemed to be contraband to be confiscated, as well as sanctioning the blockade of

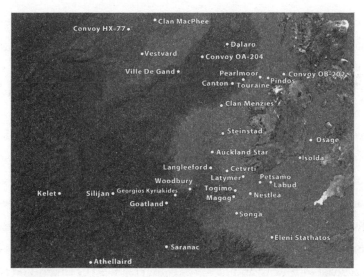

Position of ships sunk in 1940 whose survivors landed in Ireland

the North Sea, had been to impose further restrictions to the Prize Regulations. Any ship that was stopped and found to contravene these regulations was liable to be sunk or taken as a prize.

On 11 January Kapitänleutnant Wilhelm Rollmann sailed U-34 from Wilhelmshaven for a mine-laying operation off Falmouth. A couple of days later, Kapitänleutnant Victor Schütze departed in U-25. The contrast in the fortunes of these two boats explains the sense of urgency the latter demonstrated when he finally returned to sea on 13 January. Rollmann had been at sea when war was declared and he had accumulated a respectable tally of ships to his name.[3] Schütze, however, had a slightly delayed start to his war and did not sail on his first patrol until 18 October 1939, managing to account for only one ship before a mechanical failure forced his U-boat to return to base. His second patrol in December 1939 was abruptly cut short when an oil leak forced him to port again after only one day at sea. There were further delays before the leak was identified and repaired, which postponed his sailing until 13 January 1940.

Both boats headed north for the Shetlands and the entrance to their area of operations, which lay to the south and west. Schütze was first into action when he sank two ships in quick succession off the Shetlands on 17 January. The following day, as he continued south towards his designated patrol area, he sank another ship off North Rona Island. The eager crew of U-25 gorged themselves on every target that presented itself. When no other ships were found in the vicinity they continued south, heading towards the west coast of Ireland and onwards to an area west of Biscay and the Spanish and Portuguese coasts.

Entering the fray came the Norwegian steamer *Songa*, under the command of Captain Otto Lie. The ship was bound for Rotterdam from New York, with 4,000 tons of general cargo. The harsh winter weather persisted as the ship neared the Western Approaches. (The severity of the conditions was such that the sea had frozen over around Castletownbere Harbour in Co. Cork.)

The *Songa*'s crew could testify to the menace of the war at sea, as several had already experienced it at first hand. Chief Engineer Karl Boe and Second Officer Brynjulf Homnes had been on board another Norwegian ship, *Lorentz W. Hansen*, when it was stopped and sunk by the German surface raider *Deutschland*. The survivors were taken on board the warship, only to be transferred fourteen hours later to another Norwegian vessel.[4] As soon as they arrived home, both men were immediately thrust back into the maelstrom of the Atlantic shipping lanes.

Another crew member, Thomas Murray, was born in Preston to

Irish parents originally from Co. Kildare. He began his career in telegraphy at an early age, although initially on dry land. In 1904, he was teaching field telegraphy at the British army camp at the Curragh in Co. Kildare. During the First World War he found himself at sea, working as a wireless operator with the White Star Line. His career with the prestigious passenger-ship company was not without incident. While sailing on the troopship *Cymric* in May 1916, the ship was torpedoed and sunk – with minimal loss of life. Next, Murray joined the converted AMC *Laurentic*. In December 1916 it was on a special mission carrying gold ingots to Canada. After departing Lough Swilly on 25 January 1917, the ship hit two mines and quickly sank. On this occasion the loss of life was far greater, many of the deaths being attributed to exposure as the survivors fought against the wintry conditions of the north Atlantic.

Murray moved to the USA after the First World War and was hired by the federal government. His adventures continued as his proficiency in telegraphy was put to use tracking gun-runners and smugglers along the Mexican border. Times changed, however, and in 1939 he found himself in New York with little prospect of a job. With the outbreak of war in Europe and a shortage of wireless operators, Murray had found ample employment. As he later said, 'It is hard to live in New York when money is not coming in and radio operators are in very great demand on Norwegian boats.'[5] Now on board *Songa*, Murray was returning to the waters of the Western Approaches, near to where *Cymric* had met its fate twenty-three years before.

By 22 January the winter gale had abated and, with a moderate sea running and fair weather prevailing, the lone Norwegian vessel entered the Western Approaches on the final leg of its journey. Before entering Rotterdam, Captain Lie would be obliged to stop at the Contraband Control anchorage off Deal. This was part of the Navicert system imposed by the British government on shipping that intended to trade with certain countries, including Belgium and Holland. All ships were to be inspected to determine if the cargo might be contraband destined for Germany. These restrictions were unavoidable and, although not particularly onerous, added additional days to the voyage.

Around midday, those on the bridge heard the unfamiliar yet unmistakable sound of gunfire. A large splash ahead of the ship confirmed their fears and keen eyes scanned the horizon for the source of the hostile display. About 4 miles off the port bow, the silhouette of a submarine was sighted. Three further shots from the unknown assailant were more than enough for Captain Lie to stop his ship and order all the crew into the lifeboats. As the men hurriedly prepared the two boats, the unknown submarine slowly moved closer to *Songa* and stopped. Kapitänleutnant Schütze was waiting to interrogate the ship's crew before deciding whether to sink their ship, the fourth of this patrol.

With both lifeboats lowered to the water, the sailors rowed clear of the stationary ship and headed reluctantly for the waiting U-25. Schütze stood patiently in the conning tower as he observed the evacuation; once the lifeboats came alongside he questioned Lie regarding the voyage and the nature of the cargo, then made his assessment of the situation. Satisfied that the ship was a legitimate target, he informed Lie, 'We are going to torpedo you.'[6] By this period Schütze was empowered to sink *Songa* under the German Prize Regulations, because it was destined to pass through the

English Channel.[7] Lie responded by saying that his was a neutral ship and that they were carrying cargo for a neutral port (neither Norway nor the Netherlands were involved in the war at this point). His protestations were futile; Schütze simply replied that he would torpedo the ship anyway.

The lifeboats were ordered to stand clear and then, with one torpedo hit amidships, Songa broke in two and immediately began to sink. With Songa gone, the U-boat commander decided it would be prudent to depart from the scene. Before leaving the two lifeboats to their fate, Schütze offered a consolatory gesture of goodwill: each lifeboat was given a bottle of rum and told to steer an easterly course to the shipping lanes, where they could expect to be picked up.

They were alone and over 200 miles from land, but they had been lucky to have been allowed to depart their ship in good time, with no injuries to the crew. Both lifeboats were in good condition and amply stocked with rations and stores. Captain Lie and ten others manned one lifeboat, which was equipped with a motor. Chief Officer Erickson and the remaining twelve men manned the other. With the motor boat towing the second lifeboat, they set off east and, they hoped, towards safety, but the fairer weather continued only for the briefest time. After just twenty-four hours a strong gale began to blow hard, forcing the lifeboats to heave to and stream their sea anchors. The men sheltered under the canvas lifeboat covers, sitting tightly together as they tried to keep warm and dry. The lifeboats were constantly shipping water as they rode over each successive wave, the canvas covers never quite managing to keep out the sea and rain water. Wet through and shivering, their misfortune was only compounded by the events that followed.

During the early hours of the second night, the tow rope holding the two lifeboats together broke under the constant strain of increasingly high seas. The situation was exacerbated when the tail shaft on the motor was damaged, rendering it useless. There was nothing to do but wait until the weather moderated, then each boat would have to continue under sail.

With the arrival of daylight the weather improved, sea anchors were hauled aboard and both lifeboats set sail. Each boat would sail independently and make its own way towards the coast. It was not long before they lost sight of one another. Chief Officer Erickson, with the larger of the two lifeboat crews, sighted trawlers on two separate occasions. Each time a flare was lit but neither trawler spotted the flare and the men continued on. In an attempt to fortify their failing spirits, Second Engineer Johansen tried to play a few tunes on the mandolin he had somehow kept safe. Yet, despite his best intentions, even Johansen had to concede defeat as the biting cold wind forced him to stop playing.

On 26 January another trawler was sighted and this time they were picked up by *Loddon* and landed that same day at Kinsale Harbour.[8] A large crowd was there to meet them. Among those waiting were the Harbour Master, members of the Irish Red Cross and Mr Eamonn O'Neill, who was the Deputy Speaker for the Dáil. The men were quickly disembarked and taken to Murphy's Hotel. The majority, despite their ordeal, were fit enough to require only a hot bath and a good meal to revive their tired and cold bodies. Two seamen required treatment at Kinsale hospital, while a doctor treated another one at the hotel for a small injury. There had been no word of any other lifeboat landing, and Erickson and his men feared for the safety of their shipmates.

Captain Lie and his men had drifted slightly further west, and by the evening of 26 January they had sighted the Fastnet lighthouse, approximately 10 miles away. With this beacon of hope now within sight, Lie set a course, but the uncooperative weather increased in intensity again and the lifeboat had to spend one final night hove to. By morning, Lie found that the lifeboat had drifted further inshore, Fastnet was seaward and the coast was now only a short sailing distance away. The sails were set, and they steered a north-easterly course, which took them into Roaring Water Bay. The jagged coast that ran from Brow Head to Streak Head prevented any landing attempt on the nearest visible shore. Their progress was slow as the wind eased off due to the shelter afforded by the bay. Sailing further into the confines of the bay, Captain Lie was oblivious to the submerged rocks and the many dangers which were known to those seafarers familiar with the waters. As they passed Streak Head, a lighthouse came into view. Rock Island lighthouse had its own dedicated keeper and, with his keen eyesight, the keeper soon spotted the lifeboat under sail. He began to signal using semaphore. Lie and his men, who had been observing the lighthouse, quickly responded to his instructions. They changed heading and followed the guidance from the shore. Progress was slow due to the light wind, but the men took up the oars and, despite their aching limbs, rowed towards safety.

Once on shore Captain Lie and his men were taken to the lighthouse keeper's house. The local people of Goleen, Co. Cork, then opened their homes to the men from the sea. Each one was taken into a house and provided with hot food, dry clothing and a bed for the night. Third Engineer Karl Neilson was taken by car to Skibbereen hospital to be treated for exposure, but the rest of the crew were in remarkably good health, apart from swollen and stiff limbs. After a well-deserved night's sleep in Goleen, the men were taken to Skibbereen and then on to Cork.

On 28 January there was a joyous reunion in Cork as both lifeboat crews met for the first time since their enforced separation. There was relief for Captain Lie to discover that, despite the unfavourable weather conditions and the lengthy period spent in the lifeboats, none of his crew had died. Only three required hospital treatment because the crew had been given time to abandon ship, and Schütze's actions no doubt saved lives. Such admirable conduct was not uncommon during the early phase of the war, when adherence to the Prize Regulations still compelled U-boat commanders to stop and search neutral merchants.

As the crew of *Songa* departed Cork, on the morning of 28 January, another unlucky crew from a neutral-flagged ship were beginning their own tribulations. *Eleni Stathatos* was a typical Greek tramp ship built during the post-First World War boom in shipping. This stalwart of the tramping business had diligently plied its trade wherever the cargoes and profitable charter rates offered the best return. At the outbreak of the war it had been trading in the Pacific, but the demand for shipping and an increase in freight rates soon brought it back to more profitable European waters.

At the beginning of November 1939, the British government realised that there was an urgent requirement to charter shipping from neutral countries. Securing additional tonnage for the import and export of British materials would help to offset the delays caused by the introduction of the convoy system that were affecting the British war economy. Exploiting this sudden surge in shipping, Greek shipowners had sold or chartered many ships to England. This opportunistic shift in trade policy did not go unnoticed in Germany. With so many Greek ships now aiding their enemy, orders issued on 30 December 1939 decreed that all Greek ships were to be regarded as hostile when found within an area surrounding the UK. They could, therefore, be attacked without warning.

In November, *Eleni Stathatos* passed through the Panama Canal and then continued up to the Florida Keys where a grain cargo was loaded for the UK. Before making the voyage to Europe, the crew painted the Greek flag on both sides of the ship and spotlights were fitted so that the large painted flag would be clearly illuminated at night. An uneventful crossing of the Atlantic followed, with only the weather and the continuing pessimism of the wartime news casting gloomy shadows over their voyage. The cargo was destined for two ports in England. The first of these was Sheerness on the Isle of Sheppey, which meant that they would be obliged to transit the Western Approaches. As the cargo was to be delivered to a British port, being a neutral-flagged ship would not provide any protection if they were stopped by a U-boat. However, they were fortunate and made it through to their destination without incident. When the Sheerness discharge was completed, *Eleni Stathatos* sailed back down the English Channel to complete the discharge at Plymouth.

As they were nearing completion of their discharge, Captain Gratsos received his new orders. The charter rate on this last cargo must have been very good as the owners had instructed him to proceed back to the Florida Keys to load another cargo for the UK. This was a welcome return voyage back to the balmy southern

US state. However, with the recently imposed unrestricted areas now being enforced by the Germans, the waters around the UK were becoming increasingly perilous for all merchant vessels. *Eleni Stathatos* faced the same perils as the ships of any of the belligerent nations. Only a timely transit through the disputed zones and entry into the vast open Atlantic would reassure the crew that their ship was no longer in any danger. Prior to departure for Florida the old Greek steamer called at Newport docks to load coal into its empty bunker holds. Once fully supplied for the voyage Captain Gratsos prepared to take his ship back to sea.

At midnight on 28 January, *Eleni Stathatos* was about 90 miles south-west of Fastnet. The overcast sky blocked any light from the waning full moon that might have illuminated the ship. Darkness and anonymity were characteristics that Captain Gratsos happily accepted, as they were still in an area known to be patrolled by U-boats. The illusion of security provided by the darkness quickly vanished, when, at 0252 hrs, the dull thud of a torpedo impact caused the ship to shudder along its length.

The crew quickly mustered at their boat stations. Captain Gratsos stopped the engine and told the men to stand by to lower the lifeboats. They were not overly concerned, as the ship seemed little affected by the first torpedo strike. As a precautionary measure, Gratsos ordered the lifeboats swung out and made ready for immediate embarkation. The ship had taken on a small list but otherwise seemed none the worse for the damage inflicted. The chief officer went forward to assess the damage while the crew waited at their muster stations. Suddenly, a tanker came up from astern of *Eleni Stathatos*. It did not attempt to signal the stopped Greek ship and, just as quickly as it had appeared, the mystery ship moved away. It was a brief, although somewhat puzzling, distraction from their own predicament.

When the chief officer returned from his inspection of the damaged hold, he reported to Captain Gratsos that the flooding was contained and that the bulkheads appeared to be holding. Encouraged by this report the captain instructed the second engineer and a fireman to return to the engine room and to restart the engine. If the ship could proceed under its own power then there was every chance that they could reach a safe port. The rest of the crew would remain at the lifeboat embarkation decks, a sensible precautionary measure in case the situation deteriorated. Steam was soon raised, and the damaged ship was under way again. Captain Gratsos was careful not to go too fast; with the heavy swell that was running, any violent movement might exacerbate the damage to the hull causing the flooding to spread to other cargo holds.

No sooner had the crew felt the hum of the engine turning beneath them than a second, more violent, explosion devastated *Eleni Stathatos*. Those on deck felt the ship lift bodily out of the water before settling back, now with a more pronounced list. The torpedo had slammed into No. 2 cargo hold. On deck the explosion wrecked the top of the wheelhouse and the wireless masts, sending splinters of debris flying across the bridge deck, injuring the chief officer and the wireless operator. Captain Gratsos was blown off the bridge and landed heavily on one of the bunker hold hatches, injuring his head, chest and arms. With this second torpedo hit, the ship finally submitted to the damage sustained and slowly began to sink.

A short distance away, Kapitänleutnant Rollmann watched his latest conquest finally sink after he had expended his final torpedo on it.

The men of *Eleni Stathatos* wasted no time in boarding the two boats and lowering away. The port lifeboat was first into the water, although, for some unknown reason, only six of the thirty-three crew were on board this boat. With the lifeboat falls released they began to row away from the side of the sinking ship. Unable to see the starboard boat, they were unaware of the calamitous situation developing. As they rowed away from the ship, shouts for help were heard from the other lifeboat. They steered for the starboard side and, as they rounded the stern, they saw men struggling desperately in the water. The other lifeboat had been cut in two and was useless as any kind of survival craft. In the seconds that followed the port lifeboat lowering and rowing away, the overloaded starboard lifeboat had managed to get waterborne but had then drifted under the stern and become ensnared in the still-turning propeller. Miraculously, all twenty-seven men were eventually pulled from the water. The entire crew were now in the critically overcrowded sole remaining lifeboat, and the majority of those on board were soaked through and in shock.

In the aftermath of the ship sinking, the solitary lifeboat found itself in a precarious situation. It was overcrowded and what few rations were on board would not last long. The weather was very unfavourable, and the biting wind chilled each man to the bone. Waves breaking against the gunwales filled the boat with water. Captain Gratsos organised his men so that room could be made for the oars to be shipped. They set off, steering east in the hope of meeting a passing ship. After a few hours a moderate breeze blew up and so the sails were set. Those not bailing water from the bilges kept a lookout on the horizon, but for two days there was nothing.

What meagre rations they had were passed around daily and the men tried to shelter as best they could under the canvas covers. On Monday night the weather picked up, with a strong wind sweeping heavy rain showers over the huddled men. With the temperature near freezing, the strong wind and wet weather conditions, the crew slowly declined into a state of hypothermic madness.

Tuesday morning dawned, and the rain and strong wind continued unabated. As the day slowly dragged on, the deprivations endured by some of the men reached a critical point and the life within their battered bodies slowly drained away. That night the first two bodies were gently slipped over the side. The next twenty-four hours saw a succession of deaths as men succumbed to the extreme conditions. The misery of those left was compounded when they made the fateful decision to drink seawater. Described by the survivors as 'turning mad', the thirst-crazed men became a menace to everyone in the lifeboat. One became so delirious that he tried to bite someone and had to be restrained by several men sitting on him.

By Thursday morning the remaining crew were in a pitiful state, their rations almost gone, and they struggled to maintain control of the lifeboat. Two more men had passed away overnight, and, summoning their last reserves of strength, their shipmates slipped their bodies over the side. With their situation seeming hopeless, the dark conical shape of Skellig Rock appeared on the horizon. The strong prevailing wind and ocean current had taken the lifeboat north towards the Kerry coast. Desperately weak they steered for a headland to the east of the Skelligs. Shortly after noon, a motor fishing boat drew alongside. Michael Casey, a local fisherman, had spotted the drifting lifeboat and, gathering seven other fishermen, he set out to assist. Looking into the lifeboat Casey saw the wretched men lying in a heap in the bottom of the boat. He attached a tow line and, with his fellow rescuers, took the lifeboat into Portmagee.

It had only been four days since *Eleni Stathatos* had sunk, but, starved of sufficient rations and exposed to the extreme conditions, the twenty survivors who reached Portmagee were so weak that they had to be carried into the village. The following day, as Captain Gratsos recuperated in hospital, he wept bitterly as he recalled the harrowing tale of suffering and hardship his crew had endured.

Eleni Stathatos would not be the last neutral ship during February 1940 to have its crew forced to abandon ship and then subsequently to land in Ireland. The Swedish owned *Dalarö* was taking a cargo of linseed from Buenos Aires to Gothenburg. Captain Neilson was under orders to avoid calling at a British control port and having his ship and cargo inspected. By this the owners were attempting to demonstrate complete impartiality in the event of an encounter with a zealous U-boat commander. Neilson planned to take his ship over the north of Scotland before turning east across the North Sea and into the Skagerrak.

As dusk descended on 12 February, the lone neutral had reached a point approximately 200 miles north-west of Donegal. Chief Officer Grönlund and Captain Neilson were on the bridge for the evening watch. Grönlund thought he heard the sound of gunfire, quickly followed by an explosion. He took this to be a warning shot and, leaving the captain on the bridge, he went below decks to warn the crew. In the meantime Neilson brought the telegraph to stop and the ship began to slow down. Grönlund had just reached the boat deck when there was a terrific explosion. A single torpedo struck *Dalarö* amidships, bringing the ship to a halt and causing it to take on a list. The crew mustered and wasted no time in preparing both lifeboats. Grönlund stood by and supervised. When he noticed that the captain had not yet mustered and heard that nobody had seen him, he returned to the bridge, where he found Neilson lying on the deck. He had been knocked down by the powerful force of the explosion and was unable to move. Grönlund lifted his wounded captain onto his back and carried him down the stairways to the boat deck. There was a moment of consternation when they found that both lifeboats had been lowered and were moving clear of the ship. Without any regard for his own personal safety, Grönlund took off the life jacket he had been wearing and put it on the captain. Then, calling back the nearest lifeboat, he gently slid Neilson into the water. Satisfied that the lifeboat was coming back for the captain and mindful of keeping the numbers even in each survival craft, he then jumped into the water himself and swam toward the second lifeboat.

Almost half an hour after the torpedo impact, both lifeboats watched as U-53 fired ten rounds from its deck gun into the still floating *Dalarö*. The obstinate Swedish ship refused to sink and remained afloat for another two hours. With their ship gone and in the darkness of the night, the lifeboats drifted apart. The injuries sustained by Captain Neilson proved to be fatal and, shortly after being picked up by the lifeboat, he died. As a mark of respect the crew did not bury him at sea but kept him in the lifeboat in the hope that he could be buried ashore. Only seventeen hours after taking to the lifeboats, all the survivors of *Dalarö* were picked up by the Belgian trawler *Jan De Waele*.

The skipper of *Jan De Waele* radioed ahead to Buncrana, Co.

Donegal, to say that he would soon be entering with survivors. On the morning of their arrival, a sizeable crowd was waiting for the trawler, including a team of doctors and nurses. The people of Buncrana had prepared meals to be served at the local hotel, but immediately after arrival the Swedish crew were escorted onto waiting buses and driven to Londonderry.[9] Only Chief Officer Grönlund spent one night in Buncrana, along with the remains of his captain. A brief inquest was held into the death the following morning. On their departure, the coffin of Captain Neilson was draped with a Swedish flag that had been stitched overnight by Miss Maureen Watson.[10]

The unnecessary loss of *Dalarö* was yet another grim chapter in the story of the neutral shipping that became embroiled in the war at sea. It is not known why Korvettenkapitän Harold Grosse made the decision that resulted in the loss of a ship and the death of its captain.[11] What makes the entire episode more perplexing is that a warning shot had been fired. Perhaps Grosse had underestimated how long it would take the crew to lower the lifeboats and abandon ship. Irrespective of this, the U-boat commander was still obliged to check the stopped ship's paperwork before deciding whether he was justified in sinking it. In April the Swedish government protested about the sinking of *Dalarö* through the Swedish legation in Berlin.

Such impetuous actions as those committed by Grosse were isolated instances. Most U-boat commanders still operated within the Prize Regulations. However, as the war in the Northern and Western Approaches intensified, U-boats were placing themselves at considerable risk when they stopped a neutral ship in accordance with the Prize Regulations. Inevitably in war mistakes would be made and people would die. *Dalarö* was only one of many.

On the same day as the abandoned crew of *Dalarö* drifted off the Donegal coast, at 0817 hrs to be precise, the Norwegian-flagged *Nidarholm* was sighted by U-26. Initially the U-boat had dived for a submerged attack, but when the lone merchant was identified as being Norwegian, Kapitänleutnant Heinz Scheringer surfaced and ordered two warning shots, which splashed ahead of the ship. *Nidarholm* stopped accordingly and the crew began to abandon ship, but their captain ordered an SOS message to be transmitted stating that they were under attack. On hearing that the Norwegians were transmitting an SOS message, Scheringer was left with no other option but to sink their ship.[12]

Scheringer's judicious actions in his first encounter with a neutral ship, marked him as a commander who intended to comply with the Prize Regulations. Two days later, he scored his second success of the patrol when he sank the British-registered *Langleeford.* The cautious U-boat commander remained submerged for the remainder of the day after this attack. After sunset, he surfaced once again, and lookouts on the conning tower searched the horizon for the darkened silhouettes of the enemy. At 1912 hrs, a merchant ship displaying navigation lights was sighted in the distance. Scheringer remained undetected, a respectable distance away, as his officers set about establishing the course and speed of the as-yet-unidentified ship. Once these had been calculated, Scheringer decided to commence a surface night attack and began to run in to launch his torpedoes. As the range between the hunter and his unsuspecting prey closed, those on the conning tower could make out illuminated markings on the ship's side: the unmistakable flag of Norway. Scheringer called off the attack, but, rather than retreating from the scene, he decided to follow the Norwegian ship through the night and to stop it for inspection in the morning. By now the trailing U-boat had been spotted from the bridge of the Norwegian ship. Not knowing the U-boat's intentions, an apprehensive Captain Nilsen maintained the course and speed of *Steinstad*. Outwardly confident that, as a neutral ship, he was not in danger, and wary of provoking a reaction from its unwelcome escort, *Steinstad* continued through the night as U-26 followed patiently behind.

Sailing from Turkey with a cargo of ore for Norway, *Steinstad* was careful to ensure that its brightly lit national flag was on display during the hours of darkness. This precaution had already paid dividends as Scheringer had aborted his first attack. On 15 February, as dawn slowly heralded the day, Scheringer decided it was time to stop the Norwegian ship for an examination of its paperwork. At 0750 hrs, two warning shots were fired from the U-boat's deck gun, sending ominous fountains of water splashing ahead of *Steinstad*. There was no reaction from Captain Nilsen, who maintained his ship's course and speed. The uneasy standoff was broken when, at 0837 hrs, Scheringer ordered another warning shot fired at the unresponsive Norwegian. After this third shot, Nilsen turned his ship about. As *Steinstad* altered course, a Morse lamp signal from the U-boat's conning tower ordered the merchant ship to send over a boat with the ship's documentation for inspection. *Steinstad*, however, did not acknowledge the signal and continued to close rapidly. What's more, Nilsen did not appear to be slowing his ship down and Scheringer grew increasingly wary about the actions of the supposed neutral ship, fearing that the ship would attempt to ram his submarine. A final warning shot was fired close to *Steinstad* as Scheringer attempted to stop the ship and bring the situation under control. On board *Steinstad* Nilsen took this last warning shot to mean that he and his crew should abandon ship or risk being blown up. It was a tense time for both crews. Increasingly concerned about the actions of the ship in front of him, Scheringer suspected that it may yet turn out to be a British Q ship.[13] The wary German commander was then surprised to see what looked like the entire crew taking to the lifeboats. Surely, if the captain was sending over the ship's documentation, only one boat with no more than half a dozen men would suffice. Scheringer regarded Nilsen's actions with great mistrust and, fearing a trap, submerged beneath the waves, away from any possible surprise attack. On the surface, Nilsen and his men saw the U-boat disappear, but, unsure of what would happen next, they continued to row away from *Steinstad*. Then, after what seemed like only the briefest of interludes, a terrific explosion erupted as a single torpedo tore into the side of *Steinstad*. An immense cloud of water spray, debris and cargo engulfed the fast-sinking ship. Within minutes it had disappeared completely, leaving only flotsam scattered over the surface. Scheringer remained submerged, preferring not to interrogate the crew for fear of a possible air attack.

Captain Nilsen called the lifeboats together to discuss his intentions. *Steinstad* had been sunk just over 90 miles west of the Galway coast. The captain's motor lifeboat would tow Chief Officer Engebretsen's sail-equipped lifeboat and with this arrangement they would reach safety without much delay. As the day progressed the western horizon took on a deeply dark and threatening tone. The wind steadily increased, making steering the boats more difficult and straining the towline as each boat yawed and pitched continually. With nightfall the wind had increased to near gale force, and the boats were failing to make any headway. Conditions slowly descended into crisis for all twenty-four men as the deteriorating weather triggered a series of fatal calamities. Unable to endure the stress any longer, the towline holding the lifeboats together parted. Mountainous waves crashed over the open lifeboats while the men struggled desperately to maintain control over their craft. A violent wave crashed over the motor lifeboat's gunwales, knocking everyone down and sweeping Captain Nilsen and trimmer Viktor Vidala into the sea. Several attempts were made to manoeuvre near to both men and eventually they got close enough to Vidala to haul him back into the lifeboat. Nilsen was heard calling for help over the cacophony of the raging wind and crashing seas, and occasionally they caught a glimpse of him clinging to an oar. The crew made a final effort to reach him, but in that state the sea proved to be an insurmountable obstacle and gradually the cries for help faded until they could no longer be heard.

The morning of 16 February brought no respite as the appalling weather conditions continued. Second Officer Harris Nilsen was now in charge of the motor lifeboat. There was no sign of the chief officer's lifeboat that day, and little progress was made. The men would have to endure another three days of hardship as the lifeboat was pushed steadily north by the gale-force wind. On 20 February visibility improved during the morning and the bitterly cold men rubbed their salt-caked faces and peered out over the eastern horizon. Ahead they saw the central peaks on Arranmore Island. With land sighted, their spirits rose and they summoned their last reserves of energy. Steering for these conspicuous landmarks, the lifeboat was soon within sight of the western shore of the island. By early afternoon they were ashore and being helped by the locals.[14] Despite their pitiful state, all the men wanted to know was whether anything had been heard of the second lifeboat and their captain. The authorities were informed, and an air and sea rescue was conducted over the following day. The thirteen missing men were never found – a tragic loss of over half the ship's crew.

For the lucky survivors their ordeal was at an end and they had come through relatively unscathed. Only Viktor Vidala required serious medical treatment, as he had developed bronchitis, and he was subsequently treated in hospital. The remaining crew were fit enough to travel to Dublin on 22 February. Accommodation was provided at the Seaman's Institute in Dublin while the Norwegian consulate made travel arrangements. It was during this time in Dublin that one of the crew became seriously ill and had to be transferred to hospital. Petter Quitzau had an ulcerated stomach and his recent travails had greatly strained his weakened system. Sadly, on 10 March, Petter passed away. The port missionary Mr W. J. Simpson was by his bedside during his final hours. His coffin, draped in the Norwegian flag, was taken back to the Sailor's Rest on the North Wall, the last home Petter had known before his untimely passing. The funeral took place on 12 March, and Quitzau was laid to rest in Mount Jerome Cemetery.[15] It was a sad coda to the story of *Steinstad* and its hapless crew.

6

THE HAPPY TIME

The unprecedented number of ships sunk in June 1940 heralded the beginning of a period that would be known to the U-boat commanders of the Kriegsmarine as the 'happy time'. The ineffectual response by the British to the U-boat threat in the South-West Approaches had dire consequences for the merchant seamen serving on board the ships attempting to run the German gauntlet. Although the British had established the convoy system in the very early stages of the war, there still remained a substantial number of merchant ships that were routed independently. It was from these unescorted ships, as well as from stragglers and poorly defended convoys, that the U-boats were gaining their greatest success.

Typical of the losses in June was that of the Yugoslav ship *Labud*, sunk on 19 June just 30 miles south of Galley Head, Co. Cork. *Labud* was sailing independently when it was stopped and sunk by U-32. The entire crew escaped the ship unharmed and followed the beacon of Galley Head lighthouse throughout the night. Early the next morning, both lifeboats came ashore on the remote Red Strand in Dirk Bay, Co. Cork.

Further out into the Atlantic, the inadequacies of the convoy system were highlighted when ships dispersed from outbound convoys were attacked and sunk. On 25 June the British tanker *Saranac* had just dispersed from the unescorted convoy OA-172, when it was attacked and sunk by U-51. Adrift over 300 miles south-west of the Fastnet Rock, two lifeboats made it safely to the Irish coast where they were both picked up on different days by the steam trawler *Caliph*.[1]

Keen to share in the success of this happy time was Kapitänleutnant Otto Kretschmer, who had just taken command of the newly commissioned U-99. The U-boat's first patrol of the war got off to an inauspicious start, when, on 21 June, the U-boat was attacked by a seaplane from the German battleship *Scharnhorst*. The damage to the attack periscope and starboard regulating tank meant that Kretschmer was obliged to return to Wilhelmshaven for repairs. The repairs only took two days and by 27 June U-99 was back at sea. This was to be Kretschmer's first foray into the Atlantic since the beginning of the war. He had spent the early months of the conflict in command of U-23, which was a smaller type-IIB U-boat assigned to patrolling the fringes of the North Sea. The combination of the new larger type-VIIB U-boat and Kretschmer's assertive attitude would be a potent striking force amid the North and South-West Approaches.

The transit through the Hebrides was uneventful and by 5 July U-99 had taken up a patrol line covering the South-West Approaches. A fresh wind and only moderate visibility looked set to hamper their chances of detecting shipping, when a telltale stream of funnel smoke was sighted approaching from the south. Kretschmer dived and manoeuvred underwater as he prepared to attack. U-99 lay at periscope depth as its commander patiently waited for the target ship to come within firing range. Then he gave the order to fire a single torpedo.[2] As the minutes passed by without the sound of the expected detonation, it was becoming apparent that the torpedo had missed its intended target and frustrated the attack. Kretschmer was unwilling to let this lone merchant ship escape, and the order was given to surface and man the deck gun. Soon several shots were sent whizzing past the merchant ship's bow.

Captain Doughty of the Canadian ship *Magog* had been on the bridge instructing his lookouts on their correct duties when the first shots splashed into the sea ahead of the starboard bow. *Magog* had originally been part of convoy HX-52 which had sailed from Halifax on 21 June. By nightfall of that first night *Magog* had dropped so far astern of the convoy, as a result of not being able to maintain speed, that the ocean escort signalled that *Magog* would have to proceed independently. The lone ship had made it across the Atlantic unhindered and, as the ship neared the dangerous seaways off the south-west coast of Ireland, Doughty had taken to frequenting the bridge more often to ensure his crew were fulfilling their duties.

When the shots fell ahead of the ship, Doughty cast a hurried glance astern and confirmed the presence of a chasing U-boat. *Magog* was unarmed, but its captain was not prepared to submit to Kretschmer just yet. Doughty ordered a distress message transmitted while he began evasive course alterations in an attempt to confuse the German gunners. The much faster U-boat closed the distance and soon the gunners had found their target. Direct hits on the quarterdeck and foremast convinced Doughty that any further resistance was futile. The crew began to abandon ship in good order despite the continued shelling from U-99. From his conning tower, Kretschmer spotted the men clambering down into the lifeboats and ordered the gunners to cease fire. *Magog* drifted away, smoking from the gunfire. Three more rounds from the deck gun finally sent the Canadian ship to the bottom.

Kretschmer closed on the lifeboats to question the survivors. There followed a terse conversation between a proud and self-assured man on one side facing a stubborn and determined man on the other. Having gleaned enough information to know the name and cargo of the ship, Kretschmer gave the lifeboats a course to steer and then turned around to depart from the scene. The distress message from *Magog* was bound to attract the unwanted attentions of any RAF Coastal Command aircraft in the vicinity. As expected, a Sunderland flying boat was sighted within an hour of the sinking, and U-99 dived beneath the waves to reload its torpedoes. The aircraft spotted the lifeboats and, after circling the survivors, it proceeded westward in search of assistance. It was not long before the Sunderland returned and signalled to the survivors that help was on its way. This was the Finnish ship *Fidra*, which soon picked up all twenty-three Canadians. The following day, the Canadians were landed in Cobh. The men from *Magog* would enjoy an unexpected holiday in Dublin while they awaited repatriation back to Canada.

Although they had suffered three injured men when the ship was shelled, Doughty and his crew had a lucky escape. Adrift only 90 miles south-west of Cape Clear, safety was already nearby when the Finnish rescue ship appeared. The Canadians enjoyed an indulgent Irish capital for the remainder of July, while out at sea Kretschmer continued to add to his tally of conquests.

Elsewhere in the South-West Approaches on 5 July, another

U-boat, patrolling further east, sank the first ship of its latest patrol. Kapitänleutnant Wilhelm Rollmann, in command of U-34, sank HMS *Whirlwind*, and so began a succession of victories that would earn this aspiring U-boat ace the coveted Knight's Cross award. Rollmann continued to add to his success over the coming days with three more merchant ships sunk by 10 July.[3]

U-34 was searching the waters just south of Ireland when another lone merchant ship was sighted and Rollmann began to seek out an advantageous firing position. He stalked his intended target for over four hours before he was finally in a position to launch an attack. By this time the coast of Cork was within sight. It was beautiful calm day with clear sunny skies. A single torpedo was fired which struck the engine room of the Finnish cargo ship *Petsamo*. The ship remained afloat long enough to allow the crew to abandon ship without too much risk to their safety. It took *Petsamo* just under an hour to finally disappear, then the surviving crew headed north towards the Irish coast where they landed that evening at Baltimore. The west Cork village had not seen any survivors from the war at sea since the crew of *Cheyenne* had landed in September 1939.

Both Rollmann and Kretschmer would register remarkable success in the South-West Approaches and the first half of July truly was a happy time for these successful U-boat commanders. By 17 July Kretschmer had sunk four more ships and captured another. An unsuccessful night attack on an unidentified merchant ship on 16 July left U-99 with just a solitary torpedo. He did not have long to wait to find a use for it. In the fading twilight of 17 July the darkened outline of a merchant ship was seen through a passing rain squall. The sighted merchant steamer was *Woodbury*, which was proceeding independently from the Cape Verde Islands towards London. Kretschmer decided to attack, but it took some time before he could manoeuvre U-99 into a suitable firing position. Choosing the right moment, the U-boat raced in on the surface towards the unsuspecting merchant ship. The visibility was good that night, but a mainly overcast sky obscured the moon and Kretschmer deliberately took advantage of the darkness to attack. The last remaining torpedo was fired when they got to within 900 metres. The deadly payload slipped through the water towards *Woodbury*.

On the bridge, Captain Norman Rice received a sighting report of the conning tower just abaft his starboard beam. Reacting instantly, Rice shouted an order to the helmsman to steer away from the U-boat. There was little time for the quartermaster to react to the order from the helm as the torpedo struck the starboard side. The impact initially appeared to have produced no significant damage and it seemed to the crew on board as if they had gently knocked against some unknown submerged obstacle. Aside from some deck rigging toppling over, there were no other immediately visible signs of damage. Fatal damage, however, had indeed been inflicted on *Woodbury*, as a large gaping hole allowed seawater to fill the cargo holds. It was not long before the ship took on a worrying list and Captain Rice ordered all lifeboats away.

Some of the crew had slept through the explosion and only woke up when the whistle was sounded for lifeboat stations. While they prepared the boats, Kretschmer closed on the sinking ship and passed round the stern. On board *Woodbury* a lapse in concentration led to the port lifeboat being launched hastily with many of its occupants thrown out into the sea. The starboard lifeboat was then launched with too many on board. Kretschmer drew closer to question the nearest lifeboat. Satisfied with the ship's name and port of origin, the solicitous German commander advised the occupants that they should pick up the remaining men who had been ejected from the port lifeboat into the sea and distribute the survivors more evenly among the lifeboats. Then, after providing the lifeboats with a course to steer towards Ireland, Kretschmer wished the men good luck and departed.

Both lifeboats kept together that first night and headed for Ireland the following morning. They eventually lost contact with each other, but would both reach safety at Waterville and Castletownbere respectively. Kretschmer reported that he had expended all torpedoes and was ordered to the new U-boat base at Lorient for supplies.

With the surrender of France at the end of June 1940, the Kriegsmarine acquired the use of its strategically important west-coast ports and it soon established several U-boat bases along the eastern rim of the Bay of Biscay. The northern bases of Brest, Lorient and Saint-Nazaire were ideally situated for attacks on shipping transiting the South-West Approaches. However, by the second half of July, two factors conspired to ensure that there was no sudden onslaught unleashed against shipping south of Ireland. First there was a lack of operational ocean-going U-boats and the majority of U-boats were forced to return to their bases in Germany for lengthy refits. Second, since the beginning of July all convoys had been diverted away from the south and were transiting through the North Channel.

On 21 July, U-99 entered its new home port of Lorient. It was only to be a brief stay and on the evening of 25 July, refuelled and rearmed, U-99 slipped its moorings and departed in search of additional triumphs. Kretschmer was to operate off the west and north coasts of Ireland, in response to the convoys' shift away from the South-West Approaches.

One of the many ships to be rerouted around Donegal was the independent merchant *Auckland Star*. Under the command of Captain David Rattray MacFarlane, *Auckland Star* was returning from Australia with a mixed cargo of frozen beef, butter, wheat and bales of wool. With its capacious cargo holds capable of accommodating both bulk and refrigerated cargoes, *Auckland Star* was a fast, modern ship and a valuable asset to the British merchant fleet.

Captain MacFarlane was no stranger to the U-boat threat and had already demonstrated that a fast cargo ship could easily evade a surfaced U-boat. At the outbreak of war MacFarlane was in command of *Imperial Star* and was returning back to the UK after a voyage to Australia. On the morning of 17 October 1939, *Imperial Star*, with its greater speed, sighted and overtook convoy HG-3. While the much slower convoy soon passed out of view, another more ominous sighting was of more immediate concern. *Imperial Star* was being pursued by a U-boat and a chase ensued, but the fast speed and well-executed evasive manoeuvres instigated by MacFarlane negated any threat. *Imperial Star* survived the encounter and MacFarlane had gained invaluable experience in the fight against U-boats.

On the evening of 27 July, Kretschmer was proceeding north to pass along the west coast of Ireland. It had been relatively quiet since leaving Lorient, with only the occasional sighting of an aircraft breaking the routine and compelling the U-boat to dive until the danger had passed. *Auckland Star* had reached a position 90 miles west of Dingle just before 0400 hrs and was steaming north at almost 16 knots. Chief Officer Farnell had just entered the wheelhouse and was adjusting his night vision when an almighty crack and violent shudder broke the solitude of the morning. A torpedo from U-99 had just rocked the Blue Star liner. MacFarlane soon joined his chief officer on the bridge, as the telegraph was rung to stop engines and an assessment was made of the damage to No. 5 and No. 6 cargo holds. The explosion had caused serious flooding and the ship had settled quickly by the stern. Unable to control the flooding and with the ship already well down in the water aft, MacFarlane reluctantly gave the order to abandon ship half an hour after the torpedo strike. It was a bitter disappointment for MacFarlane to leave *Auckland Star*, but the optimistic captain still entertained thoughts of saving the ship. A distress message had been sent out, and it was hoped that a prompt response and tow to shore could salvage his ship.

On U-99 Kretschmer had become impatient at the stubborn refusal of the ship to sink. Almost an hour after the first torpedo, Kretschmer fired another to help expedite its demise. The second torpedo hit the engine room, but still the ship remained afloat. Observing through his periscope, Kretschmer realised that it would take another strike to provide the *coup de grâce*. To use so many torpedoes on the first ship of a patrol seemed wasteful. For the exacting U-boat commander, who expected to sink one ship with each torpedo, three seemed extravagant. However, it seemed necessary in this case and a third explosion soon rocked *Auckland Star*, which capsized shortly after and sank. The first glimmer of sunlight appeared on the eastern horizon, and the unprejudiced spotlight of daylight illuminated the scene. Kretschmer was mindful that daybreak would bring unwanted attention investigating the ship's distress message and so U-99 headed away at speed.

Left behind were four lifeboats with the entire complement of the crew of *Auckland Star*. Although a little cramped, the lifeboats were well provisioned and well founded. The Irish coast was only a short distance away and the weather was favourable.[4] They remained together until the afternoon of 28 July, when the lifeboat under the command of Chief Officer Farnell lost contact with the other three. All four would shortly reach safety, with Farnell's the first to land – on the evening of 30 July near Slyne Head lighthouse. Upon hearing the news of the arrival the local police superintendent mobilised the townspeople, and a convoy of private cars and commercial vehicles was dispatched to collect the survivors and bring them to Clifden. This was the first of many occasions when the unswerving hospitality of the residents of the small Galway village answered the call to aid those who were washed up on Ireland's rugged west coast. The remaining three lifeboats, under the overall command of Captain MacFarlane, made landfall off Dingle on 31 July, where they were met by a local fishing boat which towed them into the small fishing port. The survivors of *Auckland Star* had been fortunate to escape their ship without any loss of life.

Just like *Auckland Star*, Captain William Hughes of *Clan Menzies* was taking his fully laden ship back to the UK from Australia. Since the previous morning, when Hughes became aware of the attack on *Auckland Star*, the cautious master mariner rightly assumed that danger was stalking the Atlantic west of Ireland. Hoping to steer clear of danger, Hughes took *Clan Menzies* 90 miles west of the original course he had been planning to steer on that day. This course alteration proved to be his undoing.

Since leaving the wreckage-strewn site, Kretschmer had been busy. Not long after *Auckland Star* had sunk, the lookouts on the conning tower of U-99 sighted a periscope. Unaware of the identity of the submarine Kretschmer submerged as a precautionary measure. A little later, the detonations of two torpedoes nearby were a stark reminder that German U-boats were being hunted by their British counterparts. After this near miss, two sightings of British aircraft forced U-99 to submerge again.

However, as night fell the U-boat was in its preferred element for operating against shipping. Yet again the keen lookouts sighted the distinctive outline of a merchant ship on the western horizon. The layout of derricks fore and aft and a large heavy lift derrick forward identified the ship to Kretschmer as belonging to the Clan Line Shipping Company. The ship was steaming at almost 17 knots and it would take some time for Kretschmer to get into firing position. Just past midnight on 29 July, Kretschmer was ready to attack. The first torpedo missed, but it was shortly followed by another that struck the starboard side of the stoke hold and the engine room. The crew took to the lifeboats and eighty-eight men got away, with the only casualties those who had been on watch in the engine room.

While Kretschmer questioned the crew, *Clan Menzies* continued to float nearby. It was the second ship in twenty-four hours that had refused to sink without demanding that he expend more of his torpedoes. With two already fired that night Kretschmer was not prepared to use any more and so explosive charges were prepared to hasten the ship's end. However, they were not needed as *Clan Menzies* finally yielded and sank under its own steam.

Kretschmer left both lifeboats 75 miles west of Eagle Island, Co. Mayo, his attentions firmly fixed on restocking the torpedo hold with the spares stowed on deck. Both lifeboats were safely ashore on 1 August, one landing on Achill Island, Co. Mayo, and other at Inishcrone, Co. Sligo.

July 1940 was a remarkable debut for Otto Kretschmer and U-99 in the Battle of the Atlantic. During his two patrols he had sunk ten ships. A total of 220 survivors from *Magog*, *Woodbury*, *Auckland Star* and *Clan Menzies* reached safety along the south and west coasts of Ireland. Remarkably, there were only six casualties from these four ships – a mercifully small number.

Kretschmer went on to become the greatest U-boat commander of the war, but no more survivors from any of his attacks would arrive in Ireland. August 1940 saw a brief lull in the exploits of 'Silent Otto', while other aspiring U-boat aces wreaked havoc among the shipping in the North-West Approaches. Indeed, Donegal had become the front line in the war at sea. The inexorable succession of casualties that followed would reach the rocky northern shores on the periphery of Bloody Foreland on such a regular basis that it would constitute a crisis for the British at sea.

7

CLAN MACPHEE AND KELET

It seemed that the whole populace of Ireland had begun a mass migratory movement, as the August bank holiday weekend of 1940 enticed crowds to the popular tourist destinations. Record numbers flocked to resorts such as Salthill to take a cooling dip in the warm waters of Galway Bay. The increase in numbers staying in Salthill and Galway city emptied local shops of their produce, which, although a welcome boom for the retailers, left local residents somewhat disgruntled. In Donegal, day-trippers from across the region were drawn to the pristine beaches that decorated the rims of secluded bays around the coastline. At Downings, Co. Donegal, the ocean wavelets breaking gently against the pier enticed bathers into the waters to cool off from the afternoon sun.

The scene of tranquillity was interrupted when concerned onlookers standing on the beach observed two swimmers in difficulty offshore. Two men who were walking along the pier dived into the water. They soon reached the swimmers and dragged the near-drowned men ashore, where a third man helped revive them. Praise was lavished on the men for their heroic deed and it was later revealed that the three selfless rescuers were from the Greek steamer *Pindos*, which had been sunk on 4 August off the Donegal coast.[1] The surviving crew had been picked up by local fishermen and landed at Downings the following day.

The relaxed holiday atmosphere that pervaded along the Irish coast at the beginning of August 1940 was in stark contrast to that of the English west coast. The busy arterial ports of Liverpool and the Bristol Channel had their access to international and domestic mercantile commerce increasingly restricted. Recent air raids indicated that the Luftwaffe had identified the importance of the Irish Sea ports and intended to disrupt trade. In addition, towards the end of July 1940 work had begun on the defensive minefield across the St George's Channel that denied the southern entrance to the Irish Sea to both friendly and enemy vessels alike.

Luftwaffe air raids during the months of July and August were not concentrated and caused little tangible damage to the essential docklands and installations ashore. However, intensified mine-laying around the sea approaches to the major ports was having a much greater impact on shipping. The closure of ports while minesweepers cleared the approach channels was of paramount importance to safeguard shipping, but port authorities were burdened with congested berths and over-stretched storage capacity as ships waited for the threat from the unseen mines to be neutralised. These unavoidable restrictions severely disrupted shipping movements and were another disadvantage for the British wartime economy.

Recently returned from Canada with a cargo of iron ore for the steel works at Port Talbot, the Hungarian ship *Kelet* was delayed at Milford Haven for four days because of the danger of mines. Clearance was finally granted to resume the short coastal passage, and *Kelet* had almost reached Port Talbot when the ship was once again diverted as a precautionary measure, this time to Swansea. Finally, after a week at Swansea, *Kelet* passed through the breakwaters protecting the entrance to the River Afan and the docks of Port Talbot.[2] It had been a circuitous and protracted passage which under normal circumstances would have taken less than a day. Captain Potzner had grown accustomed to these inconveniences since commencing this voyage and tolerated the occasional detour subject to the requirements of the charterer.

By the beginning of 1940 the British Ministry of War Transport had reached agreements with most of the major maritime nations for the purchase or chartering of their available shipping tonnage. Outside of these agreements, every opportunity was taken to fix individual neutral ships on a time charter basis at the current market freight rates. In April 1940 *Kelet* completed discharging a cargo at Marseille and its owners, the Neptune Sea Navigation Company of Budapest, were keen to fix the next cargo at the best possible terms.

At the Baltic Exchange in London the agent for the company soon had *Kelet* fixed on an agreed time charter to the Ministry of War Transport and orders were received to load a cargo at Algiers. This latest charter must have aroused some apprehension amongst the multinational crew, who instinctively had reservations about entering a declared war zone. It was widely publicised throughout the newspapers of Europe that German U-boats had sunk neutral shipping in the North Sea and Western Approaches. However, Captain Potzner had an obligation to the owners to prepare his ship for the voyage.

Prior to sailing from Marseille, the Hungarian national flag was painted on each side of *Kelet*. This was expected to protect the ship from attack; however, the agreed time charter with the

British Ministry of War Transport implicated *Kelet* in assisting a belligerent nation and any German would therefore regard the Hungarian as a legitimate target.

At Port Talbot large grabs worked frantically throughout the day to unload the iron ore. (The enforced blackout prevented working during the hours of darkness.) On 6 August the discharge operation was completed and the crew set about securing the holds in anticipation of returning to sea. One last task remained and that was to load bunkers for the passage across the Atlantic. *Kelet* moved from the eastern dock wall to Margam wharf and positioned itself under the large chutes where coal filled its empty bunker holds. On 11 August *Kelet* steamed out into Swansea Bay and headed west towards Milford Haven, from where the assembling ships waited expectantly for the next OB series convoy to depart.

In addition to the disruption caused to the Bristol Channel ports, the strategically important port of Liverpool was also adjusting to life under the watchful presence of the Luftwaffe. As was the case further south, the limited air raids and reconnaissance flights over the River Mersey, which were a feature of July and August, caused only minimal damage to the surrounding city and docklands. Nevertheless, it was rightly assumed that any further escalation of aerial attacks by the enemy would seriously impede the flow of trade and disrupt convoy sailings. The Liverpool section of an OB series convoy was normally the largest and usually contained the convoy commodore. Departures were scheduled for every second day although this could be amended depending on circumstances. Once at sea the Liverpool section would rendezvous with the Milford Haven section and finally the Clyde section, then all three would combine into a single force.

During the early morning hours of 12 August, the Luftwaffe was busy dropping mines into the mouth of the Mersey. Reported sightings of mines in the vicinity of the Queen's Channel forced the authorities to close the port of Liverpool for most of the day.[3] As a result, Convoy OB-197 was delayed and the ships had another twenty-four-hour wait before heading back to sea. Among those waiting for OB-197 to sail was the veteran steamer *Clan MacPhee*. Under the command of Captain Thomas Cranwill from Dublin, the ship was on a return voyage to the south and east coasts of Africa. Despite the age of his ship Cranwill knew he could rely on his engine room to provide an impressive turn of speed once at sea. This, combined with its large capacity, made *Clan MacPhee* the ideal ship for conducting trade with the furthest reaches of the empire. Since the beginning of the war the ship had sailed in several convoys departing from the UK or Freetown, and they had all been uneventful. Some of Cranwill's officers, however, had been exposed to the war at sea. Wireless operator David Murray was a former crew member of *Athenia* and was on board at the time of the sinking.[4] Murray had been ready to board the Norwegian rescue ship *Knute Nelson* when he was transferred instead to a Royal Navy destroyer and landed at Greenock. Almost a year later, Murray had been promoted to senior wireless operator and life at sea had settled into habitual routine.

On the morning of 13 August the Liverpool section of OB-197 got under way and travelled down the channel, which had been swept clear of mines the previous day. Following were the escorts HMS *Mackay* and *Heartease*, which would remain with the convoy until it reached its dispersal point. The procession of ships moved north-west towards the Isle of Man, where later that afternoon they were joined by the Milford Haven section, which included *Kelet*. The Clyde section joined the convoy just before sunrise on 14 August and the combined formation headed out through the North Channel and into the waiting maelstrom. There was a total of fifty-four ships in OB-197 and, as they formed into twelve columns, they presented a broad front over 2 miles wide.

The two escorts were stationed ahead of the leading ships in the outside columns. This left the convoy vulnerable to attack from several directions. Defence was supplemented in daylight hours by Coastal Command aircraft flying from Aldergrove on convoy escort patrols. On the afternoon of 14 August, during the transit through the North Channel, a Coastal Command aircraft provided a reassuring presence around the advancing perimeter of OB-197. At twilight the air escort was obliged to return to base, leaving the protection to *Mackay* and *Heartease*.

The final moments of daylight extended the visibility just far enough for a periscope to be sighted between the leading ships of the first and second columns. The detonation of a torpedo close to the centre of the convoy failed to inflict any damage, but it shook the crew of the ship nearest to the explosion. Both escorts searched the area where the periscope had been sighted, but the U-boat had ample time to make good its escape.[5] The sighting of the U-boat had caused considerable alarm throughout the convoy, in spite of its ineffectual attack.

Tensions were less by daybreak on 16 August, as two nights had passed without enemy interference. As the convoy neared its designated dispersal point a cautious optimism grew that the transit through the North-West Approaches would be without any loss of shipping. There was no cause for congratulatory backslapping just yet, however, as, with the arrival of daylight, *Mackay* and *Heartease* departed OB-197 to rendezvous with convoy HX-63. With only a few hours remaining before the dispersal point, this reallocation of the escorts was considered prudent, as the protection of an inbound convoy, with its laden ships, was a higher priority.

As both convoys had been originally routed to pass close to each other, the Admiralty had amended the route of HX-63 so that it passed 50 miles further north of its original course. In addition, German radio intelligence was aware that an eastbound convoy was due to pass through a designated position on 16 August, and BdU had instructed several U-boats to converge on this position for an attack. The Germans had the upper hand as their numerically superior forces assembled for an attack that had been carefully orchestrated by Dönitz himself. Success against the laden ships of HX-63 seemed assured. However, fate decreed that it would be the unwitting ships from OB-197 who faced a concerted enemy attack without protection, not those of HX-63.

Events quickly unravelled for the convoy when Korvetten-kapitän Hans Rösing, in command of U-48, sighted them on the morning skyline. The reduced visibility obscured the majority of the convoy, but, as the U-boat approached to attack, Rösing could appreciate the full extent of the target convoy. The absence of any escort and the prevailing weather conditions allowed Rösing to approach the convoy undetected, before submerging and manoeuvring between the columns of merchant ships. Despite the difficulties in maintaining depth and avoiding the ships in each column, Rösing was able to attack the Swedish merchant *Hedrun*, which sank quickly after a single torpedo. Further attacks by U-48 failed, and Rösing dropped astern and attempted to overtake the convoy. Meanwhile, Oberleutnant zur See Endrass and U-46 were attempting to gain a satisfactory position for an attack. Frustrated by the worsening sea conditions and by having to use the air-search periscope for submerged attacks, Endrass was finally gifted a firing solution on three overlapping targets. The attack was a partial success as only the Dutch steamer *Alcinous* was hit. The torpedo started a raging fire that soon engulfed the entire forward section of the ship. There was little the convoy could do to counter the unseen enemy other than execute a series of emergency turns in an attempt to shake off the shadowing U-boats.

Undoubtedly the poor sea and weather conditions prevented a far greater number of ships falling victim to the dogged attacks of Rösing and Endrass. Both U-boat commanders withdrew and attempted to reposition themselves for more favourable attacks in the afternoon. The ensuing respite lulled the nervous merchant ships into thinking that they had successfully evaded the enemy.

At 1600 hrs, the expected signal was hoisted aloft from the commodore's ship instructing the ships to disperse. There was a gradual loosening of the columns as individual ships steered diverging courses away from the convoy.

Below deck, in the stoke holds of *Clan MacPhee*, the rate at which coal was hurled through the furnace doors increased with the demand for additional steam to propel the ship to its full sea speed. With no other ships ahead and additional sea room available for greater manoeuvrability, Chief Officer Chadd ordered the helmsman to steer the first leg of the prescribed zigzag pattern. It was a welcome relief for both Cranwill and Chadd to have their ship under their control once again. Both men took a moment to look astern at the smoke-enveloped outline of *Alcinous* still visible on the northern horizon. It was a poignant reminder of the fate that might still be theirs should the enemy be nearby. Throughout the day the wind had been freshening and by late afternoon the sea was quite rough, although this did not prevent *Clan MacPhee* from opening up a considerable margin on its less able counterparts. The engineers had successfully worked the boilers up to maximum pressure and the speed was a very respectable 12 knots.

As Chadd discussed with his captain how their chances had improved since leaving the convoy, a sickening thud from the port side dispelled any further thoughts of safety. The explosion sent cascading shock waves through the ship that completely wrecked the amidships living quarters and reduced the wheelhouse to an unrecognisable layer of collapsed bulkheads. The impact also destroyed the engineering compartments and the tremendous force of inrushing seawater quickly flooded the compromised spaces. Captain Cranwill, who had been knocked off his feet by the force of the explosion, pulled himself up and assessed the fast deteriorating situation. Stunned crew members rushed on deck and instinctively made their way to the lifeboat embarkation points. Cranwill sensed that they had little time left and immediately gave the order to abandon ship. In the debacle that followed, only one lifeboat managed to launch and clear away successfully from the sinking ship. Another was launched but was woefully undermanned and, once waterborne, became flooded and practically useless as a survival craft. The remainder had either been destroyed by the torpedo explosion or through negligent handling while being launched.

Both Cranwill and Chadd were left on board along with those who had been unable to force their way onto the crowded lifeboat.

They still had the life rafts, which were quickly thrown over the side. Staring down into the churning seas that tossed the rafts further and further away from the ship, each disheartened man prepared himself for the leap. Plunging deep below the waves, the men kicked frantically to reach the frothing surface. Stinging sea salt blurred their vision as they strained to catch sight of a life raft.

Chadd swam towards the nearest one he could see and was soon joined by two more survivors. Together they held onto the raft while they recovered from their exertions. Tired and in a state of near shock they coughed involuntarily as swallowed seawater burned their throats. Chadd regained his composure sufficiently to look around for the others who had followed him into the sea. No matter in which direction he looked, he could see no sign of anybody else. This was a particularly bitter blow, as Chadd knew that the captain was one of the last to jump from the ship. Lost amid the chaos of the seas and the sinking ship, Captain Thomas Cranwill was never seen again.

The final U-boat to muster that morning for the anticipated encounter with the Halifax convoy had finally struck. Kapitänleutnant Fritz-Julius Lemp had sighted the convoy at approximately the same time as the other two U-boats. While Rösing and Endrass proceeded with their attacks, Lemp decided to overtake the convoy before diving ahead of the oncoming ships and attacking targets as the opportunities presented themselves. Throughout the afternoon Lemp struggled against the weather while the emergency turns of the convoy forced him to refine his angle of approach. Finally he was satisfied with his position, dived and prepared to unleash his carefully conceived attack. Two attacks on different ships from the dispersed convoy had failed. The third, however, yielded better results, the single torpedo registering a direct hit on *Clan MacPhee*.

It was not long before Lemp sighted his next target. Through the powerful optics of his periscope he could clearly see the Hungarian flag on *Kelet*'s side in his cross hairs. Unsympathetic to neutral markings on a ship sailing in an enemy convoy, Lemp gave the order to fire. This, his fourth torpedo attack of the day, failed. The attack on *Kelet* was quickly followed by another unsuccessful attack, this time on the British ship *Trelawny*. Cursing the foul weather and his bad luck for missing four ideal firing opportunities, Lemp remained submerged while his crew reloaded the empty torpedo tubes before renewing the attack.

The failed attack on *Kelet* had gone completely unnoticed by Captain Potzner and his crew. Since dispersing, the Hungarian steamer, along with several other less capable merchantmen, gradually assumed a position at the rear of the convoy. Potzner had witnessed the destruction of *Hedrun* and had seen how the raging flames had engulfed *Alcinous*.

By late evening, lookouts on the bridge wings spotted the evidence of recent violence nearby. Twisted flotsam was seen scattered about on the sea, and shortly afterwards they saw the eerie glow of life-jacket lights huddled together in a perilously overloaded lifeboat. Potzner altered course towards the lifeboat from *Clan MacPhee* and tried to manoeuvre close by, but with the rough seas and the fading light the task proved difficult. Nevertheless, the lifeboat stayed alongside long enough for the transfer of the mainly Indian crew to be completed.

A short distance away, the life raft supporting Chadd and several others twisted violently as it was caught in the heaving seas.

Skilfully, Captain Potzner manoeuvred his ship close to the raft, allowing the survivors to grab lines thrown from the decks above. Slipping the heavy messenger around his torso, Chadd was last to be hoisted on board and to feel the solid decks of *Kelet* beneath his numb limbs. Although only on the raft for a comparatively short time, the whole experience had been enough to test the hardiest of seafarers.

The decks bustled with men from both ships, and the rescued were attended to by the crew of *Kelet*. The pitch-black night, combined with a thick veil of mist, had reduced visibility considerably, but the lookouts on *Kelet* were just able to make out the low silhouette of an approaching vessel. Stunned silence gripped the crowd of men and they stared fatalistically at what revealed itself to be the conning tower of a German U-boat.

It was just before midnight when Lemp was ready to surface. When *Kelet* was sighted close by, it seemed he had been given one more chance to recoup some of the honour he had lost earlier in the day. The U-boat closed to within 400 metres before firing a single torpedo. Lemp looked dejectedly across the short distance of dark sea as he realised that, yet again, another precious torpedo had been wasted on a target that in better sea conditions would surely have been destroyed. Not willing to expend any more ordnance on a ship that had twice proven to be elusive, Lemp abandoned the attack and turned his attention to a partially flooded lifeboat his lookouts had spotted.

The six men inside could provide little information other than their ship's name. Observing their pitiful condition, waist deep in water in a lifeboat that would not withstand any more punishment, the German commander felt compelled to seek the assistance of

Kelet in securing their rescue. Once within hailing distance Lemp called out to the apprehensive figures standing on the bridge. He was succinct, informing Captain Potzner about the men in the flooded lifeboat.[6] Then the U-boat turned away and disappeared behind the cloak of darkness.

Lemp would later write in the war diary for U-30: 'It was the blackest day for the boat that could have been the most successful.' It was a sentiment that was shared by Rösing and Endrass, who also failed to capitalise on their initial successes against OB-197. For the survivors of *Clan MacPhee*, rescue had been relatively swift and, although they had lost thirty-three men when their ship sank, the majority had escaped unharmed and were safe on board a friendly ship. But it was the brief encounter between U-30 and *Kelet*, and in particular Lemp's compassion for the men in the floundering lifeboat, that would be remembered most vividly by those who were witness to it. Perhaps their view of the night's events would have been slightly different had they known how close they had themselves come to destruction at his hands.

The alleyways and public rooms on *Kelet* were crammed with the survivors from *Clan MacPhee*. Their dishevelled appearance and sober mood attested to the traumatic experience they had endured. Only a handful of men required basic medical treatment, with the exception of Second Officer William Manderson, who had a badly injured leg caused by his jump from the decks of *Clan MacPhee*. It was only practicable to land the survivors at the nearest available safe port, so Potzner decided to head for the Azores before continuing on to his final destination. Although the west coast of Ireland was closer, Potzner was guarded about running back along the gauntlet from which he had just escaped.

The north Atlantic had become a significantly more dangerous place, with orders issued to all U-boat commanders in respect of an extended declared area west of the British Isles.[7] Within this declared area, U-boats considered themselves permitted to attack all shipping without warning.[8] This was a significant escalation of the blockade of Britain that had far-reaching consequences on the conduct of the war at sea.

Just over 700 miles south, Kapitänleutnant Hans Cohausz was taking U-A north along the western border of the declared area.[9] The German commander, sailing in a U-boat originally intended for the Turkish navy, was heading towards an encounter with a certain Hungarian ship under charter to the British government.

Kelet continued on its diversionary passage south, with its guests making themselves as comfortable as possible. The first two days had been uneventful and the stormy weather that had made the rescue so difficult had abated. Cohausz was also enjoying the fine weather: the light northerly breeze and good visibility were ideal for spotting distant ribbons of smoke from the funnels of potential targets.

Early on the morning of 19 August, lookouts on the conning tower of U-A spotted the navigation lights of an approaching vessel. Cohausz assessed the unknown vessel and decided to wait until dawn before taking any further action. Eventually the eastern horizon lit up sufficiently for him to make out *Kelet*. The unmistakable shape of the gun mounted on the stern caught the particular attention of the suspicious U-boat commander. Cohausz ordered a warning shot fired, which was shortly followed by a signal instructing the merchantman to send over a boat with its official papers for inspection.

The mood on board was tense as Captain Potzner hastily briefed his chief officer before sending him over to the U-boat. It was hoped that the ship's neutral origins would prevent any belligerent action; furthermore, the boat crew was composed entirely of Hungarian nationals. Potzner told Chief Officer Kehrer that he should mention the ship's humanitarian mission and that it was carrying many survivors from another ship. As the boat rowed across to the waiting Germans, anxious onlookers from both crews gathered at the handrails to watch events unfold.

Cohausz examined the paperwork thoroughly and gave his verdict to the elderly Hungarian chief officer. As the ship had been engaged on a charter for the British government, Cohausz was duty bound to sink it. Despite Kehrer pleading for clemency, Cohausz would not deviate from his ruling and gave the Hungarian delegation one hour to return to *Kelet* and organise the crew to abandon ship. There was great dismay once the news was relayed, and with the stipulated time limit fast running out, the remaining lifeboats and rafts were expeditiously launched.

Cohausz dispatched the ship with a torpedo followed by gunfire before departing the scene. The seamen, adrift over 500 miles from the Irish coast, found themselves facing several obstacles to their survival. For the men of *Clan MacPhee* it was a bitter blow to find themselves once more thrust back into the ocean.

The two senior officers from each ship drew near to each other and discussed their options. Captain Potzner initially proposed sailing for the Iberian Peninsula, but Chadd suggested that using the prevailing wind and current to head for neutral Ireland would be a more prudent option. With the Irish coast agreed as their destination, the provisions and navigation instruments that had been taken from *Kelet* were evenly distributed between the two senior lifeboats. Chadd and a mixed contingent from both ships were in one, while Potzner and the remainder of the crew from *Kelet* were in the other. The Indian crew from *Clan MacPhee* occupied two rafts which would each be towed by a lifeboat.[10]

During the first day the weather was favourable and, although neither lifeboat made much headway, they did steadily drift apart as Captain Potzner's command headed in a more easterly direction. After an uncomfortable night spent either rowing or bailing out, Chadd calculated that the distance travelled had been less than 10 miles. For the effort exerted, and given how far there remained to go, it was decided to release the tow. The lifeboat would travel ahead in search of rescue.

The weather picked up and, with a good wind blowing, Chadd was able to make considerable distance over the next forty-eight hours. Then, on 24 August, when the lifeboat had reached a position 400 miles west of Ireland, the Norwegian steamer *Varegg* sighted it and collected all twenty-five crewmen. Captain Iversen decided to divert to Galway where the survivors were landed.

It was a happy occasion for all twenty-five men when *Varegg* passed through the lock gates of Galway Harbour. Waiting to greet the survivors were the customary dignitaries who took the men under their charge and provided for their every need. While the survivors were glad that their sorry adventure was over, they expressed concern for those shipmates who remained adrift. In fact, the survivors from the other *Kelet* lifeboat and one raft with twelve Indian crew from *Clan MacPhee* which it was towing were both picked up and landed at Gibraltar. The other raft was never found.

For one survivor, the arrival in Galway was long overdue, as Wireless Operator David Murray explained to the waiting reporters about his experience on *Athenia* and how he had nearly boarded *Knute Nelson*.

After a well-deserved night's rest in Galway, those men fit to travel caught the morning train for Dublin, while Second Officer William Manderson remained in hospital in Galway. The British nationals were allowed to leave on the afternoon ferry bound for Liverpool while other seamen from *Kelet* were accommodated at the Seaman's Institute in Dublin.

8

DISASTER OFF DONEGAL

With the closure of the South-West Approaches and St George's Channel sea lanes, all convoys crossing the Irish Sea were obliged to navigate through the only approach that remained open. As a result, throughout the early days of August 1940, the North-West Approaches and the North Channel assumed a greater degree of importance in the Battle of the Atlantic.

The ill-prepared and under-strength RAF Coastal Command had yet to make any appreciable impact in the war against the U-boats patrolling the seas between Rockall and the Irish coast. The allocation of aircraft capable of accomplishing long-range anti-submarine (AS) patrols, combined with the lack of an effective weapon to use against the U-boats, reduced considerably the nuisance value of Coastal Command's AS operations.[1]

However, it was the lack of effective escort vessels that especially hampered Western Approaches Command. In response to the increase in enemy activity in this area the Royal Navy attached additional AS trawlers to the flotilla based at Belfast. This urgently needed force was immediately deployed in conducting AS sweeps through the North Channel and into the Approaches and in escorting convoys through the North-West Approaches. Although the converted trawlers lacked the speed and the many ancillary features of dedicated warships, they were an indispensable addition to the hard-pressed Western Approaches Command.

With concern mounting over the increase in U-boat attacks on convoys in the North-West Approaches, senior Royal Navy and RAF officers based in Northern Ireland gathered to discuss how they could best respond.[2] As a result of this meeting, greater cooperation between the Royal Navy and Coastal Command was established in an effort to wrest back the initiative from the enemy and to disrupt their operations in the North-West Approaches. In charge of AS surface units was Captain Ruck-Keene, who was based on HMS *Titania* in Belfast. Two RAF liaison officers were to assist Ruck-Keene, who would personally fly patrols with Coastal Command aircraft and direct the surface units while airborne. When not in Belfast or flying over the Northern Irish coast, Ruck-Keene commanded HMS *Wanderer* and took part in convoy escort operations and U-boat hunting.

With these improved measures in place, it was hoped that enemy attacks on shipping could be significantly reduced. The continued sustainability of the North Channel convoys was reliant on these improvements. The north coast of Ireland had become the new front line in the Battle of the Atlantic.

* * *

Commodore Eliot stood on the bridge wing of *Patia* and watched the leading ships of the Bristol Channel section join the rear of his convoy. *Patia* had sailed with twelve ships in the Liverpool section of convoy OB-202, passing the Bar light vessel on the afternoon of 22 August. They were to rendezvous with the Bristol Channel contingent at a junction further north than originally expected. Eliot signalled his ships to reduce speed to allow the Bristol Channel section to catch up. A day later and he was still waiting impatiently when the delayed section finally approached from the south. As the two sections merged together, the Bristol Channel escort signalled that the best speed achievable by those ships arriving was 7½ knots, a report that Commodore Eliot acknowledged with a hint of scepticism. Three hours later the remaining Clyde section arrived and took up station within the convoy's eight columns, bringing the total number of ships in OB-202 to twenty-seven.

Eliot's frustration at the delay was further aggravated by the poor station-keeping and undisciplined signalling from the foreign-flagged merchant ships sailing with the convoy. It was only with the help of the escorting warships and by communicating terse instructions through the ship's megaphone that the commodore finally gained control over the convoy. By early evening all three sections were sailing together, albeit in a somewhat imprecise fashion. They were still in the restricted waters of the North Channel, with the dim outline of Rathlin Island just discernible on the western horizon.

As the narrow waters of the channel were left behind, the convoy had more sea room to commence an evasive zigzag course. Commodore Eliot noted the speed the convoy was making and calculated that the first leg of their manoeuvre could commence at midnight on 24 August. He signalled all ships accordingly. For the remainder of the evening the convoy maintained a steady course north-west. They had worked up to a speed of 8½ knots, but, as expected, some of the ships were finding this difficult to maintain and gaps began to emerge within the columns as ships dropped astern. In particular, three Norwegian ships belonging to the Bristol Channel section, *Bur*, *Veni* and *Brask*, lagged dangerously.[3] Poor station-keeping also affected those at the head of the columns. *St Dunstan*, which was leading the starboard wing column, found itself astern of station. Not far away, *Cumberland*, which was the second ship in the sixth column, was also astern of station. As a result, an unfavourable situation developed on the starboard side as the close protective formation of the convoy slowly unravelled, presenting a clear opportunity to any attacker.

The convoy escorts maintained a vigilant presence around the perimeter. They were positioned at each apex, with HMS *Winchelsea* and *Primrose* on the port and starboard bows respectively, while the smaller AS trawlers *Man o' War* and *Ullswater* took up station on the port and starboard quarters. HMS *Witch* patrolled ahead, sweeping across the line of advance. Although the convoy had yet to commence zigzagging, the escorts took the judicious action of following their own independent zigzag course.

It was a dark night, with no moon. On the horizon to the south a solitary beacon from the lighthouse on Inishtrahull Island flashed out across the sea. As midnight approached, a mute stillness prevailed across the convoy.

The ships of OB-202 were not alone that night and sharing the view of Inishtrahull lighthouse with them was Oberleutnant zur See Erich Topp in command of U-57. This U-boat was one of the smaller type IIC designs. It had a smaller radius of operations than the larger type VII boats and carried only five torpedoes. However, its small size made it very manoeuvrable and it was quick to dive should it be surprised on the surface. For this reason, the type IIC boats were retained for operations in shallow areas such as the North Channel, while the older type II designs were retired from active service.[4] Despite the limitations of the boat's offensive capability, it was a powerful striking weapon when under the command of a competent commander, which Topp certainly was.

The low silhouette of U-57 went unnoticed by the ships of OB-202, and Topp watched the silhouettes he had seen on the horizon grow steadily larger. Once the targets were selected, Topp gave the order to fire and three torpedoes sliced through the opaque waters towards their intended destinations.

On *St Dunstan* there was no warning of an impending attack. Men were thrown from their sleep as the torpedo impact reverberated throughout the ship. The explosion had blown away the shell plating on both sides of No. 1 cargo hold and had dashed the hatch boards to pieces. While the crew mustered to assess the level of damage, others in the immediate vicinity were startled out of any complacency they might have had regarding their safety. Lookouts doubled their search for the telltale signs of a torpedo track or a surfaced U-boat.

Less than a minute after *St Dunstan* was hit, the second torpedo found its mark and exploded against the starboard side of *Cumberland*. The missile struck right aft and the resulting explosion tore away the outer shell plating. Its captain, Williams, gazed at a scene of utter devastation. The stern had collapsed into a void, its ragged remains now awash with seawater.

Two ships lay crippled as the third torpedo from the deadly salvo continued through the water unseen. It had missed its intended target and passed ahead and astern of several ships before finally finding the starboard side of *Havildar*. This ship was pennant No. 32: the torpedo had travelled right through the centre of the convoy before hitting the unlucky British merchant. The explosion caused serious damage to *Havildar* and it took on a large list to starboard, while its deck was a tangled mess of hatch boards and toppled derricks. Peering through the acrid smoke Captain Palmer assessed that a fatal blow had been dealt and feared *Havildar* might sink at any moment.

In less than five minutes, three ships lay halted in the water and seriously damaged after receiving a single torpedo hit. Both *Cumberland* and *Havildar* broke radio silence and signalled that they had been torpedoed. For *Havildar* the message was a lucky one as neither Commodore Eliot on board *Patia* nor any of the escorting ships were aware that it had been hit.

Eliot ordered an immediate emergency turn to port to steer the convoy away from the invisible threat from the north. On hearing the explosions, *Winchelsea*, which had taken up station on the port bow, increased speed and altered course to pass ahead of the convoy and down the exposed starboard side where it met HMS *Ullswater*. *Witch* also swept down the starboard side, but neither of these searches turned up any evidence of the attacker. *Witch* continued and searched the stern side of the convoy. As *Winchelsea* proceeded back towards the main convoy, a U-boat conning tower briefly appeared ahead.[5] Contact was gained on the ASDIC, and a full pattern of depth charges was dropped. The hunt for the U-boat continued for several hours.

As *Patia* guided those ships still in contact with the flagship away from the danger zone, *St Dunstan*, *Cumberland* and *Havildar* lay strewn across the sea behind them, although *St Dunstan* was still making some headway. The twisted wreckage of steel plates and beams grated together discouragingly as the damaged ships moved under the influence of a moderate swell. The crew of *St Dunstan* had managed, with some difficulty, to abandon ship, leaving only the captain on board. Realising that the ship was in no immediate threat of sinking, the chief officer had his lifeboat crew row after the runaway ship. Once alongside, he and the chief engineer reboarded *St Dunstan* and stopped the engine.

The crew of *Cumberland* had also abandoned ship without any mishaps, although Captain Williams feared that some of his crew had been killed by the initial explosion. With visibility reduced by the rain that had started falling, Williams remained close by his stricken ship, hoping that it might yet be reboarded and saved. The starboard lifeboat had ventured further away and, amid the continuous misty rain, they drifted astern and were lost from sight. However, help was close by, as the *Copeland* appeared out of the murk and soon had all the men safely on board. Not long after picking up the men of the starboard lifeboat, *Copeland* found the abandoned *Cumberland* with its master dutifully beside his ship. Williams decided that were his ship to survive its ordeal he would require his crew to assist and the men who had been picked up by *Copeland* were transferred into the port lifeboat.

Further to the south, *Havildar* remained in a critical condition, with No. 4 lower hold flooded and the deck plating badly distorted. Captain Palmer ordered all but one of the lifeboats away. The evacuation went smoothly despite the alarming list the ship had developed until only Palmer and a handful of others remained on board. Keeping a close watch on the water ingress and the integrity of the other compartments, it was soon discovered that the water level was continuing to rise and had entered into No. 4 tween deck. Certain that the demise of his ship was imminent, Captain Palmer and the remaining crew lowered the last lifeboat. Shortly after, one of the Norwegian stragglers came into view and took them on board. *Gyda* had found itself lagging behind as darkness fell and, luckily for the crew of *Havildar*, soon had all the British crew on board, apart from twenty-seven men whose lifeboat had slipped away unseen in the rain. While their shipmates were taken safely to Gourock in Scotland by *Gyda*, these twenty-seven sailed the short distance to Inishtrahull Island.[6] Once ashore they were greeted by the lighthouse keepers and taken up to the keepers' house where they enjoyed a hot drink and dried themselves as they waited for a boat from Moville to come and take them to the mainland.

Back alongside *Cumberland*, Captain Williams asked for volunteers to reboard the ship and assess its condition. With no shortage of willing hands, he picked out deckhands and a wireless operator. In the meantime, *Witch* had come into view and had asked after their safety. Williams, seeing that he had enough men available, agreed to let the rest of his crew board the destroyer. Williams did not immediately reboard himself, but instead waited for daylight and the possibility that a tug might arrive on the scene and tow his ship to safety. Unknown to Williams, the damage inflicted had been decisive and *Cumberland* was slowly sinking. The torpedo had hit the stern, causing flooding in No. 5 cargo hold, and the unseen damage beneath the waterline was equally devastating. The shock waves from the explosion had spread through the rear of the ship, buckling and distorting the plating of the shaft tunnel and the adjoining compartments. Using the shaft tunnel as a conduit, seawater poured into any space which had its buoyancy compromised by the explosion. This steady flooding of adjacent compartments eventually led to the loss of the ship.

As sunlight infiltrated the low cloud cover, Williams could see the other disabled ships through the rain, each gently rolling on an otherwise empty sea. Another destroyer approached the men in the lifeboat: Captain Ruck-Keene and *Wanderer*, which had just arrived on scene after receiving orders to assist with the hunt for the attacking U-boat. Williams wanted to explore whether his ship might be saved. He boarded *Wanderer* and discussed the matter with Ruck-Keene, who was not in favour of reboarding *Cumberland* at that time and who expressed his view that it would be better if the remaining crew came on board the destroyer. Williams declined the offer and opted instead to wait for the arrival of the rescue tug. *Wanderer* sailed away to continue the search of the area, leaving the dutiful twenty-two men behind to watch over *Cumberland*.

By late morning, it was obvious that the ship would not survive much longer and another lifeboat headed south to the safety of the Irish coast. They sailed the short distance to the north Donegal coast in just over six hours, passing through the narrow entrance to Lough Foyle and landing at Moville.

Rescue had been quick for the convoy, with the majority of those who abandoned ship coming ashore by the evening of 24 August.[7] Out of the eight lifeboats launched, only two had to sail south towards safety. The first, from *Havildar*, arrived at Inishtrahull Island; the second, from *Cumberland*, held Captain Williams and his steadfast crew. The survivors who took the longest to reach port were those who had boarded either *Witch* or *Wanderer*. Both destroyers remained at sea for several more days investigating other U-boat reports and picking up survivors from torpedoed ships.[8]

By the time evening came on 24 August, Captain Ruck-Keene felt frustrated at the day's lack of success. The close cooperation he had fostered between his surface escort forces and the RAF Coastal Command did not seem to be paying dividends. This was clear when, on the afternoon of 24 August, while they continued to hunt for the U-boat that had torpedoed *Cumberland*, *Havildar* and *St Dunstan*, Coastal Command aircraft had mistaken the submerged wreck of *Cumberland* for a submarine and had bombed it.

What was more, the attack had diverted surface forces away from their immediate tasks. *Wanderer* still had survivors from two of the sunken ships on board when it was sent by Western Approaches Command on another mission. The inbound convoy HX-65 had just been attacked and the tanker *Pecten* sunk, and *Wanderer* was sent to join the other surface forces hunting the U-boat responsible. Heading out to where HX-65 had taken a severe mauling, *Wanderer* came across the survivors of another ship, the independently sailing *Jamaica Pioneer*. It had been returning to the UK when it was stopped and sunk by U-100 under the command of Kapitänleutnant Joachim Schepke.

This brash and flamboyant star of the U-boat service was keen to extend his tally of ships on his first patrol in command of the new type-VIIB U-boat. Joining the crew of U-100 was war correspondent Ulrich Kurz. Schepke loved the thought of his daring exploits being recorded and published for the public at home to read. At this critical juncture, when the inadequacies of convoy protection were so evidently apparent, Schepke relished the opportunities that came his way to strike at such large and vulnerable targets. As U-100 moved south, just such a convoy, OA-

204, was proceeding out of the North Channel. The north Donegal coast would once again be the backdrop for a devastating attack.

Schepke reached his new patrol area on 28 August. It had been a quiet day and there had been no sighting reports. The crew were becoming restless and wanted to see some action. Then, with the onset of evening, the faint, telltale signs of shipping began to appear on the eastern horizon. The unmistakable shape of a convoy sailing west hove into view. This was what he had been waiting for. While he calculated the mean course and speed of the convoy, Schepke kept his U-boat just beyond visual contact of the advancing enemy. Once the last trace of daylight had been extinguished from the evening sky, he started to stalk his prey on the surface. This approach was especially easy and Schepke effortlessly outmanoeuvred the single escorting warship. Selecting two of the larger freighters sailing at the head of the columns, the first officer called out bearings as he viewed the targets through the UZO.[9] Then, when all was ready, Schepke gave the order to fire, sending two torpedoes racing into the darkness and towards the unsuspecting merchant ships.

Convoy OA-204 was 180 miles west of Malin Head and was expecting to reach its dispersal point the following morning after an uneventful journey across the north of Ireland. The convoy was no longer zigzagging and, as there was no alteration in course expected, Captain Robert Richardson had left the bridge of *Empire Moose* to go below. Sailing as part of a convoy was a difficult operation and the long hours of duty took a heavy toll on the ships' crews. Richardson had steadfastly remained on the bridge while the convoy had been zigzagging throughout the day. This manifest devotion to duty helped him to exorcise the traumatic memories of his recent command, *Orangemoor*, just two months before.

Returning home in convoy through the English Channel, *Orangemoor* had been torpedoed and sank within two minutes of being hit. Richardson was rescued by a passing ship, but eighteen of his crew were not so lucky. On his eventual return to sea Richardson felt mixed emotions when he stepped across the gangway, but any thoughts other than his commitment to duty were soon dispelled, and with the sailing of *Empire Moose* from Hull in August it was back to work as usual.

The shrill ring of the cabin phone presaged a report from the officer on watch. The captain was summoned back to duty. Richardson readjusted his bridge coat, then, mindful of the chill in the air, reached for his cap and left his cabin. It took several minutes for his eyes to adjust to the dark night, but slowly the faint glow of stern lights and darkened silhouettes appeared. As they scanned the visible horizon, the captain and his third officer quickly assessed the situation. The change in aspect of the ships on their starboard side indicated that the convoy was making an uncoordinated course alteration further to the south. Richardson was perplexed by this unexpected move; they had received no instructions and no signals had been relayed by the commodore's vessel. However, it was necessary to alter course to a similar heading so as to avoid a collision. A growing sense of anxiety urged Richardson to stay on the bridge.

The escorts allocated to bring OA-204 through the North Channel to its designated dispersal point were positioned on either side of the convoy. The corvette HMS *Clematis* took station on the starboard bow, while the minesweeper HMS *Gleaner* was to port. This was a typical force given the resources available to defend these increasingly perilous waters and it could only cover limited sectors of the convoy's line of advance, leaving the rear of the convoy undefended. An astute U-boat commander could easily evade the isolated escorts to attack the convoy from ahead or from either side. On this occasion, *Gleaner* was further hamstrung by having only one boiler available, which reduced its maximum speed to just over 9 knots.

Shortly after 2330 hrs, *Gleaner*, which had been conducting a sweep out on the port bow of the convoy, sighted an unusually high volume of signal traffic originating from the convoy. This bemused *Gleaner*, which altered course so that it could ascertain what was going on. As the ponderous escort approached the port column, it became clear that the convoy was dispersing while increasing in speed. As the minesweeper exchanged signals with the first ship it came across, it was tersely informed that the commodore's ship had been torpedoed.

* * *

It had been a long day on the bridge of *Dalblair* and Commodore Smith felt a sense of relief that his convoy was almost clear of the danger area. Recent Admiralty reports indicated that all U-boat activity was concentrated further north, in the vicinity of Rockall Bank, and Smith concluded that OA-204 should arrive safely at its dispersal point the following morning. He was keen to make the best possible speed during the night, and at 2325 hrs the convoy was ordered to cease zigzagging.

The commodore and Captain Bruton were on the bridge of *Dalblair* when the night sky erupted with an explosion. *Hartismere* had been sailing just ahead in the next column to starboard when it was struck by a single torpedo. Lookouts and officers alike on *Dalblair* were momentarily transfixed by the scene, when suddenly a dull thump was heard deep within their own ship. A torpedo had struck on the starboard side, blowing a cavernous hole through the shell plating and wrecking the amidships section. In defiance, the crew manning the stern-mounted 4-inch gun fired wildly in the direction from where the attack had come, narrowly missing *Astra II*, which was leading the starboard column.

Within minutes of the torpedo impact two lifeboats were lowered and quickly cleared the sinking ship. With twenty-four on board, the lifeboat under the command of Chief Officer Hogg contained the majority of the survivors. Casualties had been light, with only four unaccounted for when the muster was called, just before the lifeboats had been boarded. *Dalblair* broke in two and sank with its bow and stern standing vertical in the water before finally slipping beneath the waves. Although the two lifeboats were close to each other, they soon lost contact amidst the rolling waves, and each acted independently for the remainder of the night.

Schepke had struck the first crippling blow against OA-204. The convoy degenerated into total confusion following the loss of its commodore. As the initial shock of the first attack subsided, small groups of ships began to scatter. While the majority turned away from the perceived threat and steered a more southerly course, *Astra II* and the other ships of the eighth column turned to starboard and headed north-west.

Meanwhile, the escorts tried to react effectively to events, but without much success. *Clematis*, which had been on the starboard beam of the convoy during the first attack, commenced a sweep ahead and out to a distance of 3 miles. *Gleaner* was unable to manoeuvre clear of the fleeing ships and was obliged to turn about and work its way around the rear of the convoy, losing valuable time and remaining oblivious to the full extent of events that continued to unravel further north. The under-strength escort screen had been rendered impotent by its own actions and by those of the fleeing convoy.

Schepke was already inside the path of the searching *Clematis*, and before long had encountered the group led by *Astra II*. Another single shot at close range completely detached the bow of *Astra II* from the remainder of the ship, which fortuitously remained afloat long enough for the mainly Danish crew to abandon it.

While Schepke was busy dispatching *Astra II*, the survivors from *Dalblair* waited patiently. They figured that rescue was close at hand. Within an hour of the sinking, the Swedish ship *Alida Gorthon* had found Chief Officer Hogg's lifeboat and had taken all twenty-four on board. A short time later, the second lifeboat from *Dalblair* was picked up. This accounted for all the survivors from the first attack.

Alida Gorthon received instructions to rejoin the fleeing ships to the south while *Clematis* would speed ahead and try to reform the convoy. *Gleaner*, which had spotted some flares in the water, proceeded north to investigate.[10] All that *Hartismere* could do was to continue with damage control and attempt to restore main propulsion.[11]

It had been almost three hours since the first attack, and, across an ever-expanding area, the remaining ships of OA-204 continued to flee haphazardly from their unseen attacker. The initial confusion had diminished and small ad-hoc columns were forming up. However, the majority of ships acted independently.

Hogg and his fellow shipmates from *Dalblair* enjoyed the hospitality of their Swedish rescuers, relieved that their recent trauma was behind them. *Alida Gorthon* had almost succeeded in catching up with a group of ships when Schepke once again intervened, outmanoeuvring the unsuspecting Swede. The torpedo impact erupted inside the engine room with a violence that stunned those on board, throwing nearly everyone into a frenzy as they hastily made their way to the lifeboats. For some of the survivors from *Dalblair*, reaching the boat deck was especially difficult as they were left to find their way through an unfamiliar labyrinth of corridors and stairways. Several crewmen from *Dalblair* reached the open deck just as the starboard lifeboat was being lowered. Hogg found himself standing alone on the deserted deck, the davits fully extended and the falls hanging limp as the lifeboat below cleared away. After a moment weighing up his limited options, Hogg took a step back then launched himself forward over the ship's side. Plunging feet first into the choppy sea, Hogg was encouraged to see that the lifeboat was heading towards him. After only a brief interval in the bracing water the lifeboat passed within touching distance and his outstretched arm grabbed the offered oar. He was hauled over the gunwale and bundled down into the bow sheets, violently coughing up swallowed seawater. As he sat shivering in soaked clothing in the cold breeze, the Swedish ship disappeared in a torrent of hissing water.

A short distance away floated the port lifeboat: upside down, heads occasionally breaking the surface as survivors fought desperately for air. In their haste to launch the lifeboat, the aft falls had been prematurely slipped, sending the lifeboat into an uncontrolled vertical slide. Almost all the occupants were thrown into the water below. In an attempt to save the lifeboat, someone had cut the forward falls. This ill-conceived action caused the boat to plunge stern first into the water and onto the unlucky men beneath. By the time the starboard boat had reached the scene, only one survivor remained to be pulled from the water. The others were needless casualties of the disorder that had overwhelmed both crews in the moments after the attack.[12] The occupants of the sole surviving lifeboat of *Alida Gorthon* assessed the situation. Their ship had been trailing behind the fleeing convoy, and the chances of another ship coming to their rescue were slim.

Since being recalled to the bridge of his ship, Captain Richardson had made a full appraisal of the situation. *Empire Moose* joined the end of a column of ships gradually taking station to form a compact group. There was the occasional explosion somewhere abaft the beam or an incandescent magnesium flare interrupting the night sky, but eventually the night's stillness was restored. Tiredness once again began to overwhelm Richardson, and, taking advantage of the apparent lull in manoeuvres, he once again went below to rest.

Once *Alida Gorthon* had been dispatched, U-100 continued chasing the straggling elements from the remaining convoy. As Schepke hunted for a target worthy of his last torpedo, a tantalising opportunity presented itself: a group of five merchant ships. Only a single ship out of this group could be selected as the final target before U-100 would have to sail for its home port of Lorient. Schepke assessed the options available and selected one of the larger ships in the group. Orders, repeated by a line of crew members, travelled down the conning tower, each precise command following in succession, then Schepke stolidly gave the command to fire. A rapid exhale of compressed air and the torpedo was gone.

Captain Richardson was awake and on his feet moments after the impact. *Empire Moose* had been irrevocably damaged and was listing ominously to port. The explosion had caused a fire to erupt from No. 5 hold, which was sweeping uncontrolled through the empty space. Once on the bridge Richardson gave the order to abandon ship, and the mustered crew prepared both lifeboats. Before leaving, Richardson hurriedly walked aft through the twisted wreckage to ensure that nobody remained on board. Looking down through the engine-room skylight he could see the sea steadily rising above the lower decks. He returned to the starboard lifeboat and was preparing to descend the boarding ladder when the painter holding the boat alongside parted. Balancing on the inclined deck, the captain looked on as the lifeboat drifted away into the black of the night. The ship settled deeper by the stern as the intense conflagration consumed everything in its path. With nowhere else to go, Richardson had to climb down the boarding ladder to avoid the fire. Caught between the inferno above and the waters below, Richardson hung on to the ladder and waited for the lifeboat to return. However, time had run out for *Empire Moose* and, as the stern submerged ever further beneath the waves, Richardson knew that he had to get clear away from the ship before its final plunge. He leapt from the ladder into the sea and after swimming purposefully to a safe distance away, looked back at his ship. The bow of *Empire Moose* was almost vertical, and the fire, driven by the draught from below, turned the upright forward section into a massive funeral pyre.

Schepke himself looked on at the magnificent torch illuminating the surrounding area, then, content at seeing the ship disappear, he gave the order to return to Lorient.[13]

Richardson managed to find a section of wreckage to cling to, from which he shouted for help. Feeling alone and dispirited after his punishing ordeal, it was only with the greatest determination that the severely tested master mariner continued to hold on to his makeshift buoy. His determination was rewarded when the starboard lifeboat returned after hearing his calls for help. Richardson was soon organising his men in an effort to regain contact with the missing port lifeboat. With the aid of flares, they were soon within hailing distance. It was decided that they would remain in the vicinity until morning and then, if rescue was not forthcoming, both lifeboats would sail towards the nearest land.

Morning revealed a skyline devoid of shipping and so each boat set sail towards the north Donegal coast.[14] Just beyond their visible horizon the sole remaining lifeboat from *Alida Gorthon* also headed for the north Donegal coast.

With the area long since vacated by any shipping previously associated with convoy OA-204, there was little to indicate that they would be rescued. Although badly damaged, *Hartismere* had managed to restore main propulsion and was soon steaming east while *Gleaner* acted as close escort. Further south, *Clematis* made a half-hearted attempt to gather whatever ships were sighted back together before leaving OA-204 to rendezvous with an inbound convoy.[15] That afternoon, the unescorted ships dispersed. Later, in the wireless room of *Clematis*, disturbing reports were received that enemy aircraft were bombing ships they had left just hours before. The North Channel had become even more perilous with the arrival of the Luftwaffe and the FW200 Condor anti-shipping bomber.

All three lifeboats made good progress towards the coast. The weather remained favourable for the following days and they had uneventful journeys south, although the general discomfort caused by prolonged inactivity in the open lifeboats would undoubtedly have given many a reason to complain. The encouraging sight of a dark band of coastline expanded across the southern horizon on 31 August.

As the lifeboat from *Alida Gorthon* neared the north Donegal coast, they sighted the rescue tug *Englishman*, which hauled all seventeen survivors on board. *Englishman* sailed into Lough Swilly and landed the relieved men at Buncrana. For David Hogg and the three other survivors from *Dalblair*, it was the end to a traumatic experience. As that fateful night of 28 August had unfolded, they had been torpedoed twice within several hours and most of their shipmates had been killed while trying to escape from the ship that had rescued them. After a night of well-deserved rest in Buncrana, all four men from *Dalblair* set off via Londonderry on the return journey to England, while the Swedish crew of *Alida Gorthon* headed to Dublin to await repatriation.

The two lifeboats from *Empire Moose* gradually lost contact with each other. (The second would eventually land in the Hebrides.) Captain Richardson guided his lifeboat south, where they sighted the Donegal coast in the early afternoon of 31 August. As they sailed into Donegal Bay looking for a landing spot, a local fishing boat sighted them and guided them to Killybegs Harbour. It was a welcome relief for the exhausted crew to set foot on the quayside. Apart from some minor medical conditions, all of the twenty-one *Empire Moose* survivors were in good health. While waiting to travel to Londonderry the crew enjoyed a night of hospitality courtesy of the folks of Killybegs.

9

ISOLDA

From the outbreak of war in September 1939 until July 1940, the Irish Sea remained relatively free of enemy activity. The forbidding coastal regions of the northern and southern entrances and the presence of Coastal Command aircraft discouraged intrusion by U-boats, which instead operated in the approaches to the Irish Sea. What was more, before 1940 German aircraft were unable to make any serious foray into the Irish Sea, as the Luftwaffe medium bombers had neither the range nor the defensive armament to fly to the Irish Sea from their German bases. Until the fall of France, the Luftwaffe conducted its anti-shipping operations exclusively in the North Sea.

Although the Irish Sea remained free of U-boats, there were plenty of sighting reports from inexperienced air crew and nervous merchant ships. These would inevitably turn out to be false, but the high level of concern about the U-boat threat kept the AS forces busy chasing ghosts.

During the winter months of 1939–40, a series of mine-laying operations were carried out by U-boats in the Bristol Channel and Irish Sea. Using the long winter nights and new-moon periods to stay longer on the surface, U-30 was able to penetrate as far as the

Mersey estuary and lay twelve mines across the river approaches. These mines accounted for six ships sunk, including the Irish Sea ferry *Munster*.[1]

With the fall of France in June 1940, the Luftwaffe acquired air fields across northern France from where attacks could be launched against shipping in the South-West Approaches and in the Irish Sea. Attacks on shipping began in July and the coastal convoys passing through the English Channel came under intense pressure. By the end of July further Luftwaffe units began operating out of Brittany and soon shipping was being attacked on a daily basis in St George's Channel and along the southern Irish coast.

The coastal shipping trading between Britain and Ireland and the fishing fleets of Milford Haven and Fleetwood were hardest hit. One of the first ships to be attacked in St George's Channel was on the morning of 31 July, the British coaster *Fleshwick*, 8 miles east of Tuskar Rock. With the installation of the recent minefield blocking the southern approach to St George's Channel, a natural funnelling effect was caused between the western limits of the minefield and the shallow waters surrounding Tuskar Rock. The sea area surrounding the rock was a focal point for later attacks on shipping by the Luftwaffe.

Daylight anti-shipping strikes by lone aircraft, or by flights of three machines acting together, continued to sweep through the Irish Sea for the remainder of 1940. Shipping navigating the south and east coasts of Ireland were particularly affected by these attacks. It seemed that as the U-boats had shifted the focus of their attention towards the North Channel, so the Luftwaffe would maintain the pressure on the south. For the few Irish-registered ships trading across the Irish Sea, neutrality failed to act as any defence. In the second half of 1940 six Irish ships were attacked by German aircraft. The indifference of the German aircrews to neutral markings led to unnecessary casualties.

Towards the end of November 1940 the number of attacks against shipping in the St George's Channel area dropped off. The Luftwaffe did remain active, however, and on 28 November the Trinity House tender *Satellite* was attacked off the coast of Cornwall near Wolf Rock. This was an isolated incident, as patrolling FW200s were having greater success along the west and north coasts of Ireland.

On the morning of 18 December, just north-east of the Arklow lightship, the British tanker *Osage* was on a voyage from Belfast to Foynes with a cargo of petrol and paraffin. The small coastal tanker was spotted by an FW200 coming from the south and was attacked with machine-gun fire and bombs. The last bomb struck the quarterdeck, completely wrecking the stern of the ship and opening the side plates so that the engine room began to flood. With no power on board and unable to control the flooding, Captain Victor Wright called on his crew to abandon ship just over an hour after the attack. The FW200 continued north, finding the ferry *Cambria* and later the coaster *Tweed*. Both ships were damaged by bombing and strafing attacks, but were able to make port. Meanwhile, Captain Wright and his twenty men spent the remainder of the day in their single lifeboat. They were picked up the following morning by the coaster *Crewhill* and taken to Rosslare Harbour.

Berthed at the quay in Rosslare Harbour on 18 December was the Commissioners of Irish Lights' (CIL) tender *Isolda*. The lighthouse tender had taken a relief crew out to the Tuskar Rock lighthouse that morning and planned to take relief crews out to the Barrels and Coningbeg lightships the following day. The air activity over the south-east corner of Wexford had been seen and heard by the crew on board, but it had remained at a distance from the tender and did not raise much concern.

Transporting relief crews between the lighthouses and lightships was a routine operation for the tender. The Irish crew, who were from Dublin and Dun Laoghaire seafaring families, were a close-knit group. Family connections were not uncommon, with successive generations of father and son working on board the tenders operated by CIL. One of the youngest crew members on board was seventeen-year-old Sam Williams, whose father was a quartermaster on another CIL ship, *Alexandra*. Sam had sailed to the Caribbean and back, and a love affair with the sea was forged on the voyage. Shortly after returning home, he got a job on *Isolda* – the previous boy had failed to find his sea legs.

At the other end of the crew list was Captain Alan Bestic, who was acting as temporary relief master. Bestic was a vastly experienced mariner who had served on board ocean-going sail ships for the early part of his career. At the outbreak of the First World War Bestic was working for Cunard, and he was on board the *Lusitania* when it was torpedoed off the Old Head of Kinsale in May 1915.

The threat of attack from German U-boats seemed little more than a fanciful idea for Bestic and the *Isolda* crew, as their work rarely took them outside Irish waters. The belligerent nations officially respected the territorial sea limits of Ireland, which prohibited the entry of any aircraft or naval craft within 3 miles of the coast. For this reason, aircraft attack was unlikely, although not impossible.

Early on 19 December, the relief crews for both lightships began arriving from their homes in Wexford to board *Isolda*. By 0900 hrs the lighthouse tender had rounded the massive stone breakwater that protected Rosslare Harbour. The first call was to the Coningbeg lightship and the expected journey time was just over two and a half hours. There were no stores to land on either lightship and so it was not anticipated that *Isolda* would take long to complete the transfer of personnel.[2] It was a beautiful crisp winter's morning with only the slightest breath of wind disturbing the sea. Second Officer Jocelyn O'Hehir was on watch and he was joined by Quartermasters Mark McDonagh and James Horan. Elsewhere the ship's crew were engaged in routine duties. Captain Bestic and First Officer Ernest Thornton were in their cabins, while Chief Engineer Thomas Whyte was busy compiling the annual stores list for the ship. Once clear of Tuskar Rock, Second Officer O'Hehir put *Isolda* on a course towards their first destination.

In the pre-dawn darkness of that same morning, an FW200 had taken off from its base at Bordeaux-Merignac. The intended patrol area would take the aircraft past the Isle of Man to the northern limits of the Irish Sea and then south to exit through St George's Channel. The FW200 passed west of Cornwall and proceeded north into the Irish Sea. The seas, however, appeared empty of prey and no attacks were carried out on the northern leg of the patrol. On the return leg, the movements of the FW200 were reported by the Coast Watching Service. Lookout posts from Dublin all along the east coast to Rosslare sighted the large aircraft flying low over the sea. At Greenore Point the FW200 altered course and turned to follow the coast west towards Hook Head. Just east of the headland, the Irish merchant ship *Lanahrone* was back at sea having left Waterford earlier that morning. From the bridge, Captain Hanrahan watched the FW200 come into view around Carnsore Point and circle his ship twice. The Irish neutral markings on *Lanahrone* were clearly seen by the German aircrew and they headed south, where they spotted another ship.

On the bridge of *Isolda*, Second Officer O'Hehir reported the sighting of the strange aircraft to Captain Bestic. The second officer and quartermaster watched as the unknown aircraft turned and passed ahead of the ship. On the foredeck the gathered lightship men watched the large aircraft fly low out ahead of the ship and then turn in a tight circle back towards them.

Captain Bestic had joined O'Hehir on the bridge when the lookout shouted that the aircraft was heading directly at them. The FW200 came roaring in just above mast height and flew over the ship from port to starboard. The first bombs fell short and exploded in the water off *Isolda*'s port side. The ship juddered under the concussive force of the near misses. It was unclear to Captain Bestic what damage had been sustained but he knew that further attacks would follow, and as First Officer Thornton and Bosun Edward Johnston reported to the bridge they were told to get the lifeboats ready. The FW200 circled around and made a second attack. This time a bomb sliced clean through the port lifeboat where it hung in the davits. The 250-kilo bomb continued on and burrowed deep into the steel decks before exploding.

The order was passed down from the bridge to abandon ship and the crew began to make their way to the boat deck. In the engine room, Second Engineer Best had stopped the engines while Chief Engineer Whyte went below and cut off the fuel supply. The near misses and single direct hit had sent the small tender reeling and the damage sustained was terminal. Yet above the high-pitched screech of escaping steam and the shouts of men, the frightening drone of the FW200 could be heard approaching once again.

After the first attack, the lightship men had been caught exposed on the foredeck. As the FW200 circled around they found shelter where they could. Below decks Sam Williams made his way forward to the forecastle to retrieve his life jacket. As the young boy contemplated his next move, the FW200 made its second attack. The explosion rocked the ship so much that its bell became dislodged and fell onto the steel foredeck. The deafening roar gave Williams such a scare that he ran for the boat deck where attempts were being made to launch one of the ship's cutters. Smoke began to billow from inside the ship as the explosion ignited fires that spread unchecked. Some of the access ladders leading from the lower decks had been fractured as the ship had trembled under the intensity of the explosions, and this slowed down the escape efforts of those men who had still not made it to the boats.

Williams reached the boat deck just in time to see a cutter already lowered into the water on the starboard side. The youth never hesitated and jumped for the knotted lifeline hanging above the cutter and climbed down. Williams was only just in the cutter when the FW200 was seen approaching for one final deadly pass over *Isolda*. The aircraft approached from astern with the bay doors opened to unleash a further stick of bombs. The last direct hit on the ship wrecked what remained of the bridge. The ship lurched to one side and took on an unnatural list.

The attack had lasted less than fifteen minutes.

Only Captain Bestic and his first officer remained on board. Fighting to regain an upright stance against the angle of the list, both men made their way to the boats. The crew had managed to launch the ship's motorboat and a single cutter. Both cleared the sinking ship and took stock of their situation. While the motorboat searched the sea for those men who had leapt from the decks to take their chances in the water, the cutter waited a short distance off and those on board tried to make the several wounded men amongst them more comfortable.

Captain Bestic instructed the motorboat to make fast a towing line to the cutter and then, with both boats tethered, they proceeded north towards Kilmore Quay. There was a sombre mood in the silent cutter. In addition to the injured men it was apparent that several of the crew had been killed in the attack. The realisation that fellow shipmates had been lost, and the intense ferocity of the brief encounter would have stunned any shipwrecked seaman. As the survivors steered north, the merchant ship *Lanahrone* and the lifeboat from Kilmore Quay headed out to the scene of the attack to help. At Kilmore Quay, ambulances were waiting to take the injured men to hospital. The remainder of the crew headed to a local bar where they waited for transport to take them into Wexford town and the train home. Young Sam Williams was considered too young and was not allowed a drink. He took himself off on a walk around the village to reflect on the events of that morning, while his shipmates took solace in the public house.

Soon a succession of cars and taxis arrived to drive the men into Wexford town. From here they boarded the afternoon train for Dublin; they would alight at Dun Laoghaire. The families of the crew had been notified in advance and were waiting on the platform as the train pulled in. There were emotional reunions as concerned loved ones embraced fathers and husbands who had returned safe from the loss of *Isolda*. It was left to Captain Bestic and his officers to break the tragic news to the families of those crew members who had been killed in the attacks. The heartrending scenes of relief and despair enacted on the platform that evening were emblematic of the war at sea.

Following the loss of *Isolda* there was much speculation as to why the ship had been attacked and whether the attack had taken place inside Irish waters. The work carried out by those dedicated to making the seas safer for all should have exempted them from attack. As such, these ships were clearly marked. *Isolda* had the words 'LIGHTHOUSE SERVICE' in white letters 5 feet high on each side. However, the attack on the Trinity House tender *Satellite* the month before had shown that this marking did not exempt any ship from attack. In any event, the German pilot later reported that he had attacked a ship with the lighthouse-service mark, so it was hardly a case of mistaken identity. Other suggestions put forward for the attack were that the *Isolda* flew a British blue ensign at the time, which the German pilot would have recognised as a British merchant-navy ensign.[3] Regardless of the reasons for the loss of the lighthouse tender, the fact was that six innocent Irish seamen were killed.

Following leave, Captain Bestic and the *Isolda* officers were employed on the other CIL ship, *Alexandra*, which continued to serve the lightships off the Wexford coast. In the aftermath of the attack on *Isolda*, additional protection against air attack was given to *Alexandra*, including defensive armaments and armour protection around the wheelhouse.

The ratings from *Isolda* were given shore jobs working in the Trinity House depots in the south of England. However, after a brief spell in England, and as the bombing of English cities continued, the Irishmen preferred to return home.

Sam Williams was released from service at the end of January 1941. He remained connected to the sea and joined Palgrave Shipping in 1943 as an ordinary seaman. In 1948 Sam was re-employed by CIL and joined *Discovery II* in London. His long and successful career had its beginnings with *Isolda* and the harrowing events of 19 December 1940.

10

NO SAFETY FOR STRAGGLERS

In November 1940, with the onset of another winter in the Atlantic, Dönitz decided to move the few remaining U-boats on patrol out of the North Channel. Operations were shifted towards the west in a move intended to give the U-boats more time to manoeuvre into an attacking position. However, this new plan was hampered in its effectiveness and actually resulted in fewer sinkings: first, there were simply too few U-boats on patrol and not enough encounters with convoys and, second, the winter weather impeded the effectiveness of those U-boats in the operational area. There were some positive results in December with an extremely successful action against convoy HX-90. However, after this encounter no U-boat succeeded again in intercepting a convoy sufficiently far west to allow a large number of U-boats to reach it before it entered the confines of the North Channel.

Even though bad weather and poor visibility hampered the efforts of his commanders at sea, Dönitz remained convinced that operations in the north, where the shipping was most concentrated, should continue. But he was also conscious that operations further south should not be overlooked and agreed that two U-boats be sent into the central Atlantic. This would divert the overstretched

Royal Navy while providing valuable experience to the U-boat crews.

* * *

Explosions echoed around the relatively quiet waters of Freetown as Korvettenkapitän Von Stockhausen, in command of U-65, wreaked havoc amongst the poorly protected merchant ships off the West African coast.[1] For convoys departing Freetown the protection afforded to them was limited at best, as escorts were simply not available to northbound convoys for the entire voyage. A local escort composed of destroyers and AS trawlers could provide limited protection for a few days only before they were obliged to return to port for refuelling. The situation regarding ocean escorts was even more critical and half the northbound convoys leaving Freetown in January 1941 had no ocean escort at all.[2]

One other trend troubled Western Approaches Command during January 1941. At the beginning of the year they felt that a combination of bad weather, enhanced counter-measures and diverted convoy routes had significantly reduced the number of sinkings by U-boats. However, this favourable outcome had been offset by the knowledge that German air attacks on shipping in the North-West Approaches had sunk just as many ships as their U-boat counterparts over the winter.

Ships particularly prone to attack were those sailing independently or stragglers who had become detached from their convoy. With a defensive armament that was practically ineffective, these lone ships were easy prey for the voracious FW200 which cast an ever-increasing shadow over the bleak wintry North-

West Approaches. The first two convoys to sail from Freetown in January 1941 each lost two ships to aircraft attacks – all four were stragglers that had lost their convoys when poor weather scattered them or less able ships that had fallen astern.[3]

* * *

Just after sunrise on 8 January 1941, HMS *Pretoria Castle* entered the outer channel approaching Freetown Harbour. After several days searching for German surface raiders, the AMC was ordered to return to the port to refuel and load stores in preparation for its next assignment. The large converted liner manoeuvred smoothly through the myriad of merchant ships and warships lying at anchor in the crowded harbour. Congestion in the port was particularly bad because of the troop transport convoy WS-5A, which had been forced to delay its onward journey to South Africa owing to a lack of fresh water at Freetown. The shortage was finally alleviated when the tanker *British Zeal*, which was carrying a cargo of fresh water, arrived under tow into Freetown, having been damaged when attacked by Von Stockhausen.

Shortages of fresh water, bunkers and victualling were a constant logistical worry at Freetown. Although supplies of stores and fuel would arrive from the UK and South Africa, the lack of small local tenders to transport them to the waiting ships inevitably led to delays. Yet, despite these shortcomings, the naval and port facilities had improved considerably since the beginning of the war. The port defences had been built up steadily and by the end of 1940 the entrance to the harbour was protected by substantial AS boom defences and coastal gun batteries sited at prominent points overlooking the harbour approaches.[4]

As the starboard anchor from *Pretoria Castle* was let go, merchant ships in the harbour speculated correctly that perhaps this might be the ocean escort for the next scheduled convoy, SL-62. Many of the waiting ships were already veterans of the long journey north as part of an SL convoy, including the Norwegian cargo ship *Austvard,* which had previously sailed as part of SL-33. That journey had passed without incident and *Austvard* had an uneventful convoy experience on its voyage to Limerick. Also due to sail from Freetown was the Belgian ship *Olympier*, which, like *Austvard*, carried a full cargo of iron ore.

On the morning of 10 January, the captains of the merchant ships in SL-62 were transported ashore for the briefing. In total, thirty-one vessels would sail from Freetown, with another joining from St Vincent. The commodore would sail in *Adda.* Acting as ocean escort would be the recently arrived *Pretoria Castle*, while HMS *Kelt* and *Turcoman* would provide a local escort from Freetown. During the briefing, Commodore Burke stressed the need for each ship to maintain position within the convoy and, where circumstances permitted, to fill any gaps that appeared in the columns. The importance of maintaining the ordered speed was imperative, as was the proper identification of signals issued by the commodore's ship.

Later in the afternoon the harbour echoed with the sounds of ships preparing to depart. Thick black ribbons of soot billowed out of funnels as steam was raised for the engines, while sailors mustered on forecastle decks and prepared to heave up the anchors. Commodore Burke and *Adda* were the first to get under way, then the remainder of the ships passed through the boom defences in close prearranged procession. By the time the last ship had cleared the outer channel and the convoy had formed up into columns, the sun was already low on the western horizon. The convoy steered west, away from the coast and out into the north Atlantic. Ahead lay a three-week voyage and it was one shrouded in uncertainty.

The following days were uneventful as the convoy settled into a pattern of zigzag courses and speed adjustments. Commodore Burke frequently exercised the ships in evasive steering and visual signals, making the best possible use of the good weather and relative safety afforded by the southern latitudes before the convoy entered the critical leg of the voyage. On 13 January the local escorts parted company with SL-62 and returned to Freetown. With only *Pretoria Castle* remaining until the rendezvous with the local escorts of the Western Approaches, the convoy would be defenceless in the event of a U-boat attack. There was also the aerial threat – in such an eventuality each ship would employ its own guns. It was expected that a combined defensive barrage from the convoy would repulse any attack from the air.

By 22 January progress had been good, with minimal disruption, and the convoy had now reached a position just 100 miles south-west of the Azores. That day, however, menacing signs loomed large on the western horizon as the weather conditions gradually deteriorated. Dense opaque bands of rain swept across the skyline in squally torrents, momentarily concealing ships behind a curtain of water. The freshening breeze and moderate swell steadily increased in intensity, which made station-keeping especially difficult as helmsmen struggled to maintain a steady heading. Nevertheless, despite the conditions thus far, the convoy was still making a very respectable speed of 9 knots. The continued good progress did not last long, however, and just after midnight on 23 January the wind increased to near gale force. Swell waves in excess of 4 metres, combined with the heaped-up seas, made the movement of each ship more erratic as they fought stubbornly against the worsening conditions in an attempt to maintain position within the convoy. Concerned that the severe conditions might cause damage to some of the ships, during the early hours of the morning Commodore Burke decided that the convoy should heave to.

For the manoeuvre to be executed successfully the lead ships of each column were required to alter course together. Then each ship in the columns would follow the one ahead. Under normal night conditions such a manoeuvre would have posed a considerable challenge to any experienced master conning his ship. With tempestuous seas spilling around the ungainly ships, and reduced visibility, it proved almost impossible. The turn began when the lead ships altered course to port, turning from a heading of 335 degrees to the new heading of 280 degrees while simultaneously reducing speed. The rectangular outline of the convoy slowly turned into the weather, its solid mass of close-sailing ships like a cloak being swept forcibly around into the wind. As the cloak twisted and stretched against the worsening gale so the fabric holding it together ripped apart. Those ships that fortuitously remained close to the commodore desperately tried to maintain station, but the majority were dispersed amidst the heaving seas and continuing downpours.

As dawn broke over the scene, the remaining convoy continued to ride out the bad weather while Commodore Burke assessed the meteorological situation. Satisfied that the winds had eased sufficiently, he decided to resume his original course. With so many ships scattered over such a wide area, *Pretoria Castle* began to search for those that had lost contact during the night and by late afternoon had managed to locate all but a few stragglers. One of those which found itself alone was *Olympier*, which had been trying to regain contact with the convoy since daybreak. Assuming that they would probably return to their original track, the captain of *Olympier* wisely did the same.

The weather continued to improve into 24 January, the wind having reduced to a gentle breeze with a moderate swell dominating the sea. Time had been lost, and both *Pretoria Castle* and Commodore Burke were mindful of the need to ensure that the convoy was not delayed for its rendezvous with the Western Approaches local escort. As noon approached, *Nestor*, which was leading the fourth column, spotted a ship ahead of the convoy. *Pretoria Castle* increased speed and continued on to investigate. The vigilant escort closed on the unidentified ship, and they exchanged recognition signals. It was *Olympier*. The convoy quickly caught up with the lone Belgian, which gratefully retook its position within the formation.

That afternoon SL-62 passed to the west of the Azores, completing over half the voyage. Weather permitting they would arrive on time for the rendezvous with the local escorts. They made good progress throughout the following days, although the cyclonic weather conditions lingered on. Progress was halted once again by the weather when, on the evening of 26 January, Commodore Burke was obliged once more to turn the convoy and heave to. The lead ships began to alter course, with those following behind endeavouring to remain in position, although the worsening sea conditions and the poor visibility again increased the difficulty of the manoeuvre. Once again, for one reason or another, some ships could not keep station and lost contact with the convoy. The extent of the situation became clear when, just before 0300 hrs on 27 January, the largest grouping *Pretoria Castle* could find was of six ships only. The remainder were scattered over the surrounding area, some in smaller groups of twos and threes, with individual ships dispersed over a large area. With daylight and visual contact regained, ships began to make their way back to the main group and to reform into some semblance of an organised convoy.

Pretoria Castle was busy all morning rounding up stragglers, but by noon only thirteen ships had been accounted for. *Austvard* was one of the many ships to have lost contact with the main convoy during the night, but it had located *Clan MacIver* and *Clan Murdoch*. The trio were found by *Pretoria Castle* and guided back towards the main group.

Improving sea conditions had allowed the convoy to resume its course, but it was imperative that there be no further delays and that the best possible speed be maintained by all. On the evening of 28 January, just prior to *Pretoria Castle*'s departure, only nineteen ships were still in convoy. Neither *Olympier*, which had not been sighted since 26 January, nor *Austvard* had been able to keep up.

Within the coming days the convoy would enter the critical phase of the voyage. On 28 January FW200 aircraft had attacked two ships in the approaches to the North Channel and, in the early hours of 29 January, another homeward-bound convoy, SC-19, was attacked, with the loss of five ships. Its escort of two destroyers and two AS trawlers had failed to prevent the losses, and the U-boats had evaded detection, slipping away unscathed.

Later that morning there was relief throughout the ships of

SL-62 with the sight of masts on the horizon. An advance escort force comprising the destroyer HMS *Mallow* and two AS trawlers, *St Elsk* and *Northern Dawn*, formed up around the convoy. The remainder of the escort group, consisting of destroyers and corvettes, would arrive the following day and would significantly increase the defensive screen. No further stragglers caught up with the convoy and those ships unaccounted for were to remain independent for the rest of the voyage.

On 30 January the ships of SL-62 were stretched out over a wide area of the Atlantic, with the main body at the western extremity of an extended line. Approximately 200 miles to the east sailed *Austvard*, and in between was *Olympier*. Not too far off from the Belgian ship was another straggler, *Rowanbank*. Although both ships were within visual sight of each other, there was little in terms of mutual defence that either could offer the other in the event of an attack.

The isolation of the morning was abruptly interrupted when an FW200 flew in low over the decks of *Olympier*. The large aircraft had managed to stalk its victim without detection until it was almost directly above the ship. As the surprised crew looked up, the German dropped a stick of bombs and raked the decks and wheelhouse with machine-gun fire. The aircraft flew over the ship twice before flying off. Thankfully, the ship had escaped serious damage and was able to continue steaming. The sudden attack had shaken the crew into the grim realisation that, as a single ship, they were extremely exposed. The captain ordered a radio message be transmitted stating that they had been attacked by an enemy aircraft. They had been fortunate that the aircraft had flown off and had not waited to assess the full impact of its attack, but the

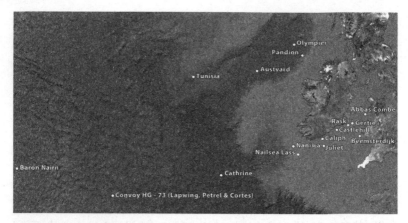

Position of ships sunk in 1941 whose survivors landed in Ireland

FW200 was fishing in a barrel, and it would not be long before another attack on an unsuspecting straggler would be made.

Just over an hour after the attack on *Olympier*, the German FW200 caught *Austvard* completely unawares. Two low-level attacks scored five direct hits on the ship. Three bombs ploughed through the ship's hull at the waterline, tearing the steel plates apart and causing catastrophic flooding of the adjoining cargo hold spaces. The ingress of water combined with the heavy iron-ore cargo overwhelmed *Austvard* and sealed its fate. The remaining two bombs hit the boat decks, destroying two lifeboats and badly damaging another. As the FW200 flew over the ship it raked the decks with machine-gun fire, hitting the radio room and putting the equipment out of action. On top of the devastation caused by the attack, five crewmen were missing or dead. Those who still had their lives hurriedly prepared to abandon ship as *Austvard* settled deeper into the water. The rate at which the ship slipped beneath the encroaching waves speeded as successive cargo holds began to flood, causing the decks to take on an unnervingly acute angle.

It only took ten minutes for *Austvard* to sink, leaving those men who had managed to abandon ship adrift in a handful of survival craft. Only one lifeboat had escaped total destruction in the air attacks and, although afloat, it had been damaged and needed repairs right away. In addition to the damaged lifeboat, the crew had launched two life rafts. Those men who had jumped from the decks began swimming towards these. Materials from both rafts were used to repair the lifeboat and to make it as seaworthy as possible. It was necessary to transfer some of the lifeboat crew to the rafts while the repairs were carried out. Once completed, the lifeboat was able to accommodate only eight men while the remaining crewmen had to make do with a place on one of the rafts. Once they had stabilised their situation and assessed their options it was decided to sail for the Irish coast. The lifeboat would lead under sail while both rafts were taken in tow. It would be a slow and cumbersome journey eastward, but with no other options available and an early rescue looking unlikely, they set off.

On 31 January the lookouts on *Olympier* scrutinised every sector of the horizon. The clear skies and good visibility threatened that more air attacks would follow. That day's inevitable attack followed a similar pattern to the day before, only this time the FW200 was spotted before the attack began. *Olympier* was brought to an immediate stop when three direct hits inflicted crippling damage and caused it to lurch violently, also killing some of the crew. Damage reports of uncontrolled flooding were soon relayed to the bridge and it was clear that the ship was doomed. Orders shouted down instructed the lifeboats launched and this was accomplished in good order and without any panic. Both lifeboats rowed a safe distance away and the surviving crew watched the last moments of *Olympier*. The groaning steel plates beneath the waves merged with the high-pitched hiss of escaping air. As this din gradually faded, the crew in the lifeboats could just make out the drone of the FW200 in the distance as it attacked *Rowanbank*.

The Belgian crew were fortunate to have abandoned ship in good order in well-founded lifeboats. Several men who had been seriously wounded in the attack were made as comfortable as possible, but the first-aid kits could not provide any real relief for them. Urgent medical assistance was required to improve their chances of surviving their ordeal. With only 100 miles to the Irish coast, both boats set off together. During the night they drifted apart and by daylight on 1 February they had lost contact.

As the lifeboats of *Olympier* began their journey towards Ireland, the survivors from *Austvard* were not making as good progress as they had hoped. Towing the rafts was very slow work and little headway was being made. After a brief deliberation, a decision was made that the lifeboat would carry on without the rafts. On reaching safety, the lifeboat crew would notify the authorities and send help for those on the rafts. Cast free from the burden of towing the rafts, the lifeboat was able to sail at a respectable speed.

The first survivors of the FW200's attack to make landfall on 2 February were those on one of the lifeboats from *Olympier*, under the command of Chief Officer Geirnaert, who, despite badly swollen legs and feet, managed to pilot his craft into the safety of Carrigart, Co. Donegal. Of the fifteen occupants, five were in a serious condition and the attending doctor insisted that they convalesce at Carrigart. Two more seamen were taken directly to

Letterkenny hospital with leg and feet injuries. The remaining eight were generally in good spirits after their ordeal and enjoyed the generous hospitality of the people of Carrigart that night. The following day, arrangements were made for those fit to travel and they went by bus to Londonderry for onwards repatriation to England. It would be some time before the men who remained behind for medical attention would be considered fit to leave Donegal. One of the longest temporary residents of Carrigart was Chief Officer Geirnaert, who stayed for thirteen months.

Rescue attempts were launched to locate the remaining missing men. During the early morning of 2 February the rescue ship *Toward* picked up twenty-two survivors from a lifeboat off the north Donegal coast. As the exhausted men were hauled on board and given hot drinks and blankets, they were able to tell their rescuers that they were from the Belgian ship *Olympier*.

The lifeboat from *Austvard* had made steady progress since it was released from towing the unwieldy life rafts. However, the repairs carried out immediately after *Austvard* sank barely managed to keep the boat afloat and its buoyancy was precarious. It fell to First Officer Knut Dykesten to maintain the boat in a seaworthy condition. The deteriorating physical health of the crew members gradually took its toll. Over the course of those early February days, the bodies of two crewmen who had succumbed to the effects of exposure were quietly slipped over the gunwale. For the remaining six men it seemed that unless they were rescued soon they might share a similar fate.

Salvation was just over the horizon when, on 4 February, the outline of Dingle Peninsula greeted the weary men's eyes. Dykesten beached the lifeboat on a remote landing between Sybil and Dunmore Heads, and the survivors were cared for by the few local people who lived close by. Transport was arranged to take them to Dingle where medical attention could be administered. One critically ill seaman was admitted to Dingle general hospital on arrival. Regrettably, despite the best efforts of the medical staff, Alfred Andersen did not recover and the following day he passed away. As each man regained his strength, he travelled to Dublin, where he would wait for the Norwegian consulate to arrange his passage across the Irish Sea. Only five crew members from *Austvard* survived to leave Ireland, a pitiful number considering the original crew numbered twenty-eight. The life rafts were never found.

11

TUNISIA

The demands on merchant seamen were such that survivors of ships lost through enemy action quickly found themselves back at sea. Just as the replacement of lost shipping tonnage was critical in the effective prosecution of the war, so too was it crucial to have a pool of suitably skilled men to work on board the merchant ships. Those who had endured the ordeal of escaping a sinking ship and making it back to friendly shores were left with little alternative but to report to the shipping office and have their names placed back in the operational pool of seamen.

All too often the call to join a ship was received after only the briefest of periods at home. Those failing to report for duty could face fines or even imprisonment. The fortitude of those seamen, who despite their previous experiences continued to man the merchant ships during the bleakest periods of the war at sea, is nothing short of inspiring. Each seafarer who survived a sinking had his own story to tell. For some, a prompt rescue meant the whole incident passed without significant consequence. For others less fortunate, the journey from abandoned ship to friendly shore might last for months or even for years. An extended voyage at sea in a small open lifeboat might end with the survivors landing on a remote stretch of unfamiliar coastline, which might even prove to be unfriendly and lead to incarceration by one of the Axis powers. For these men, their physical and mental strength was tested to the limit.

On 1 April 1941, the cargo ship *Tunisia* lay alongside at Barry docks and waited for its new crew to board before sailing into the hazardous seas beyond the Bristol Channel. *Tunisia* had been part of convoy SL-67 from Freetown, which had been attacked by U-boats on the night of 8 March, with the loss of five ships. The following morning, as the convoy recovered from those losses, another more imposing threat had appeared on the horizon in the guise of two German battleships. *Scharnhorst* and *Gneisenau* had been directed towards SL-67 by the attacking U-boats and were on an intercept course. However, the powerful raiding force withdrew when it realised that the British battleship HMS *Malaya* was part of the convoy escort. It was a day of high drama for *Tunisia*'s Captain William Shute and his seasoned wartime crew.

Shute had sailed in several coastal convoys while in command of his previous ship, *Marsa*, which had worked its way around the east and south coasts of England under the constant threat of German attack by air and by S-boat. But it was a collision with another ship, HMS *Godetia*, that proved its most dangerous encounter at sea. *Marsa* was badly damaged and needed lengthy repairs, but *Godetia* was less fortunate and sank shortly after.

Five months after this incident Shute's *Tunisia* crew included several former crew members from *Marsa*. Chief Officer Arthur Parry, Second Engineer William Allen and Third Engineer Walter Smith had formed a healthy working relationship with their captain over their time serving together. Deck ratings Ernest Haysham, Patrick Hamilton, John Benson and Thomas Atwell had been on board the cargo ship *Herport* when it struck a mine in the River Thames on 14 March. Within ten minutes it had sunk. All four escaped and a fortnight later they were walking up a gangway again, this time to board *Tunisia* for the first time. For Ernest Haysham, the loss of *Herport* had not been his first experience of escaping from a sinking ship. Twice before his ships had been torpedoed and each time the lucky youngster had escaped unharmed.

One of the youngest members of the crew to join *Tunisia* while it was loading at Barry was eighteen-year-old William Pook, whose wartime exploits were as remarkable as any, in spite of his age. During the invasion of Norway in 1940, Pook was serving on board the British ship *Mersington Court*, which was trapped in Narvik Harbour when the Germans landed. Unable to escape Narvik, the merchant seamen were forced to make a long and arduous trek across the bleak landscapes of Norway and Sweden before being interned by the Swedish authorities in the northern town of Jörn. Towards the end of 1940, a plan was conceived by the British for five interned Norwegian ships to sail from Sweden to the UK with vital war materials.[1] As many of the Norwegian crews were unwilling to be part of such an audacious operation, fifty-eight British seamen from Jörn, including William Pook, volunteered to man the ships. The plan was given the code name Operation Rubble and, despite the steep odds against its success, on 25 January 1941 all five ships arrived safely at Kirkwall after the thrilling dash through the Skagerrak.

Pook had spent eight months marooned in Scandinavia and, with the extra pay earned from Operation Rubble, he spent the next two months enjoying himself. His shore leave finally ended though and, with the fervour of youth on his side, Pook returned to sea. At the shipping office in Barry the newly promoted ordinary seaman was assigned to *Tunisia.*

With a cargo of coal destined for Freetown, *Tunisia* sailed once more for the Atlantic. The OB convoy series had continually shifted the dispersal point further north and west in response to German air and U-boat attacks. The Atlantic had become an uncompromising battleground and a long serpentine route had become necessary to avoid the attention of the enemy on the extended voyages to West Africa. Once the convoy dispersed, *Tunisia* proceeded independently south towards Freetown. It was an uneventful voyage with no interference from the enemy. For Captain Shute and his crew the monotony of steaming through an empty Atlantic was an enjoyable interlude.

The arrival at Freetown ended the illusion of peacetime sailing, as *Tunisia* sailed through the boom defences into a harbour choked with ships. With such large numbers at anchor, delays were inevitable at the overworked wharves that served the small port. Days of inactivity lapsed into weeks as *Tunisia* waited for the opportunity to discharge its cargo of coal, but finally the last load was hoisted over the side and onto the waiting barge.

For its next cargo, *Tunisia* did not have to leave the port limits of Freetown. It would proceed upriver to the small port of Pepel and load a full cargo of iron ore. Once complete, it would be back to the anchorage to await sailing orders with the next homeward convoy. By this time *Tunisia* had spent almost nine weeks at anchor and Captain Shute was concerned about the best speed his ship could make. Having been stationary in the warm waters of Freetown Harbour for so long, a sizable amount of marine growth had accumulated on the ship's hull. The extra friction would have a negative effect on the ship's maximum speed, which in turn would have serious repercussions for maintaining position within a convoy. At the ship masters' conference prior to departure Shute estimated the best speed of *Tunisia* at 8½ knots. This was an optimistic approximation and the only way to tell with any degree of accuracy would be when the ship was at sea and the commodore performed speed trials. The speed set for the forthcoming convoy was between 7½ and 8 knots. Captain Shute's estimate did not leave much room for manoeuvre.

The day of departure finally arrived on 15 July 1941, when *Tunisia* set sail as part of convoy SL-81. Commodore Tate on board *Abosso* weighed anchor and passed through the protective boom of Freetown Harbour just before midday. By the afternoon the convoy had formed up and the escorts had taken up station. The weather was fine, with clear skies and good visibility. The convoy was off to a good start. With over three weeks remaining before they were safely docked in England, those on board hoped that the smooth sailing and favourable weather conditions would last for the duration of their voyage.

The convoy made steady progress over the following days, with a slow but steady average speed of 6½ knots up to 19 July. Since the ship left Freetown, *Tunisia*'s chief engineer, Johnson, and his engine-room staff had been busy dealing with several mechanical defects. Despite the problems, Johnson still managed to coax enough steam out of the machinery to maintain the required speed. The pace was picked up the following day when Commodore Tate ordered an increase of speed to 7½ knots. As Shute watched from the bridge, he was dismayed to see that *Tunisia* was unable to respond to this increase of speed and immediately began to drop astern. The toll taken by the extended time in Freetown combined with the mechanical breakdowns became all too evident.

Throughout the day *Tunisia* continued to fall behind, until by the evening it was 3 miles astern of the convoy. The convoy reduced speed to 6 knots to allow *Tunisia* to catch up, but it took until early morning on 21 July for the ship to regain its position. Although the convoy maintained an average speed of just over 6 knots for the rest of the day, Shute and Johnson were facing a difficult situation on board. The exertion of the previous day had put a strain on the machinery and it was now becoming a serious issue. The engineers worked tirelessly to keep the engine going, but on the morning of 22 July *Tunisia* dropped astern again with engine trouble. By the afternoon the convoy was out of sight and *Tunisia* was alone, with no escort and with serious machinery problems. Shute considered the limited options available to him and decided that the only sensible approach was to try and resume course at the best available speed. The standard practice once contact with the convoy was lost was to sail for the rendezvous position for the following day. Shute followed these instructions and set a course at the best speed available to him, hoping to catch up with SL-81. There was still no sign of the convoy on 23 July and Shute was left with no alternative but to continue on course. With a little luck and a change in the prevailing conditions he might increase speed and gradually reduce the distance between his ship and SL-81.

On the morning of 24 July the Admiralty sent a message to HMS *Moreton Bay*, which was acting as ocean escort for SL-81. Due to the threat of U-boat activity ahead of the convoy's route, an amended routing instruction was issued. The convoy would now deviate from its original course, hoping to avoid enemy contact further north. Captain Shute was completely ignorant of this alteration and continued on his original course. *Tunisia* and SL-81 were now on diverging tracks and the probability of them meeting up was diminishing rapidly.

For the next few days *Tunisia* continued on its search, without regaining contact with any of the other ships. On 26 July the skies were overcast and the anxiety felt by Captain Shute increased as he neared more hostile waters. Finally, on 27 July, in an attempt to regain contact with any friendly forces in the area, Shute ordered a coded message to be broadcast, giving their position and requesting assistance from any British warship. The message was received on board *Moreton Bay*. The commanding officer, Captain Bell, reviewed the signal and deduced that the only straggler from the convoy under his care was just over 300 miles to the west. Instead of being behind its parent convoy, as would be expected, the lone merchant ship was tracking on a parallel course ahead and to the west. Engineers Johnson, Allen and Smith had done their utmost to keep the engines going and had it not been for the deviation in the convoy's route they would have succeeded in catching up.

Shute's immediate concern was the safe completion of the voyage. The further north he took his ship the greater the likelihood of his encountering the enemy. There was cause for hope on 1 August, when a signal was received from the Admiralty requesting the position and updated details of *Tunisia*. Relieved that contact had been established, Shute had the information transmitted. It was followed by another Admiralty signal giving new routing instructions. Shute was reassured that this guidance would lead his ship away from known U-boat activity. So far, by following the convoy's original course, *Tunisia* had kept well to the west and had evaded the attentions of any patrolling U-boats.[2]

The threat from the air remained and on their final approach towards the North Channel Captain Shute entered the realm where the predatory FW200s patrolled. Lone merchant ships and stragglers were favourite targets and with the protection of the convoy gone, Shute knew that the threat of an attack was a credible one.

On the same day Shute received the revised routing instructions, the weather began to deteriorate. Freshening winds and the onset of overcast skies pointed to a depression moving in from the west. By 4 August the wind was near gale force, with the skies remaining dark, but visibility was good and the lookouts had an unimpeded view across the white-streaked seascape. However, those posted on the port side of the bridge and on the monkey island did have to contend with the freshening wind, which blew in their faces and impaired their vision.

Shute ordered the defensive steering pattern stopped, as the rough seas caused the ship to roll precariously on the parts of the zigzag where the stern was exposed. The kite, which was used as a defence against low flying aircraft, was up, but the strain on the tether cable caused by the high winds proved too much and the cable parted.[3] The crew set to work repairing the damaged cable and attaching a second kite. This took just over two hours and as preparations were being made to launch it, the lookout on the port side entered the bridge to inform Third Officer John Stone that he had just seen large splashes off the port beam. Bewildered deckhands, who had also noticed the splashes, joined Stone on the port bridge wing.

An FW200 suddenly appeared, breaking through some low cloud and closing rapidly. In silence, its engines turned off, it glided in a shallow dive on the ship. It had fired its forward machine guns as it dove and the bullets falling short were what had caused the splashes seen by the lookouts.[4] The initial stunned reaction of the crew at seeing the silent marauder turned to frenzied action. The ship's guns were manned, and two Parachute and Cable (PAC) rockets were fired, but they failed to halt the FW200 as it swooped over its target.[5] With its engines roaring back into life, the pilot circled around for another attack. Shute ordered a distress message sent out immediately. Meanwhile, the crew reloaded the PAC rockets.

The aircraft came in low, lined up for a bombing run. It approached from astern with the bomb bay doors opened and a stick of four bombs fell. They splashed into the water right along the port side of the ship. Although the pilot's aim was slightly off, the explosions were nonetheless devastating. As the falling seas drenched the exposed decks and those standing on them, below the waterline the ship's port side was irreparably damaged. Side plates from the turn of the bilge up to the waterline groaned under the strain of the underwater shockwaves. Rivet joints split open and seawater flooded into the lower holds. In the engine room, the main bilge injector valve became dislodged from its seating and here, too, seawater flooded in. Whole sections of steam lines around the engine room leaked as the joints fractured, and propulsion as well as electrical power were lost. In the pitch black of the engine and boiler rooms, men shouted to each other over the screech of escaping steam and the unnerving sound of flooding seawater. Without power the engineers could not pump out the seawater flooding their crippled ship. There was nothing to be done but try and make it to the upper decks.

Those on deck prepared for the next deadly pass of their attacker. The German aircraft had circled and approached once again from the port side, this time on a diagonal run across the ship. The gunners on *Tunisia* opened fire as soon as the large target came into range. They scored hits, but the German pilot was undeterred and pressed home his low level bombing run. Shute watched the bombs from the aircraft fall towards the aft end of his ship. The first smashed through the hatch boards of No. 4 hold and the second hit the poop deck. The explosions sent violent reverberations throughout the ship, causing further damage in the already condemned engineering spaces. The death knell had sounded for *Tunisia* and no hope of saving the ship could be entertained.

Surveying the damage and how ineffective their own defence was in dissuading the aircraft from making further attacks, Captain Shute ordered the crew to abandon ship. Instinctively the sailors went about the duties they had drilled so many times before. Remaining on the bridge throughout, the captain, along with Third Officer Stone, watched as the hurried crewmen prepared the lifeboats for lowering. Some were still half dazed from bomb concussions, while others were completely absorbed in the preparation of the boats and seemed oblivious to the shouts and gesticulations around them.

The radio officers reported to the bridge: they had managed to transmit a distress message but no acknowledgement had been received. Perhaps they would receive a response on the lifeboat radio set once they left the ship.

Tunisia was dead in the water and already settling by the stern. As the last of the lifeboats cleared the ship, Shute finally left the bridge and made his way to the main deck. Standing by alongside was the port jolly boat; the sailors manning the oars had been instructed to wait for Shute and Stone. Having done all he could, Shute stepped into the waiting jolly boat. *Tunisia* gradually disappeared beneath the waves.

The lifeboats were scattered around where the ship had been, and they caught occasional glimpses of each other as they crested the waves. Shute called them together to assess their situation. Rational thinking and sound seamanship were needed to prevail under these circumstances and there was little time for melancholy. A preliminary evaluation of their condition seemed favourable: they had managed to launch three of the four lifeboats and both smaller jolly boats. However, closer inspection revealed that both port lifeboats had been badly damaged by the explosions on that side. They were leaking badly and could not be used as effective survival craft. Furthermore, in their haste to launch the lifeboats, stores that were not lashed to the thwarts were lost overboard as the boats rocked in the davit falls. Shute had the men from the port lifeboats distributed between the remaining intact starboard lifeboat and the second jolly boat. The sea threw around the lifeboats and each man had to steady his nerve before attempting the perilous jump from one gunwale to the other.

For the rest of the day the boats tried to stay in close proximity to each other. It was hoped that the lifeboat radio set would receive a response to the distress message transmitted earlier. With the possibility that a rescue ship was en route, it made sense for the boats to remain in the locality of the last position sent out. But the lifeboat radio set, a relatively new item of equipment for merchant ships, was not robust enough for the conditions to which it was subjected, and the survivors of *Tunisia* did not find out whether their distress message had indeed been received.[6]

The weather on that first day made it very difficult for the lifeboats to remain in contact. As night fell and the temperature dropped, the darkening night soon blotted out any remaining view that Shute and his men had of the two companion boats. The atmosphere in the jolly boat was subdued but not dispirited. Along with the captain and the third officer were Seaman John Gillies and his two shipmates from *Herport*, John Benson and Ernest Haysham, who had survived the sinking of two and four different ships respectively.

The next morning, Shute and his men found that they were alone. The other two boats had drifted out of sight during the night. Without any sea anchor, their boat would have drifted along with the strong winds and the north Atlantic currents. Under these conditions, any time spent just waiting for a rescue ship to arrive would undermine their chances of survival. The only realistic option was to attempt a landfall on the west coast of Ireland. This in itself was going to be difficult. The jolly boat was not fitted with a mast and sail, leaving the men with the most unenviable task of rowing if they wanted to make any headway. However, with two navigating officers on board, they felt that there was a good chance they could navigate to safety. The men were up to the task, and they set out, each taking his turn manning the oars, while the captain took the tiller and steered them across the persistently rough seas.

The men's stamina was severely tested by rowing throughout the day. Shute knew it was important to keep the men focused and organised each man into a routine of watches and rowing duties. Positive leadership and an unyielding belief that they would come through the ordeal spurred the men on through each weary day. For the first few days, the men tried to maintain their strength by eating the standard lifeboat biscuits and tinned meat. To the annoyance of the hungry men, the rations only accentuated their thirst. As the days wore on so the men ate less, until only two half-starved sailors were managing to consume their rations while still being able to discipline their craving for water.

Eventually the cumulative effects of exposure and lack of proper rest and food began to affect all five of the survivors. Exhausted, they could not summon the energy to pull another stroke. As aching muscles and swollen limbs forced a halt to their progress, Shute suggested jury-rigging an oar and blanket into a rudimentary mast and sail. If successful it would relieve the men from rowing duties while still propelling the boat closer to Ireland. The men set to work preparing the rigging, swollen and numbed fingers clumsily grasping at blanket and rope. Once completed, the makeshift mast was stepped and lashed into position. Then, with a sense of satisfaction and relief, the spirits of the five shipmates were lifted as they saw the blanket fill with wind and the jolly boat heaved forward under the power of sail.

On 11 August the lookout surveyed an empty horizon shrouded in a translucent veil of shadows and darkness. At first, it appeared as nothing more than a partial outline, but as his eyes adjusted and he could see with clearer definition, a shadow on the horizon slowly developed into a coastline. By daybreak on 12 August the coast was much closer and each man was scanning the shore for anywhere they might beach the jolly boat.

Standing on the beach at Dog's Strand, Clifden, Co. Galway, were some holidaymakers from Dublin, who spotted the small boat out to sea. Shute steered the boat for the beach and, after navigating into the small rocky bay, the wooden keel finally ran aground on the soft sand. The excited tourists ran down to the boat to help the five exhausted men. The survivors were driven to Clifden and admitted to hospital, although mercifully nobody was seriously ill. Captain Shute apprised the Shipwrecked Mariners' Society agent of the incident and informed him that there were two other lifeboats of survivors from *Tunisia* still at sea. Naturally the captain was eager to find out if there had been any news about these boats, but no other survivors had come ashore in Ireland.

Once nursed back to health, Captain Shute and his four companions set off for Dublin and the return journey to England. By early September there was still no word on the remaining two boats, but Shute remained optimistic that they would be found. He had left them in good order and there was no reason why they would not have followed a similar route to Ireland. As the weeks passed with no sign, the men were officially declared missing. Only the five had survived the sinking of *Tunisia*.

Each had a short leave period before again returning to sea. Ernest Haysham, who had survived four sinkings, was back at Barry docks on 18 September to join his next ship. For the remainder of his wartime career his ships remained afloat. Captain William Shute was honoured for his actions in defending *Tunisia* against air attack and for bringing the four other crew members safely ashore. In January 1942 he was awarded an OBE in recognition of his actions. However, the unrelenting war eventually caught up with him. In August 1942 he was in command of the cargo ship

Hamla, which was torpedoed en route to Freetown with all hands lost. Of the other three survivors who landed in Ireland, both Stone and Gillies would survive the war, but John Benson died at sea in February 1943.

The rugged coast of Galway had once again hosted the arrival of unfortunate merchant seamen caught in the Battle of the Atlantic. As the kindly residents of Clifden bade farewell to the survivors of *Tunisia*, elsewhere on the ocean events were set in motion that would bring more men from the sea to the small Galway village.

12

ENGLISH NAVVIES IN IRELAND

During the winter of 1940, the contentious issue of air reconnaissance for U-boat Atlantic operations remained unresolved. The political wrangling between the Kriegsmarine and the Luftwaffe hindered any close cooperation between the services. In January 1941 bomber wing Kampfgeschwader 40 (KG40) was made operationally subordinate to BdU.[1] Admiral Dönitz had high hopes that this new collaboration would yield great success. After some initial setbacks by the aircraft of I/KG40, the first notable results came in February when a combined attack by six FW200s and U-37 on convoy HG-53 resulted in the loss of eight merchant ships. Hopes of repeating this success were, however, never realised because of the limited numbers of aircraft available and inaccurate position reports from shadowing FW200s.

There was limited success against Gibraltar convoys during the first half of the year, albeit without significant U-boat involvement, but convoys had increased their defences against the FW200 threat. The situation improved for the Germans in July when a shift east in the patrol areas of U-boats permitted greater opportunities for combined operations.

The sea lanes between the UK and Gibraltar were vital and

had to be kept open for the duration of the war. In addition, the bay at Gibraltar acted as a staging post for ships sailing into the Mediterranean or heading south down the West African coast. Military personnel being transferred to new postings made a brief stopover there before heading to their final destinations and a lively passenger trade was still active between the UK and the neutral countries of Spain and Portugal. Trade routes between the Iberian Peninsula and the UK were essential, and there were sound economic reasons to ensure that these remained open. The revenue from selling British coal and other goods was desperately needed to buy materials such as cork, potash, pyrites and iron ore – all vital to the British war economy.

Despite the routing being constrained by the war, the shipping trade itself was similar to that of peacetime, where a ship might find itself on a round voyage sailing outward to Gibraltar with coal and then returning with Portuguese pyrites or Spanish iron ore. From Gibraltar the ships followed the coastal routes either east into the Mediterranean or west back out through the Straits and round to the ports of Portugal and Spain, ensuring they kept within the safety of the neutral Iberian territorial waters. It was this trade that Dönitz set out to disrupt during the latter half of 1941.

Since summer 1940 the OG and HG series of convoys had been obliged to take the long circuitous route through the North-West Approaches and far out into the Atlantic in order to avoid the Luftwaffe, which was now based along the French west coast. The threat from marauding FW200s was constant, as the long-range aircraft had the ability to reach the OG and HG convoys for the greater part of their extended ocean voyage.

The convoys between the UK and Gibraltar had the reassurance of a strong naval escort for the entirety of the voyage. The Royal Navy had introduced the fighter catapult ship and in December 1940 the seaplane carrier HMS *Pegasus* began to escort Gibraltar convoys.[2] Each escort force was supplemented by a local escort operating out of Gibraltar or Londonderry. Increased defensive armaments on merchant ships also helped to improve the ability of a convoy to defend itself against attack from the air. As a result, after the attack on HG-53, the previously indomitable FW200 suffered a series of losses while attacking HG convoys. The increased risk eventually forced the Luftwaffe to abandon low-level attacks against the heavily defended OG and HG convoys. Instead, the FW200 provided reconnaissance for U-boats.

On 13 August convoy OG-71 sailed from Liverpool for Gibraltar.[3] Originally scheduled to depart on 9 August, an attack on SL-81 and the subsequent anti-U-boat operations and rescue work postponed its departure by several days. Twenty-two merchant ships sailed. Four of these, *Lapwing, Petrel, Starling* and *Stork*, belonged to the General Steam Navigation Company (GSN). This long-standing shipping company had been operating a fleet of small near-continental trading ships for over 117 years.

The GSN ships were no strangers to war. In June 1940 several were involved in the evacuation of the British Expeditionary Force from Dunkirk. The passenger steamer *Royal Daffodil* brought back 8,500 troops over five days of hazardous cross-channel crossings. On board at the time was Second Officer John Bingham Wood-house, who earned a commendation from the King for his actions when the ship came under attack. By August 1941 Woodhouse had been promoted to chief officer and was on board *Lapwing* under the command of Captain Thomas Hyam.

After Dunkirk, *Stork* was involved in the evacuation of military personnel and civilian refugees from Saint-Nazaire and Bordeaux, and, since July 1940, it had been engaged in shipping military stores between Belfast and Preston. *Starling* was a regular trader to Spain and Portugal, and had been attacked by aircraft on 12 October 1940 while approaching Cadiz Harbour. Among the GSN ships, only *Petrel*, under the command of Captain John Klemp, had sailed more times than the *Starling, Stork* and *Lapwing* in OG and HG convoys.

Many of the crew on the GSN ships would have been long-standing permanent staff. The bonds between these shipmates prevailed throughout those anxious times when an attack from the air or from beneath the waves tested the resolve of all on board. This unwavering camaraderie extended beyond the crews of individual ships and bound each company ship together in shared strength.

The original route proposed for OG-71 was amended on 14 August in response to a build-up of U-boats west of Rockall. As a result, the convoy sailed closer to Ireland and within the operating envelope of patrolling FW200 aircraft. Two days after leaving the North Channel, the convoy was spotted by an air reconnaissance unit patrolling the area west of the Porcupine Bank. Dönitz ordered four U-boats to move against this convoy and later that same day the first made contact.[4] In the ensuing battle, which lasted until 23 August, six merchant ships and two naval escorts were torpedoed and sunk.

During the night of 19 August, *Petrel* rescued twenty-five men from the torpedoed *Ciscar.* Captain Klemp slowed down his ship and two lifeboats were sent out. *Petrel* meanwhile remained motionless and vulnerable to attack. As the convoy and escorts drew further away, Klemp and his men waited anxiously for the lifeboats to return. Two hours later *Petrel* had completed its mercy mission and made its way back to the convoy. On the final night of the battle *Stork* was hit by a single torpedo. The explosion ignited its cargo of petrol, setting the entire ship ablaze from stem to stern. Miraculously, three crew members managed to escape from this floating inferno. Second Officer Wolley and Ship's Carpenter Stanley Smart jumped from the port bridge wing into the water, while Second Engineer Maxwell had to jump through a porthole to escape the burning vessel. Smart had to tow Maxwell out through a lane of burning petrol and place him on a raft. They were rescued by the corvette HMS *Campion* and eventually landed at Gibraltar. With the losses steadily mounting and the escort incapable of preventing further U-boat attacks, the Admiralty ordered it to proceed directly to Lisbon and the safety of neutral territorial waters. Convoy OG-71 and its heavy escort had been trounced.

The port of Lisbon swelled with the unexpected arrival of so many vessels, but it was only a temporary surge as many of the ships would later proceed independently towards other ports. Once the survivors from *Ciscar* were ashore, *Petrel* left Lisbon and headed north along the coast for Oporto where its cargo of coal and general goods was due. *Lapwing* and *Starling* turned south towards Cape St Vincent and the Spanish port of Huelva.

At Oporto, *Petrel* loaded bales of cork and general goods in place of its coal when it had been sent ashore. In addition to his cargo, Captain Klemp took on board one passenger who would return with the ship to England: Roy Wearne, who worked for the sherry producers Gonzalez Byas & Co. At Huelva, *Lapwing* and *Starling* remained long enough to discharge their cargoes before returning to Lisbon, where they each loaded a full cargo of pyrites. On 15 September the three GSN ships were reunited at Gibraltar. After a short spell at anchor there, in the late afternoon of 17 September, the gathered merchant ships and escorts of convoy HG-73 sailed out past Europa Point and turned west into the Gibraltar Straits.

The convoy consisted of twenty-five merchant ships. These were protected by a strong close-escort force of one sloop, eight corvettes and a catapult fighter ship, which was complemented by a powerful local escort of fast destroyers from Gibraltar. It was an impressive protective screen and its powerful presence reassured the merchant ships as they were shepherded out into the Atlantic. During the afternoon of 18 September the familiar silhouette appeared of an FW200 stalking the convoy from a safe distance. In response to this threat, HMS *Springbank* flew off its catapult fighter. The Fulmar succeeded in chasing away the Condor, which escaped undamaged while the Fulmar returned to Gibraltar.

Now that HG-73 had been located by the Axis forces, the task of maintaining contact with it was handed to a patrol line of Italian submarines operating nearby. Further sighting reports between 19 and 22 September allowed BdU to direct U-124 and U-201 towards the northbound convoy. Both these U-boats had been involved in the successful attack on the well-defended convoy OG-74 and had sunk five merchant ships over a two-day period. Emboldened by their recent exploits, both U-boat commanders relished the chance of striking against another convoy.

The Admiralty issued two routing amendments to HG-73 on 22 and 24 September in an attempt to evade the approaching U-boats. It was a futile effort, and in the early hours of 25 September Kapitänleutnant Johann Mohr, in command of U-124, made contact with the convoy. Mohr had sighted *Springbank* steaming out ahead of the convoy and, after reporting the sighting back to BdU, decided to attack. The torpedoes missed *Springbank*, which meant that the presence of U-124 went undetected, and the opportunity to attack an escort and a large merchant ship presented itself an hour later. There was frustration yet again for Mohr when the attack on the escort missed, but this was offset by his pleasure when the British ship *Empire Stream* became the first casualty from HG-73.

With the breaking of dawn on 25 September, the convoy realised that the U-boats that had steadily encroached upon their position had finally engaged despite their efforts to evade them. While the survivors from *Empire Stream* were rescued from the water, the hunt for the unseen assailants continued without success. On board the surrounding ships, merchant seamen embraced the welcome sunrise, assured that with daylight came the relative safety of freedom from U-boat attack. Throughout the day U-124 continued to shadow the convoy from a safe distance and it was joined in the afternoon by U-203, commanded by Kapitänleutnant Rolf Mützelburg. The stream of radio position reports back to BdU from both shadowing U-boats was monitored by the Admiralty, which had a growing feeling of foreboding that another attack was imminent.

After an uneasy and tense day a dispiriting cloak of darkness enveloped the convoy once again. Commodore Creighton on board *Avoceta* ordered another significant alteration of course in the hope that it would turn the convoy away from any U-boats that may be lying in wait. On board *Petrel* Captain Klemp remained on the bridge with Third Officer Ivan Philips. *Petrel* was leading the first column and therefore lay in a particularly exposed position.

Lookouts were briefed and posted at each side of the wheelhouse, with particular emphasis placed on keeping a lookout to port. At the rear of the first column Captain Hyam and his men on board *Lapwing* were equally alert as they kept an all-round lookout for any possible threat. Both these veteran crews were accustomed to the long nights of convoy sailing and the rigours they demanded of the lookouts. For those on watch the weather conditions were far from ideal for spotting an object low in the water. Although the visibility was generally good, the thick cloud cover had obscured the minimal moonlight available and a fresh north-westerly wind combined with the moderate swell running made the seas very choppy. Under these prevailing conditions a prudent U-boat commander would make his attack on the convoy's port side which put *Petrel* and *Lapwing* in the line of fire.

Just before midnight on 25 September, the stillness of the night was torn apart by large explosions at the centre of the convoy. The sky was lit up by the fiery glow, which was followed shortly after by distress flares that shot upwards and burst into a brilliant crimson glow. In this daring opening attack, two ships succumbed almost simultaneously to the boldness of Rolf Mützelburg. Taking position ahead of the convoy and inside the escort screen, Mützelburg selected the leading and second ships of the fourth column. From a spread of four torpedoes, one had hit the commodore's ship *Avoceta*, while two more found the Norwegian bulk carrier *Varangberg*.

Roused to immediate action by the attack, Captain Klemp ordered all his crew on deck with their life jackets. If an attack on his own ship should occur then this precautionary measure would save precious moments if they had to abandon ship.

The convoy's escorts began to fight back when HMS *Larkspur* sighted U-203 on the surface. The muzzle flash from *Larkspur*'s gun alerted the U-boat, which soon disappeared beneath the waves. On board *Lapwing* and *Petrel*, the men on watch did not allow the battle to detract from their responsibility to ensure the safety of their own crew. Lookouts intensified their focus, and every sector of the horizon was scrutinised through binoculars for a sign of approaching danger. After their experience in August, everyone expected there to be at least one more U-boat stalking them. Indeed, the enemy was closer than they would have liked, and U-124 attempted to break through the escort screen that guarded the port flank of the convoy. Mohr manoeuvred at high speed on the surface and tried to slip through and attack any targets of opportunity.

As midnight passed, the weather conditions deteriorated. Out to the west rain squalls moved across the seas and created dense curtains of precipitation that obscured everything behind them. There followed a moment of nervous calm amongst the crews who listened to the depth-charge attacks of *Larkspur* against U-203. For now at least the second anticipated attack did not materialise.

Captain Klemp had by this stage been on the bridge for much of the day. Confident that he could leave his experienced second officer, Alec Bruce, on watch unassisted, the tired captain left the bridge and retired to his cabin.

Meanwhile, Mohr had successfully manoeuvred U-124 through the defensive screen when he finally sighted the vulnerable ships of the convoy. He assessed the situation. The men in the conning tower fixed their attentions on a group of three ships leading the column immediately in front of them. Using the prevailing weather conditions to his advantage, Mohr kept within the passing rain squalls that camouflaged his whereabouts. He selected the leading ships of the column and fired a single torpedo at each one.

Second Officer Alec Bruce and his lookouts were afforded a good unobstructed view of the sea on either side of the ship. As he looked astern Bruce saw that *Cortes*, the second ship in the column, had closed the distance slightly between them. Noting the change in position, he returned to keeping a lookout ahead, when the quiet night was abruptly shattered by the explosion of a torpedo striking *Cortes* amidships. Bruce barely had time to digest the full extent of this attack when seconds later another torpedo found its mark and struck his own ship on the port side, right aft and in way of the engine room. The muffled explosion sent up a plume of water from the point of detonation. The damage caused by the explosion allowed a deluge of water to immediately flood the machinery spaces. Those unfortunate enough to be on watch in the engine room became the first casualties of the unfolding disaster. The men on deck took whatever shelter they could find as water and debris from the explosion rained down on the decks. As Captain Klemp rushed on deck, the ship started settling quickly by the stern and it was clear it would founder. The lifeboats, which were located on the poop deck, remained attached to the davit arms and were already being dragged beneath the water.

With little time to spare, the men on deck hurriedly launched the life rafts and then scrambled over the side. Captain Klemp remained on board long enough to ensure that his crew had all jumped overboard. As the sea embraced *Petrel* and pulled it steadily under the waves, Klemp joined his crew in the water. Apart from the engine-room staff, the remainder of the crew were able to successfully abandon ship. The inspired order by Klemp to have his off-duty men assemble on deck with their life jackets doubtless saved lives. With the lifeboats lost, the men clung desperately to the few rafts scattered amongst the wreckage. Klemp and eight others clung precariously onto one raft. In the distance they could see the red life-jacket lights of other men in the water.

From the bridge of *Lapwing*, Captain Hyam had witnessed the devastating attacks on *Cortes* and *Petrel*. The devastation and rapid sinking of both ships indicated that the loss of life was probably high. Without a moment's hesitation Hyam ordered Chief Officer Woodhouse to take charge of the starboard lifeboat and prepare to rescue survivors. The sinking of *Stork* the previous month and the loss of so many GSN men was a terrible blow and with the survivors from *Stork* returning home on board *Petrel*, Hyam was determined to prevent any further loss of life. He manoeuvred his ship to windward of where *Petrel* had sunk, thus providing a lee for the starboard lifeboat to launch. With a crew of five others Woodhouse then set off in the lifeboat to where they could see the red life-jacket lights.

The sea had become a confused mix of men and cargo, and the survivors from *Cortes* and *Petrel* drifted together among the floating bales of cork that had escaped from the holds of *Petrel*. This flotsam presented the lifeboat crew with difficult obstacles in addition to the unfavourable sea conditions. They pressed on towards a group of men on a life raft.

As the lifeboat approached, Captain Klemp and the others called out to Woodhouse telling him to pick the men out of the water first. The spirits of the men on the raft were buoyed by the knowledge that rescue was now at hand.

Rowing the ungainly lifeboat on the rough seas was proving difficult and tiring. Progress was slow, and maintaining a steady heading was difficult. Nevertheless, Woodhouse and his crew continued on with the lifeboat, steering an erratic course as they went to each man in the water to pull him on board. After almost three hours of arduous rescue work, Woodhouse and his men had picked twenty men out of the blackness of the night. They returned to *Lapwing* to disembark these rescued men before returning to the remaining men on the raft they had initially sighted. The soaked and cold survivors struggled up the side of the ship: seventeen from *Petrel* and three from *Cortes*.

For Captain Hyam, the time the lifeboat took to rescue the men must have seemed an eternity. His thoughts must have turned to the possibility that the U-boat might still be lurking in the vicinity and might yet discover the stationary *Lapwing*. The battle was still very much in progress and the convoy had moved well out of sight. Further south, *Larkspur* had engaged the submerged U-203 for almost three hours before finally losing contact and deciding to return to the convoy. As the corvette proceeded at its best speed back towards the convoy, it passed the stopped *Lapwing*, observed rafts and a lifeboat in the water and assumed the ship had been a victim of an earlier action. As it appeared that the ship was not in a sinking condition, *Larkspur* continued on but cut loose a small cutter to assist.

Woodhouse and his exhausted lifeboat men set off into the darkness once again on the final leg of their rescue mission. They summoned their last reserves of energy to reach the survivors who waited patiently on the raft. Since Captain Klemp had first seen the lifeboat and had sent it off for the other men, the raft that had provided sanctuary after his ship had sunk itself began to sink. The men had managed to reach another raft and, despite this too being in a partially submerged condition, they had lashed the two together. The result provided sufficient buoyancy for the nine survivors. They were all very much relieved when the lifeboat returned and each man was taken on board. It seemed that their ordeal was finally coming to an end. However, unseen and resolute, Kapitänleutnant Rolf Mützelburg was about to make a dramatic reappearance.

Since the attack on *Avoceta* and *Varangberg*, Mützelburg had successfully evaded the chasing *Larkspur*. Confident that the escort had given up the search, Mützelburg surfaced and immediately set off searching for the convoy, which by now had moved off to the north-east. It was not long before an escort, which could only have been *Larkspur*, was spotted and promptly attacked. However, the attack was unsuccessful and U-203 dived once again, not to escape the attentions of the vengeful corvette but rather to reload its torpedoes and prepare for another attack. When the search resumed, the crew on the conning tower spotted a lone stopped merchant ship.

This was an unmissable opportunity. Mützelburg pointed the bows of the U-boat towards his next target and fired a single torpedo. Watching the target through his powerful Zeiss binoculars, Mützelburg scanned across the port side of the ship as it rolled and pitched in response to the movement of the waves. Hidden from view on the starboard side were the men of *Lapwing*, anxiously awaiting the return of Chief Officer Woodhouse and the lifeboat.

Woodhouse steered his rescue craft towards *Lapwing*, but, as it neared the starboard side, the welcoming view suddenly disintegrated as *Lapwing* was hit just aft of amidships on the port side. The force of the explosion caused the hatch covers to blow skywards, while on the poop deck cowlings were shaken from their foundations. There was no time to launch the remaining lifeboat as the aft decks were soon awash. Those men not killed or injured in the explosion would have to jump overboard and take their chances. Stunned at the ferocity of the explosion, the rescued men from *Petrel* and *Cortes* were compelled to hurl themselves back into the sea for the second time that night.

Lapwing disappeared beneath the waves in less than two minutes, taking Captain Hyam and most of its crew. Left behind on the surface was a scene of devastation and human suffering. The sea was strewn with the wreckage from three ships. Those men lucky enough to jump free of *Lapwing* each faced his own personal struggle for survival.

Klemp and Woodhouse in the lifeboat set about searching for the familiar red lights from the life jackets. There were the occasional cries from the injured that signalled in which direction the boat needed to go. After searching through the wreckage it was painfully apparent that *Lapwing* had taken many of its crew and rescued seamen down with it when it had sunk. From the surrounding debris the lifeboat managed to find a fireman from *Petrel*, Harold Weeden, and the boatswain from *Cortes*, Alfonso Pimentil. Both of these men had previously been picked up by the lifeboat and placed on board *Lapwing*. Weeden had suffered terrible leg and feet injuries as a result of the *Lapwing* explosion.

For the men who had manned the oars throughout the night, their physical exertions had taken their toll and they could go no further. The sea anchor was streamed, which allowed the men to rest while they waited for a rescue ship to return. They huddled together for mutual warmth as persistent rain squalls added to their general discomfort. There was a cautious sense of optimism with the arrival of daylight and the possibility of sighting a rescue ship. However, the prevailing weather conditions were far from ideal and visibility was poor. Then, through the veil of rain, the dark grey outline of a corvette appeared nearby. Men started to shout and wave their arms while others ignited signal flares to attract the attention of the warship. In an effort to make the flares more conspicuous, two were tied onto the end of a boat hook and then ignited. But the unknown corvette failed to notice the distress signals and disappeared from view through another heavy rain squall. The lifeboat did manage to spot a small group of men on a life raft who had also burned signal flares, yet they too had failed to attract the attention of the corvette. As quick as the raft had come into view it disappeared again and was never seen again by the men in the lifeboat.

Some time before midday on 26 September the lookouts in the lifeboat sighted the cutter from *Larkspur*. Occasionally one of the occupants would appear to stand up to take a look around, watching, like those in the lifeboat, for any signs of rescue. With no sign of a ship returning from the convoy, the cutter rowed over towards the larger lifeboat. The five men were all survivors from the explosion that had sunk *Lapwing*. They included two Arabian firemen from *Cortes*, and two stewards and a gunner from *Lapwing*. The total number of men in the lifeboat was now twenty-two: three from *Cortes*, ten from *Petrel* and nine from *Lapwing*.

As the weather showed little sign of improving, Klemp and Woodhouse decided to remain adrift with the sea anchor streamed for the remainder of the day. The provisions from both lifeboats were consolidated and it was found that, provided they adhered to a sensible rationing system, the stock water and rations should be enough for twenty days' sailing. The cutter had been well stocked with provisions, including plenty of fresh water, corned beef and tins of condensed milk. The corned beef, however, was found to be unfit to eat as the tack nails used to hold the packing cases together had pierced the tins.

Next, the hierarchy within the small survival craft was formally decided. Captain Klemp of *Petrel*, Chief Officer Woodhouse and Third Officer Dawson of *Lapwing* would be in charge of the lifeboat. Although between them they had a considerable number of years' experience at sea, none had any practical experience of sailing a small boat and they lacked any navigation aids or instruments to assist them in making landfall. However, with neutral Spain nearby and with favourable weather conditions they expected to do so in less than a week.

There was little improvement in the weather on the second day adrift. A strong north-westerly breeze was blowing and the sea state was far from ideal for sailing. With a strong wind from behind, the lifeboat pitched and lurched freely between the dark-blue Biscay rollers. It was decided that they should step the mast and run before the wind in an attempt to make landfall at Finisterre in Spain.

Despite the hardships they had to endure, the men did relatively well over those first days in the lifeboat. The canvas cover gave them some protection from the weather and, although not perfect, it did permit some reasonable on-board conditions. Rations were distributed amongst the men twice daily, with half a dipper of water and half a biscuit covered with condensed milk given to each

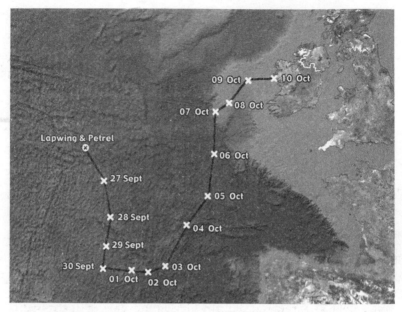

Route of lifeboat with survivors from Lapwing *and* Petrel *after their ships were sunk on the night of 26 September 1941*

man. The emergency biscuits were very hard, and some of the men took to soaking them in saltwater to soften them up and make them easier to eat. By 29 September the men were declining the biscuit ration, as the combination of soaking the biscuit in saltwater and the condensed milk was making them thirsty. That same day, Harold Weeden, who had suffered intolerable pain for three days in the damp uncomfortable conditions, finally succumbed to his wounds. His body was slipped over the side.

An unfavourable change in the wind direction on 30 September halted the steady progress of the lifeboat. The wind had backed and was blowing from the south-east, which was the heading Klemp and his officers were trying to steer. Unable to run before the wind and not wanting to attempt tacking into the strong breeze, the lifeboat hove to until a more favourable wind developed. For three days the prevailing wind blew from the south-east and denied the men any further progress towards the tantalisingly close Spanish coast.

Although they were generally in good condition, with sufficient rations, a general feeling of lassitude began to affect the morale of the men. For some, the inactivity of the lifeboat was a source of despair, while others reflected on the night upon which their ordeal began. Some had doubts as to whether they made the right decision to leave the area where the attacks occurred. However, the unfaltering optimism displayed by Klemp and Woodhouse ensured that the spirits of the men never crumbled.[5]

While at the mercy of the wind the survivors continued to scour the horizon for a ship's mast, but the bleak Atlantic proved barren during those tough days adrift. The spirits of the men would have been lifted had they known of the rescue operation that was under way for the missing ships of HG-73. When *Larkspur* caught up with the convoy after the unsuccessful depth-charge attack on U-203, it reported to the senior officer on HMS *Highlander* that it had passed a merchant ship afloat after the attacks. With every merchant ship and its cargo desperately needed, when this report reached Western Approaches Command, they decided to send a rescue tug and attempt to tow the unidentified merchant.

The chosen rescue tug, *Zwarte Zee*, to be escorted by HMS *Leith*, was ordered to proceed to where the drifting ship was last sighted.[6] *Leith* was escorting a convoy in the Irish Sea and it took another forty-eight hours to return and report for duty. So it was late on 28 September that *Leith* and *Zwarte Zee* exited the Irish

Sea through St George's Channel and proceeded en route to the scene where *Lapwing* was last sighted. Further details regarding the ship were scanty and Western Approaches Command could provide little information that might be of any use. *Leith* had devised a search pattern that took the ship's estimated rate of drift into account. Once the search began in earnest, *Leith* could only report back to Western Approaches Command that, apart from the occasional bale of cork, the reported ship had not been located. Then, late in the afternoon of 1 October, the lookouts on *Leith* sighted a life raft with a survivor on board. Once the wretched man had regained his composure, he identified himself as Leonard Lambert, formerly a fireman on board *Lapwing*.[7] *Leith* and *Zwarte Zee* continued the search for survivors through the night until the search was abandoned at nightfall on 2 October.

On 3 October the problems for the lifeboat got worse when the wind direction changed yet again. An unwelcome southerly breeze made any chance of reaching the north Spanish coast remote. Consequently, both senior officers decided that waiting for a favourable wind was impracticable. This wasted time and, more importantly, depleted their stocks of fresh water and provisions. It was decided that their best chance would be to attempt to make landfall in Ireland. This was undoubtedly a difficult decision for all to accept; after having been in the lifeboat for a week, they now faced the prospect of at least another week at sea. If their navigation was off or the winds unfavourable they might end up on the coast of occupied France.

The condition of some of the men began to deteriorate as the effects of ten days' exposure in an open lifeboat and basic survival rations took their toll. Casualties among those less able to cope under these demanding conditions were inevitable and both Arabian crewmen from *Cortes* faded and died within a short time of each other.

The general discomfort of being constantly cold and wet was unavoidable, although the boat's canvas cover did help alleviate this, especially at night. Swollen limbs and feet were also a common ailment. Those who suffered from swollen feet found that rubbing them with wave-quelling oil from the lifeboat's stores gave them some relief.[8] Chief Officer Woodhouse took to wearing no boots at all and used the oil on his feet, which worked very well for him. Thirst was their greatest torment and as they did not know how long they would be at sea, Captain Klemp had to ration the water strictly. As a precaution, Klemp and Woodhouse took it in turns to watch over the dwindling water rations every night.

By 8 October Klemp and Woodhouse estimated that they could now alter course to the east to make landfall on the Irish coast. The following day, they had the first sign that they were nearing land when a cormorant flew over the boat. The sight of the lone seabird, soaring above the masthead of their battered lifeboat, injected enthusiasm into the failing spirits of the men. Their optimistic outlook was tempered later that evening when the weather obliged Klemp to halt their eastward sailing lest they damage the boat. That night, there was a heavy rainstorm and the thirsty men took the opportunity to capture some desperately needed fresh water. They cut a hole in the canvas cover to collect the deluge, and, as they filled empty tins and passed the heaven-sent gift around to each other, 'the men took to it like mother's milk'.[9]

Early on the morning of 10 October, as the lifeboat was tossed among the Atlantic waves, Slyne Head lighthouse was sighted on the horizon, a beacon of hope. The men eagerly reached for the distress flares and lit several, but there was no answer from the lighthouse. With the lifeboat running before the wind onto a lee shore, Klemp sought out a safe landing place for them. He saw a fisherman's boat drawn up onto the beach ahead and made a careful approach. He stood in the fore part of the lifeboat and relayed helm orders back to his officer manning the tiller. It was a dangerous approach to the beach as submerged rocks lay on either side, but under Klemp's guidance the lifeboat eventually grounded gently on coarse gravel.

The elated men disembarked in a haphazard manner. Some jumped straight into the water and scrambled through the surf while others slipped over the gunwale directly onto the beach. Unaware of just how weak they had become during their fortnight-long incarceration, several collapsed onto their hands and knees. Finally, after an incredible journey, the men had found safety on a remote beach in Co. Galway.

Several local fishermen from Keeraunmore were immediately ready to assist the exhausted sailors. The wife of one brought down a large jug of hot tea to help revive the weary men. News of their arrival reached Clifden, and a Red Cross unit was dispatched with its new ambulance to assist as best they could. The ambulance took three men who were in a seriously weak condition back to Clifden. One of the weakest to be transported was Alfonso Pimentil, whose health had steadily declined over the past week. The ambulance would return for the other injured and ill men, while private cars were arranged for the remainder.

In total, eight men, including Pimentil, were admitted to the district hospital, while those who did not require medical care were lodged in the Railway Hotel. The manager, who was also the local representative of the Shipwrecked Mariners' Society, provided for their every need. The following morning a message was sent from the hospital to Captain Klemp informing him that one of his men was dying. Pimentil, who was the only crew member of *Cortes* to make it ashore, passed away shortly before Klemp arrived at the hospital. The Filipino boatswain was buried the next day at Ard Bear cemetery, just outside Clifden. Captain Klemp led the mourners at the funeral. These included most of the people of Clifden, who acted as pall-bearers and carried the coffin the whole way along the winding road up to Ard Bear. Following the funeral, those of the survivors fit to travel left for Galway and then travelled onwards by train to Dublin. From there they were put on a ferry from Dun Laoghaire. They were finally on their way home.

Captain Klemp later paid a glowing tribute to the small neutral island that served as host to so many victims of the war at sea by calling Ireland, 'that one little haven of peace in this storm-tossed world.'[10] The efforts of both John Klemp and John Woodhouse did not go unrewarded, and on 20 January 1942 both men were awarded the British Empire Medal for showing 'great courage and enterprise' while safely bringing the lifeboat through a journey of nearly 900 miles.

13

RICHMOND CASTLE

In 1934 the Union Castle Steamship Company began a large shipbuilding programme aimed at increasing its fleet of passenger and cargo ships. Orders were placed with Harland & Wolff for a series of large passenger ships to accommodate the growing passenger trade between the UK and South Africa. Emerging from Belfast during this building programme was the magnificent *Stirling Castle*, the largest ship built for Union Castle. Its impressive speed set a new record for the voyage to the Cape. At the same time that construction was in progress on *Stirling Castle* and its two sister ships, work was under way on the first of six fruit carriers. With their refrigerated cargo holds and impressive service speed, these specially designed ships were to be engaged in the lucrative fruit trade from South Africa. The first two entered service in 1935 and were an immediate success for the company. Early in 1939 *Richmond Castle* was launched, followed shortly by *Rowallan Castle*, the last ships of the class to enter service at a time when the diplomatic overtures in Europe hinted at the possibility of war.

Richmond Castle completed its sea trials in February 1939 and sailed out of Belfast Lough, down the Irish Sea to Southampton

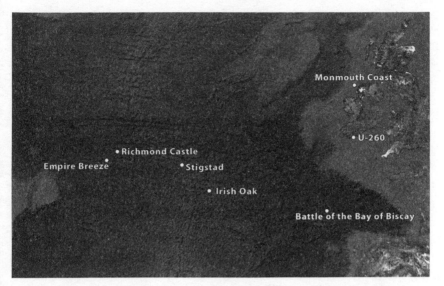

Position of ships sunk in 1942–45 whose survivors landed in Ireland

where its first cargo was carefully loaded: explosives destined for Egypt and ports in the Red Sea. It was an unconventional cargo for a ship that had been designed for a very different load, but this versatility in cargo-carrying capabilities allowed *Richmond Castle* to alter its trading patterns in the forthcoming years. The category of cargo loaded at Southampton docks was an ominous portent of future events: munitions destined to supply the outposts of the Empire implied that preparations for an impending conflict were already under way.

When war was declared, *Richmond Castle* was at the busy river port of Lourenço Marques, Mozambique, loading a cargo of fruit destined for the UK.[1] The homeward voyage was made round the Cape and calling at Cape Town, where the remaining available hold space was filled. The ship's distinctive Union Castle livery was painted over with drab Admiralty grey and it was fitted with defensive armament. As it sailed up the Mersey towards the bustling Liverpool docks, *Richmond Castle* displayed the same sullen exterior as every other merchant ship.

Throughout 1940 *Richmond Castle* and its sister ships continued trading between the UK and the South Atlantic. While other Union Castle ships were requisitioned by the Admiralty for conversion into troop transports and AMCs, these ships continued in trade. With a maximum speed in excess of many of their counterparts, they were not constrained by sailing in convoy and were routed independently. Carrying general cargoes outward from the UK or the USA, they maintained a steady trade with South Africa where vital exports were landed and indigenous goods taken back to British ports. Not all the cargoes taken back to the UK were fruit: desperately needed frozen meat from Argentina was also loaded, the refrigerated holds being able to handle any chilled or frozen cargo.

With the war at sea becoming increasingly desperate and the large volume of merchant shipping being sunk by German U-boats, *Richmond Castle* was able to deliver vital food supplies as it sailed independently across what must have seemed like empty oceans. Independent routing of fast merchant ships with a service speed in excess of 15 knots had been in force since the war began. Independently dispatched ships could perform more round voyages, thus delivering more cargo than ships whose schedules were restricted by the convoy system. Each independent sailing was given a predetermined passage plan based on the guidelines in the Mercantile Atlantic Routing Instructions (MARI). Depending on the intended route, the MARI would give specific courses and also detail areas to be avoided. The MARI were continually updated and amended to take into account the latest convoy routing and also recent surface raider developments. However, sailing independently did not give immunity from being attacked and sunk, and the loss rates for ships in convoy and those sailing independently in 1940 and into 1941 were comparable.

Throughout the first two years of the war, as increasing U-boat activity in the north Atlantic wreaked havoc among the convoys, *Richmond Castle* was as yet unscathed and had yet to see at first hand the effects of the war at sea. The only serious incident that jeopardised the safety of the ship occurred in July 1941 when returning to the UK with a cargo of frozen meat which had been loaded at Rosario, Argentina. On 20 July, the ship was involved in a collision with the steamer *City of Bangalore*. Both ships were seriously damaged, so much so that *City of Bangalore* had to be sunk the following day.[2] The badly damaged *Richmond Castle* limped as far as Trinidad where temporary repairs enabled it to sail on to Galveston, Texas, where it was dry-docked. It was several months before the repairs were affected and normal trading resumed. After finally loading at New York and crossing the Atlantic unhindered, *Richmond Castle* arrived in Liverpool on 16 December 1941.

Meanwhile, at the port of Stettin in the Baltic Sea, Kapitänleutnant Reiner Dierksen had just taken command of the newly built Type IXC U-176. For the next six months Dierksen and his crew trained intensively in preparation for their first war patrol.

In April 1942, after completing another voyage out to South Africa and returning via Buenos Aires with a cargo of frozen meat, *Richmond Castle* was preparing for another circumnavigation of the Atlantic. Loading on the Clyde the ship heaved with activity as heavy loads were hoisted from the quayside. Among the many cargoes that came on board destined for South Africa was a valuable consignment of Scotch whisky. As it was lowered into No. 3 hold to be stowed, Deck Cadet John Lester stood by and scrutinised each pallet as it came into the hold. Tasked with keeping a tally of the whisky packed tightly into the cargo space, the young cadet surveyed the scene as dockers moved about the beguiling cases. For Lester, it was an initiation into the intricacies of dealing with dockers, who, by the nature of their work, could be notoriously opportunistic when it came to such a tempting cargo. This was the young cadet's first voyage – he had completed his initial training at Pangbourne Nautical College in December 1941. He turned down a position with Canadian Pacific Lines for a berth with Union Castle – with a near relative recently retired from serving as master on board the *Stirling Castle*, it was appropriate that the family connection should continue within the prestigious shipping line.

Throughout the remainder of April the laborious task of loading goods continued. In addition to the whisky, sacks of mail were taken on board destined for South Africa. Captain Pickering was kept abreast of the status of the loading with regular reports from Chief Officer Walter Gibb. Pickering was sailing as far as South Africa, where he would leave *Richmond Castle* and take up his new appointment as master of the Union Castle feeder vessel *Rovuma*. As the loading of cargo neared completion, Pickering received a message to say that prior to sailing his ship would be given enhanced defensive protection. This would mean a delay to the scheduled sailing date as the nature of the work required shipyard labour to carry out the necessary improvements. Additional plastic armour was fitted around the wheelhouse and the ship's defensive armament was further complemented with twin Marlin machine guns on each bridge wing.[3] By the beginning of May the repair-yard workers had completed the modifications and *Richmond Castle* was ready for sea.

On 9 May *Richmond Castle* left its berth in Princes Dock and sailed serenely down the Clyde. The grey Admiralty paint may have dulled its once glistening exterior, but the elegant lines that diligent naval architects at Belfast had imparted into the design of these ships implied an elevated position among the unofficial hierarchy of the other more common merchant ships. Once clear of the Clyde boom defences, the great Firth of Clyde widened to present a horizon unbroken except for Ailsa Craig. The opening fetch of sea permitted a fresh westerly breeze to drag incrementally larger waves against the sleek bow which was slowly increasing in speed as engineers below carefully examined the main engines.

The following morning, with the North Channel cleared, the Irish coast slowly disappeared from view. Only the isolated Tory Island remained within sight. Ahead lay a three-week voyage and the ship's first port of call in South Africa. The voyage south was largely uneventful and life on board was dictated by the daily routines that govern all ships at sea. Lookouts were posted at all times on each side of the bridge, watching out over a sea vacant of all other shipping. As the ship was intentionally routed well clear of the usual shipping lanes, even the occasional sighting of land that would normally be encountered on the voyage south was omitted from the unending panoramic view. Only the changing of the weather signified to the crew that the ship was indeed heading south. As the temperature increased steadily the moderate north-easterly trades gradually gave way to light variable winds. While the ship zigzagged on a mean southerly course it intersected the demarcation between fresh trade winds and the doldrums. The partly cloudy skies would occasionally grow heavy with heavy downpours and sudden squalls enveloped the ship in a mantle of torrential rain, temporarily blinding those on watch and sending men caught out on deck running to avoid a tropical drenching.

There was a harsh reality check for those who may have lapsed into complacency, however, when one evening the wireless room intercepted an RRR coded message.[4] The anonymous sender was transmitting the position of the *Richmond Castle*. Hidden from Third Officer Allan, an unidentified merchant ship had spotted the fast-approaching Union Castle vessel and, not willing to take any chances, immediately transmitted the short letter signal. When the darkened hull of the unknown ship was sighted, Captain Pickering ordered an immediate alteration to starboard away from this suspicious character.[5]

Nearing their first destination, the unmistakable promontory of the Cape Peninsula loomed large on the horizon ahead. Sailing down the rocky and barren coast towards the southern extremity, Captain Pickering rounded Cape Point and entered False Bay on the eastern shores of the peninsula, where the first discharge port lay. There followed several port calls around the South African coast, each lasting several days as cargo was unloaded. It was at this time that Captain Pickering departed the ship to take up his new command. In his place, Captain Thomas Goldstone took the helm for the voyage back to England. Goldstone, who had been on the *Rovuma*, Union Castle's African coastal feeder trade ship, was retiring and *Richmond Castle* was to be his final command. Goldstone made preparations to take his ship on to its next destination, Río de la Plata in the Argentine.

At La Plata the ship began the process of loading frozen meat, the holds had been prepared and the refrigeration system reactivated on the passage across from South Africa. As the loading neared completion, Chief Officer Gibb had his men prepare the ship for sea. They would be crossing an area of the north Atlantic where seasonal hurricanes were liable to be encountered. The ship had to be ready for any eventuality that might arise on the voyage home. There followed a short river transit to the Uruguayan capital Montevideo for refuelling. While in port there, important routing instructions were received from the Admiralty, moving their course farther out into the Atlantic. With the increase in shipping losses around the entrances to the wider Caribbean area, shipping departing from South American ports for the north Atlantic was instructed to avoid the waters around Trinidad.[6] Goldstone and his navigator Francis Pye plotted the new course.

Once all official business had been completed, the time came to depart Montevideo, fully laden with cargo and fuel. Sailing down the channel out towards the open sea, *Richmond Castle* passed the part-submerged wreck of the German pocket battleship *Graf Spee*. For some, the sight of the German ship and the knowledge that they were about to face the most dangerous stage of their whole voyage exacerbated their sense of anxiety.[7] The fastidious captain remained on the bridge until the ship had cleared the Río de la Plata approaches, the river pilot was disembarked and the ship's course set for the voyage north.

The rest of July ebbed away quietly as the journey north took

Richmond Castle once again across the equator and back into the temperate north Atlantic. The morning of 4 August was a typical autumnal north Atlantic day. A moderate breeze gave the air a crisp clean flavour as it cooled the faces of the weary lookouts posted throughout the ship. The previous night had been quiet, with the ship maintaining its mean northerly course while zigzagging at all times. They were approaching the next waypoint on their route; from there the next course would take them to a position off Inishtrahull Island and within a day's sailing of home.

Heavy overcast skies prevented Walter Gibb taking any morning star sights. Unperturbed, he passed the remainder of his watch pacing the wheelhouse, the fresh morning wind encouraging his thoughts of breakfast. Below, John Lester enjoyed a hearty breakfast of bacon and eggs before heading to the wheelhouse for another day's duties. Making his way down to the engine room, Fourth Engineer Johnson must have been glad that they were now in more moderate latitudes. The humid equatorial climate would have combined with the already hot engine room to produce a stifling atmosphere very uncomfortable to work in. Johnson went below for another watch, monitoring the ship's refrigeration machinery.

Captain Goldstone entered the bridge to find the second and third officers already conferring with each other behind the chart table. The ship was approaching the designated waypoint and the next alteration of course. Without any sights recently they would have to rely on dead reckoning to estimate their position and when they should alter, taking into account the effect the Gulf Stream would undoubtedly have had, pushing *Richmond Castle* east as it crossed the axis of the powerful warm water current that snaked across the north Atlantic.

Goldstone reviewed the chart and the calculations laid out on the table in front of him. As he and his navigators came to an agreement as to when they should alter, Cadet Derrick Cutcliffe came running up to the bridge and reported a small vessel with what appeared to be a lug sail, two points abaft the starboard beam. Immediately all three officers joined the bridge lookout on the starboard wing and trained their binoculars on the bearing reported by the sharp-eyed cadet. Sweeping through an arc of the horizon, each man focused on finding the small vessel but failed to do so. The continuing showers that cluttered the surrounding area reduced the nominal visibility, making the efforts of those on lookout duty more difficult. The reported sighting had caused much consternation among the men on watch, yet without another confirmed sighting Captain Goldstone returned to his previous dilemma of when to alter course.

Sharing that overcast morning were Kapitänleutnant Dierksen and U-176, who had just taken up their assigned patrol station. The grim outlook for the day suddenly brightened when the mastheads of a fast-moving ship were spotted in the distance. Initial manoeuvres to gain a good firing position were hampered as the target ship altered course. The continuing line of rain squalls hampered Dierksen's efforts to relocate the ship. However, occasional sightings through the rain were enough to reinitialise the attack and, as the ship turned onto a new leg of a zigzag course, U-176 found itself in an ideal firing position. As the unidentified independent approached, Dierksen submerged the boat and prepared for an attack. Monitoring the sleek lines of the approaching ship through the periscope, he gave the order to fire three torpedoes when the range was 2,500 metres.

Shortly after the sighting report, *Richmond Castle* turned to starboard onto its new heading and, once steadied, the obligatory zigzag was resumed. As the time approached noon, the day was abruptly interrupted by the thunderous detonation of two torpedoes on the starboard side. Both missiles appeared to explode simultaneously, the first slamming into No. 3 hold while the second hit abreast of No. 5 hold. The devastation wreaked upon the ship by the explosions caused an immediate list to starboard.

In the tumultuous aftermath of the explosion, a towering wall of water rose up the ship's side, cascading back down onto the wheelhouse and decks. John Lester, who had been on the port bridge wing, was rocked by the explosion and then drenched by the falling water. Despite the violence of the attack, the sudden list to starboard and the main engines stopping, the ship still carried some headway and there remained electrical power. Radio Officer James Gillespie lost no time in transmitting a distress message while it was still possible. Regaining his equilibrium on the bridge, Captain Goldstone gave the order to abandon ship. The sense of urgency was not lost on the crew who had involuntarily begun to clear away the lifeboats almost immediately after the attack.[8]

On the starboard side, Nos 1 and 3 lifeboats were released and swung away from the ship, plunging into the fast-approaching water. On the port side, the acute angle of the list was causing serious problems for lowering Nos 2 and 4 boats. Walter Gibb, along with those mustered on the port side, had started to prepare No. 2 boat for lowering. With the gripes released, the heavy wooden lifeboat swung inboard away from the water. It was impossible for the men to keep it out over the ship's side. Struggling against the exaggerated incline of the decks, they persevered, lowering away only to have the inner side of the lifeboat's hull become snagged on obstructions on the deck. In desperation, they continued to lower and the grab rail finally tore away from the lifeboat's keel. The lifeboat ended up on the deck plating by the davits. A final slacking away of the falls and it tilted outboard, the forward end waterborne while the aft end remained hung up on deck plating despite the best efforts of the men to push it off. With *Richmond Castle* still having some forward momentum and only the forward end of the lifeboat waterborne, it was in serious danger of being forced under the water and lost. It was imperative that the whole of the lifeboat become waterborne to prevent any serious damage or loss of equipment. The men put all their strength into one final push and finally managed to dislodge the aft end of the boat off the deck and over the ship's side. Once fully waterborne, the remainder of the crew were able to board the waterlogged lifeboat. With the *Richmond Castle* listing heavily to starboard, some found it easier to stand on the ship's side while they waited to board. Others took the decision to jump into the sea, which by now was covered in a thick film of fuel oil and cork insulation granules. Sitting on thwarts up to their waists in water, those in the lifeboat frantically rowed away from the doomed ship.

In just eight minutes, *Richmond Castle* had rolled over completely onto its starboard side and quietly sunk beneath the waves. The abrupt demise of the ship had resulted in casualties among the crew, including Fourth Engineer Johnson, who never made it out of the engine room. As they assessed their precarious situation, each lifeboat crew set about bailing out their boats or retrieving oil-covered men from the sea. Walter Gibb and his men needed to lighten the load so that they could begin to bale out their flooded lifeboat. Captain Goldstone took his boat alongside so that some men could transfer over, but in their eagerness to transfer several men jumped at the same time, causing No. 2 lifeboat to capsize and throwing all the occupants into the sea. Gibb organised his men, and soon they had managed to right the lifeboat and set about bailing out the water, more men progressively boarding the boat and assisting with making the survival craft seaworthy. Navigator Francis Pye had his men row through the debris and pick up men swimming in the water.

Dierksen, meanwhile, had surfaced and closed on the lifeboats, seeking to identify his first sinking. The shout went out, asking for the name of the ship. There were a handful of sardonic replies offered such as 'Hardship', 'Queen Mary' and 'Hungry Bastard'. Only when the Second Mate's boat came closer did the German commander get the correct response. In an empathetic gesture to the seamen, Dierksen provided some provisions and medical supplies and offered to send out a distress message later that night.

With the U-boat gone, the three lifeboats started to organise themselves and to evaluate their situation. No. 2 boat had lost its sail and mast, along with all of its fresh water and small gear when it had capsized. The food provisions survived the capsizing and remained intact and fit for consumption. While the other boats searched amongst the wreckage for a mast and sail, Gibb rowed around the floating rafts to collect all their available fresh water, stores and provisions. The self-release gear of the rafts prevented these invaluable stores from going down with the ship. While searching for a sail and mast for the Chief Officer's lifeboat, Second Officer Pye made an attempt to right the capsized No. 4 lifeboat that had floated off the sinking ship, but it was not possible and so the boat was abandoned.

After waiting several hours in the immediate vicinity, Captain Goldstone decided that they should take advantage of the freshening wind and start sailing for Newfoundland. As No. 2 boat had lost its sail, it would have to be towed by the other two boats. No. 1 boat was fitted with a motor and it might have been better suited to towing, but the motor was damaged and so they too had to set sail. Good progress was made by the three boats throughout the evening, but a sudden change in weather conditions forced them to suspend their westward journey. The wind had increased, the sea was forming large foam-crested waves and the lifeboats struggled to make any headway. That night each lifeboat streamed its sea anchor, hoping to ride out the bad weather and resume sailing westward in the morning if there was any improvement in the conditions.

During the night the deteriorating weather took its toll on the already battered lifeboats. The rudder pintals on No. 1 lifeboat broke, meaning the steering oar would have to be employed once they got underway. No. 3 boat lost its sea anchor when the hawser broke, but the quick-thinking second officer set the jib sail to help maintain the lifeboat head to wind and reduce the rate of drift. When daylight broke on 5 August the wind had moderated and all three lifeboats were still visible to each other even though they had drifted apart. They managed to reassemble close to each other, and it was decided that No. 3 boat would take No. 2 in tow and the captain would proceed as best he could in No. 1.

A change in the wind direction prompted the officers to agree on changing their course to head for the Irish coast. It was a greater distance to travel when compared to the geographically closer Newfoundland, but the prevailing south-westerly winds would help sustain a good average speed that would be supplemented by the effect gained from the Gulf Stream. The towing lifeboats took the lead, while No. 1 boat, hindered by the use of the steering oar, followed behind as best it could. To make the best possible speed Captain Goldstone needed to sail with the wind on the quarter, which required him to keep the steering oar constantly at an angle to counteract the wind and keep the boat on a steady course. However, with only the steering oar this was proving very difficult as the lifeboat was inclined to run before the wind, which resulted in a reduction in speed and a tendency for the lifeboat to yaw. There was also the added danger of a sudden gybe causing damage to the sailing rig and injuring the lifeboat crew.

After three hours of toiling with the steering oar, a considerable distance had opened between the lifeboats so that Goldstone and his complement of the crew found they no longer had the others in sight.[9] The unperturbed Goldstone continued to steer on their intended westerly track, acutely aware that his men were solely reliant on him to navigate as there were no other deck officers in No. 1 boat.

Progress became arduously slow as Goldstone and his men languished within the confines of their open lifeboat. Survival for the twenty-one men was a matter of enduring the inescapable weather conditions and summoning the will to continue despite their inevitable physical decline. The dwindling supply of fresh water and the difficulty in consuming the ship's biscuits added to the general misery. As the strength to carry out tasks such as bailing and manning the oars drained away from swollen limbs, men who at first appeared to be sleeping slowly drifted away and never regained consciousness. Among the first to succumb to the effects of exposure was Goldstone himself and those remaining had to rely on each other's navigation skills if they were to have any chance of reaching the safety of the Irish coast. Nine days after the sinking of *Richmond Castle*, the remaining nineteen men on No. 1 lifeboat lay in disarray among the thwarts and flooded bilges. Having endured so much without any sign of rescue there was a tangible air of despondency. The Irish coast seemed as far away on this day as it had a week before.

As morning dawned on 13 August, fate intervened to bring Ireland a little closer to the hapless survivors. A silhouette appeared over the western horizon and as it drew nearer it became the unmistakable outline of a ship. Lookouts on board *Irish Pine* spotted the drifting lifeboat and in just over one hour Captain Matthew O'Neill and his crew had pulled nineteen exhausted and very weak survivors from its confines. The men were in a pitiful condition and one in particular was hauled on board unconscious and close to death. His condition proved fatal, and, despite the best efforts of the Irishmen, Cyril Patterson passed away after failing to respond to artificial respiration. That afternoon, Captain O'Neill stopped *Irish Pine* briefly to allow for the burial of Patterson.

For the remaining eighteen men, their ordeal was over. During the passage to Ireland they were treated for their wounds and allowed every opportunity to rest. On the morning of 17 August they were landed at Kilrush, Co. Clare, and taken to Limerick hospital. Before disembarking they expressed their gratitude to the captain and crew of *Irish Pine* who had rescued them when their situation was critical and hope of rescue remote. Just three months later, there was a tragic reversal in the fortunes of the rescue ship, when *Irish Pine* was torpedoed with the loss of Captain O'Neill and all the crew.

14

EMPIRE BREEZE

At the end of 1941, the war in the Atlantic was being fought far from the coastline of Ireland. The U-boat concentrations had moved further out into the central Atlantic. There, laden eastbound convoys could be located and shadowed, allowing sufficient time for coordinated wolf-pack attacks before they got too close to the North-West Approaches. Once in the Approaches, an increased air threat provided by Coastal Command hampered the fast surface movement that U-boats required to close on a target convoy.

With the entry of the USA into the war there was another shift, this time towards the American east coast and the Caribbean. Admiral Dönitz sought to inflict a serious blow against the abundance of merchant shipping trading in this region. In early 1942 U-boats would score an unprecedented number of victories, heralding what became known to the German sailors as 'the second happy time'. However, as the US Navy and Coast Guard devoted more resources to combating the U-boats, so the losses in merchant shipping began to drop. In July 1942 Dönitz decided to return the main focus of the U-boat campaign to the Atlantic. With over 100 operational U-boats available to use in the new campaign, a concerted effort against the Atlantic convoys was waged over the following months.

While morale among the U-boat crews was high after the successes of the second happy time, the situation was reversed for the merchant seamen who bore the brunt of this devastating campaign. The high shipping losses and feelings of general war-weariness saw morale among the merchant shipping crews slump to a worrying low. The need to sustain the merchant navy as a specialised and professional workforce had been identified early in the war, but it would take some time before a credible effort was made to safeguard their well-being. Legislation introduced by the British government in 1941, aimed at redressing financial grievances, and the general move by shipping companies to ensure that better life-saving appliances were fitted on board their ships were met with general approval. In a further effort to bolster flagging spirits, additional training at gunnery schools set up at the major ports imbued the seamen with a sense that they were contributing to the fight against the enemy.

Nevertheless, maintaining morale and discipline on board individual merchant ships could be a difficult task, which was ultimately the responsibility of the captain. The sometimes harsh working conditions combined with an unforgiving Atlantic did not endear newly appointed seamen to their chosen career. In the face of these adversities, the prospect of a sudden attack by an unseen enemy amplified any trepidation felt by individual crew members. As a result, discipline could suffer, and this could even prove fatal in an emergency when the whole crew was required to act in unison. It was only through the strong leadership of the captain, who could impose fines as punishment for breaches of the merchant-navy disciplinary code, that this could be controlled.

For Captain Robert Thomson, serving on board the Ministry

of War Transport ship *Empire Breeze*, faith in his crew and their abilities had been sorely tested by the end of another transatlantic voyage. *Empire Breeze* returned to the River Mersey on 31 July 1942, after a voyage to the east coast of America and Canada which took just over ten weeks. During this time Captain Thomson had had to deal with a succession of ratings who either refused to work or who failed to return to the ship while in port. His crew was a mixed bag of young, inexperienced men who had joined the merchant navy since the war began and who worked alongside a core of experienced pre-war ratings and officers. Many had already been confronted with the dangers of the war, including Chief Engineer Miller and Third Officer Robert Philips, who had both been on board ships that had been sunk by FW200s.

While the ship was still discharging along the Mersey, a group of firemen joined who had all served on the same ship, recently sunk. It was to this experienced core group that Thomson looked to ensure his ship operated properly and also to show a guiding hand to the younger members of the crew. Whatever reservations Thomson had about the commitment of his crew and their quality, he was prepared to deal with each case on board and not discharge the men ashore for misconduct. He would have been acutely aware that, with the manpower shortages, what you got on board was all that was available.[1]

The ship itself had already proven to be a resilient product of British shipbuilding. Shortly after completion in February 1941 at the J. L. Thompson & Sons shipyard of Sunderland, *Empire Breeze* was proceeding along the east coast of England when it ran aground on rocks off the Northumberland coast.[2] The damage was extensive, with its decks and sides cracked at No. 3 cargo hold and further critical damage to the engine and boilers. The grounded vessel lay on the rocks for almost a month, with nearly all its spaces flooded and open to the tidal flow of the North Sea. It was finally refloated and towed back to Sunderland for repairs. It eventually returned to service after sustaining damage that would have relegated any other ship of similar size to scrap.

After two weeks spent between Ellesmere Port and Manchester, *Empire Breeze* finally discharged the last of its cargo and was ready once again to make the return voyage to the eastern seaboard of America. The westbound convoy ONS-122 sailed from Liverpool on 14 August 1942, under the watchful presence of Captain Martin RNR, who was convoy commodore on board *Athelprince*. Once the convoy had cleared the North Channel and formed up, there were thirty-six ships making up the extended columns. *Empire Breeze* was leading the fourth column and had *Athelprince* on its starboard side. Protection was provided by the destroyer HMS *Viscount*, with the senior escort officer, Lieutenant Commander Waterhouse, in command, and the Norwegian corvettes HNoMS *Potentilla, Eglantine, Montbretia* and *Acanthus*.

Unusually for the time of year, a deep depression moving in from the west had stirred up fierce gale-force winds, which were causing severe disruption to convoy schedules. As the convoy emerged from the shelter of the North Channel, it ran into a fully developed storm. Many of the ships, including *Empire Breeze*, were in ballast and sat high in the water, which greatly affected their station-keeping abilities. Many others found themselves unable to maintain the proper speed and the convoy was soon a ragged, strung-out grouping. There seemed to be no respite from the continuing strong westerly gales and on 19 August Commodore

Martin was forced to turn the convoy and heave to before the majority of the ships became scattered.

By the following day the convoy was once again proceeding on its route and by the evening of 21 August the gale-force conditions had moderated. The convoy had passed through the advancing weather front. The morning of 22 August was settled, with forecasts looking favourable for further improvement later in the day. Keen to exploit the calmer seas, Commodore Martin ordered the convoy to increase speed. Several days of gales had delayed them and so it was imperative that any lost time should be regained. Merchant ships slowly increased their engine revolutions and the convoy began to increase speed. From the bridge of *Athelprince*, Commodore Martin could see conspicuous smoke trails coming from the funnels of the steamers at the rear of the convoy. Their thick black ribbons reached high up into the afternoon sky without dissipating. Such overt traces, which might divulge their presence to a nearby enemy, were unwelcome and stern signals were soon directed from the commodore's ship to the offenders.[3]

As ONS-122 struggled against the gales north-west of Ireland, an extended patrol line of thirteen U-boats designated Group Lohs, was waiting for the expected arrival of an earlier westbound convoy.[4] After several days of waiting, on 21 August Admiral Dönitz ordered the patrol line to move further north in anticipation of later westbound convoys.[5] Group Lohs covered a large area of the Atlantic and the length of the patrol line was over 300 miles long. At the southern end of the line was U-135, under the command of Kapitänleutnant Praetorius.

On the afternoon of 22 August, Praetorius was called to the conning tower for a sighting report. Several smoke clouds had been sighted, which might indicate a convoy. As they observed the smoke trails, another sighting report – of an escort – was more alarming. Praetorius hastily retreated away from the escort without any follow-up disturbance from the warship. This initial sighting report, followed by another report from U-135 later that same night, convinced Dönitz to commit all the U-boats of Group Lohs against this convoy, identified as ONS-122. The furthest U-boats of Lohs were converging at maximum speed and, provided that Praetorius could maintain contact with them and successfully direct them, the outnumbered convoy escorts would be overwhelmed and the helpless merchant ships left at their mercy.

HNoMS *Eglantine* was stationed on the starboard bow of ONS-122 when the lookouts in the crow's nest sighted the conning tower of U-135. Not long after the U-boat turned away, visual contact was lost and not regained. The significance of this sighting was not lost on either the convoy commodore or the senior escort commander. An engagement with the enemy seemed a foregone conclusion, so all that remained to them was to stay vigilant and to chase down any shadowing U-boats, thus preventing the convoy's exact location from being established.

For Captain Thomson and his crew, their responsibility was to stay in station and alert to any sign of danger. Knowing that the enemy was near, but not where the first blow would fall, placed a terrific mental strain on the merchant seamen. The tension escalated at night when the likelihood of attack was the greatest. It was a long, nerve-racking night on the bridge for Captain Thomson. A gentle drizzle and a cool chill in the air ensured the men on watch felt all the more uncomfortable.

As dawn broke on 23 August without any enemy infiltration, the merchant ships enjoyed a moment of reprieve. A patch of morning fog soon enveloped the convoy. Deprived of the extended visibility that they had enjoyed the previous day, the convoy was temporarily lost to the world and also, more importantly, to any lingering U-boats watching from a distance. As the fog cleared and the convoy emerged into another clear day, the situation remained tense.

The uneasiness of another night drew in once again and it was not long before direction-finding (DF) bearings indicated the presence of a U-boat off the convoy's starboard beam. For the next few hours *Viscount* and HNoMS *Potentilla* hunted two U-boats which were detected on the surface. Although U-432 and U-705 had to submerge and were subjected to prolonged attacks, they managed to escape to continue the hunt with only minor damage.[6]

When Lieutenant Commander Waterhouse returned from these attacks, he conferred with Commodore Martin and it was decided to alter the course of the convoy away from the gathering threat to the north. The thirty-six ships carried on unmolested, but the assembling force of U-boats was gradually gaining.

One of the boats closing in from the north was Kapitänleutnant Reiner Dierksen and U-176. Since sinking *Richmond Castle*, Dierksen had operated against SC-94, sinking another four ships. With the prospect of another large group attack against ONS-122, Dierksen had driven U-176 hard to get ahead of the convoy's line of advance. In the early hours of 24 August, as U-432 and U-705 were being attacked, Dierksen lay submerged and listened to the depth charges detonating in the distance. The convoy could not be far off, but an attack would not be possible in what remained of that night. Calculating the estimated course and speed of the convoy, U-176 surfaced and steered an intercept course that would bring them within striking range once darkness fell. Beacon signals from U-660, which was in contact with ONS-122, gave additional assistance in following the advancing convoy. With nightfall, U-176 and the large group of pursuing U-boats would be ready to strike in a coordinated attack.

The daily routine of shipboard life continued on the cargo ships despite the knowledge that an attack would doubtless be unleashed against them. The protection of the convoy lay in the hands of the escort screen, although the merchant ships could actively participate by listening for enemy radio transmissions. *Empire Breeze* was fortunate to have three radio officers on board and a constant watch was maintained. In the early evening of 24 August, *Empire Wagtail* reported to the commodore a DF bearing of a U-boat transmission. To give credence to this report, it was followed up within an hour by two more DF bearings intercepted by *Empire Breeze* in quick succession. Thomson was in no doubt as to the validity of the intercepted transmissions and reported both to the commodore. All the evidence suggested an attack on the convoy that night. This was confirmed by the Admiralty, who sent new routing instructions to *Athelprince*, which then plotted a track away from the trailing pursuers. However, Commodore Martin deferred the course alteration until nightfall, when it was less likely to be noticed by the enemy.

The weather conditions did not favour the defenders of ONS-122. The moon was nearly full and the bright glare permeated through the generous blanket of low cumulus. Air and sea-surface temperatures indicated the likelihood of fog, but in the meantime the visibility remained good.

The first attack came from the starboard beam.[7] From his vantage point on the bridge of *Empire Breeze*, Captain Thomson observed bright flashes erupt from the far side of the convoy. Alarm bells wailed through the compartments of the ship. Their shrill cries woke off-duty personnel and summoned all crew members on deck while the gun crews manned their stations. Rockets punctuated the northern horizon as ships illuminated the sea looking for the attacker. A series of engagements occurred along the starboard side of the convoy, as escorts chased down sighted U-boats on the surface. Lieutenant Commander Waterhouse instructed Commodore Martin to make an emergency turn to port away from the developing action. As the signal was sent to the convoy, the columns began to wheel over to port in unison. As the turn continued, *Empire Breeze* slowly crept ahead of the commodore's ship and ended up in front of the other column leaders when the new heading was reached. To correct his station-keeping, Thomson ordered a reduction in speed to allow the ship to fall back into position. The high-sided cargo ship was a prominent figure out in front and presented a clear target.

U-176 had made visual contact with ONS-122 in the late evening of 24 August. Dierksen prepared to attack when the first ships were torpedoed on the starboard beam. Manoeuvring on the surface he closed in on the convoy without any interference from escorts. As he neared the expected panoramic view of dark outlined ships pressing through the night, the men watching from the conning tower were confronted with a ship directly ahead and perfectly silhouetted against the background light. Without hesitation, Dierksen selected the large steamer as his first target. Once ready, two torpedoes were fired. It took just ninety-three seconds for both weapons to strike the steel sides of the ship. From the bridge of *Athelprince* Commodore Martin watched as a bright explosion flared up from the starboard side of *Empire Breeze*. As the stricken vessel began to slow down and veer off its original heading, *Athelprince* had to alter course to avoid hitting it. As they passed, Commodore Martin and his staff on the bridge looked on, unable to assist – and undoubtedly thankful that at least it wasn't them.

The first torpedo hit *Empire Breeze* in its No. 3 hold, just forward of the bridge, and the second hit further aft in the cross-bunker hold. It seemed like the ship had been moved by some great seismic event. Hatch boards from No. 3 hold were sent flying into the air, while seawater and escaping coal from the bunker hold littered the open deck spaces. Inside the ship, violent tremors threw everything to the deck with no fixture on any bulkhead surviving the ferocity of the explosions. From the starboard bridge wing, Thomson could see the full extent of the damage to No. 3 hold. The side plating had disappeared to leave a gaping hole running below the waterline while deck plating had buckled under the immense forces placed on the metal structure. Unsure of how long the ship would survive, Thomson gave the order to prepare the lifeboats. While the crew sprang into action, the captain surveyed further the damage to No. 3 hold and found that both bulkheads were still holding and preventing seawater cascading into the other cargo holds. The ship, however, had already settled deeper in the water and reports from the engine room were that there was flooding from the cross-bunker hold. Unwilling to risk waiting any longer, Thomson gave the order to abandon ship.

At the lifeboat embarkation deck, two people were unaccounted for since the attack. Third Officer Robert Philips had been on the bridge at the time of the explosions but had subsequently disappeared. The second missing person was Yusuf Doalay, who was on duty as a fireman. Doalay had been one of three crew members to join *Empire Breeze* in Liverpool when their previous ship had been sunk. Just three months on, fate had finally caught up with the unfortunate seaman.

All three lifeboats were launched in good order and, to the surprise of the men in the starboard lifeboat, they found Philips swimming in the water by the ship's side. After the first torpedo explosion had blown out the hatch boards from No. 3 hold, Philips, who was standing on the starboard bridge wing at the time, was knocked off balance and ended up falling into the open hold. Luckily for him the space was already filled with seawater, which softened his landing. The shock of his experience, in conjunction with several knocks and contusions, left Philips in a daze, but the spirited young officer was able to make sense of his predicament and, with quick thinking, he used the hole caused by the torpedo explosion to swim out of the flooded hold. It was an incredible escape from a situation that could easily have resulted in his death.

The rest of the convoy had continued on without stopping. Dierksen searched for another target but was forced to submerge when *Viscount* returned to the convoy. There was a designated rescue ship sailing with the convoy, *Stockport*, but it was busy rescuing the survivors from the first attack. In the *Empire Breeze*'s lifeboats, the distant din of explosions soon petered out and the gloom of the dark night was fused with a damp cold fog that cocooned the survivors from the outside world. The men were cold and uncomfortable, and as the lifeboats remained close to their ship, Thomson debated whether he should lead his crew back on board. Considering the damage sustained and the level of seawater in the known flooded compartments, he decided not to reboard during the night but rather to wait until morning and then reassess the situation.

With the first light of a new day the crew of *Empire Breeze* rowed back alongside their ship, and a small party, including the captain and radio officers, climbed the embarkation ladders. The rest of the crew stayed in the lifeboats as a precaution against the ship suddenly sinking. Teams of men were sent throughout the ship so that a full assessment of the vessel's condition could be ascertained. What was already known from the previous night was that with the engine room partially flooded there was no chance of propulsion and no electrical power on board. The wireless equipment had been damaged beyond use, but the radio officers were able to connect the emergency lifeboat radio to the ship's main aerial and send out a distress message. This radio set depended on batteries for power and the usage would have to be carefully monitored. As the reports came back from the search teams it became clear that the damage was not as bad as first anticipated and Thomson was confident that the ship would remain afloat for some time. The sturdy building techniques of the Thompson shipyard had once again proved their worth as *Empire Breeze* defied the odds by surviving damage other ships would certainly have not.

During the afternoon the radio officer managed to send out a distress message which was received by the Belle Isle station in Canada. The reassurance of the acknowledgement from the coast radio station gave everyone hope that rescue would soon arrive. Thomson was personally optimistic and even entertained thoughts of saving the ship. Time, however, was critical and the longer they had to wait the greater the chance that structural failure would claim the damaged ship. Thomson had been inspired by how his crew, in which he had previously had such little faith and had so often rebuked, had revealed their true indomitable nature over the past twenty-four hours. Every man had worked solidly and without complaint since they had taken to the lifeboats.

Checks of the hold spaces on the morning of 26 August brought disheartening news. The water levels in the engine room and No. 3 hold had increased, while seawater was also beginning to flood No. 1 hold. *Empire Breeze* was slowly sinking from under them. Another distress message was transmitted, with greater urgency placed on the ship's dire situation. Unless help arrived soon, Thomson and his boarding party would have to abandon the ship once again and take their chances in the lifeboats.

Approximately 45 miles west, the Irish cargo ship *Irish Willow* was listening to the repeated distress calls. Captain Shanks had been informed of the messages from *Empire Breeze* the previous day, but as they were still too far away and the coast station had acknowledged the call, the Irish crew decided to simply continue to monitor the situation. As the repeated calls on that morning showed the ship was in imminent danger of sinking, and with the distance considerably reduced, Shanks instructed a message to be sent asking how long they could hold out. Thomson estimated six hours. The response was immediate: 'Coming to you – with you in about five hours.' What remained was for *Irish Willow* to find the ship in distress, which, under the prevailing meteorological conditions, was not going to be easy. Prior to taking on the rescue mission, *Irish Willow* had been in fog for two days and was unable to take astronomical observations to accurately plot their position. *Empire Breeze* had been adrift for almost thirty-six hours and was also relying on dead-reckoning positions, which were relayed in the distress calls. With fog persisting over the area and unreliable positions for both ships, Captain Shanks was going to have to rely on his radio officer to obtain good DF bearings from *Empire Breeze*'s transmissions.

There was not a moment to lose if *Irish Willow* was to reach Captain Thomson and his men in time. As the rescue ship proceeded at its best speed, DF bearings were taken every half hour, which helped guide the blind Irish ship. Meanwhile, another problem threatened to undo the rescue attempt. The batteries supplying power to the lifeboat radio on board *Empire Breeze* were running low. Without these, all contact with and chance of an early rescue would be lost.

The time to decide about leaving the ship finally came for the boarding party. Almost forty hours since being struck by two torpedoes, the resilient *Empire Breeze* remained afloat, but the increasing water levels meant that to stay on board any longer would put lives in danger. Thomson decided to return to the lifeboats with the emergency radio while the batteries still had enough power to allow *Irish Willow* to take DF bearings from its signals. A message was sent to say that they were leaving the ship but would stay close by and continue to use the lifeboat radio. The strength of the final radio signals received indicated that *Irish Willow* was getting much closer and Captain Shanks had to slow down for fear of collision with the unseen derelict.

The rescue effort entered its final painstaking stage. Blind-folded by the dense fog, Shanks continued on at the safest speed that could be maintained while navigating in zero visibility. In the radio room there was a brief period when the DF signals from the lifeboat radio were lost. The low battery power was beginning to affect the signal output – plus the emergency set was at sea level and had lost the height it had enjoyed on board *Empire Breeze*. Eventually the homing signal was regained and the search continued. The afternoon dragged on and the fading light made the efforts of the Irish crew even more difficult. Finally *Irish Willow* began to pass wreckage strewn across the sea. They were getting closer, and the additional lookouts strained to see as far into the fog as they could. Then, from behind a ghostly veil of tenacious fog, *Empire Breeze* emerged, drifting in silence. It was an eerie spectacle to see the ship festooned with wisps of mist, its decks empty and forever quiet after the crew had boarded the lifeboats. However, there was no sign of these lifeboats and so the search resumed.

As darkness descended, *Irish Willow* switched on all its deck floodlights. Captain Shanks manoeuvred carefully, directed by his radio officers, who manned the radio direction finder. Two and a half hours after they passed *Empire Breeze*, all three lifeboats were finally sighted lying close together. All forty-seven survivors were taken on board. Relieved that the lifeboats had been located, Captain Shanks resumed his voyage back to Ireland.

Below decks, Captain Thomson and his crew were heartily fed, and bunks were given over for their use. Reflecting on the past forty-eight hours, Thomson reflected on his confidence in a crew that had previously been found lacking. Their steadfast commitment to the duties demanded of them while contending with a life-threatening situation had earned them his admiration.

The rescue that followed the attack on *Empire Breeze* was only made possible by virtue of the ship remaining afloat. Without the use of the ship's main wireless aerial, the underpowered lifeboat radio would not have been able to contact Belle Isle station or *Irish Willow*. The Irish crew conducted a difficult and well-executed rescue under conditions that were extremely restrictive. In addition to the fog, both ships and the lifeboats were almost certainly affected by the north Atlantic current, which swept the lifeboats away from *Empire Breeze* and delayed the final rescue. If the circumstances had been different and all three lifeboats required to try and reach safety by their own means, the chances of survival for all the crew would certainly have been drastically reduced.[8]

The days on board *Irish Willow* were spent recuperating and even the lucky Robert Philips recovered from his ordeal. Two seamen had come down with a fever, but their condition was not serious. The ship was en route to Waterford and it was decided to land the rescued crew at Dunmore East before proceeding up the River Suir. Before dawn on 1 September the bluff rocky coastline west of Waterford Harbour came into view. The stout Hook Head lighthouse across the harbour guided the ship, which shortly thereafter anchored off Dunmore East. As always, the arrival of the survivors was expected and a boat containing an advance party of doctors and Red Cross volunteers soon appeared. Its passengers climbed on board *Irish Willow* to see to the immediate needs of the rescued men. A boat from *Irish Willow* was then used to ferry all the survivors ashore, leaving the retrieved lifeboats from *Empire Breeze* on deck to be landed later on the quayside at Waterford. Waiting on shore was a full team of Red Cross volunteers who had set out from Waterford in the early hours of the morning and turned a local parish hall into a reception centre. Additional medical facilities and hot meals were provided to the thankful survivors. Two crew members who required further medical treatment were taken by ambulance to the Waterford Infirmary. Later, the remaining forty-five survivors were transported to Waterford.

For the final leg of their Irish journey, Captain Thomson and his crew were to travel to Dublin. However, with the lamentable state of public transport at this time of the war, two buses had to be authorised by the government to convey the men to the capital. As they waited for the buses, Captain Thomson and his men became the figures of intense local interest. The crew were asked to recount their stories to journalists, who were treated to the exploits of Third Officer Philips and the tireless radio officers. Their captain, however, remained reticent, preferring not to talk too much about the events subsequent to the attack. Instead, he reserved all praise for the crew of *Irish Willow* and the Red Cross volunteers at Dunmore East. Summing up his feelings, Thomson said, on behalf of his crew, 'We are very pleased to land in Eire, and we certainly could not have found a better landing.'[9]

15

Beginning of the End

During the cold, dark morning of 8 December 1941, the Rosslare lifeboat was called out after distress flares were sighted near Tuskar Rock lighthouse. The volunteer RNLI crew dutifully set out to investigate the reported flares, not sure what to expect. As they neared the reported position, a lifeboat was spotted containing eleven men. The lifeboat had come from the British coaster *Gertie*, which had struck a mine near Tuskar Rock. The large defensive minefield placed across St George's Channel was frequently the source of rogue mines that broke adrift of their moorings in bad weather. Invariably, these mines were either washed ashore along the Irish south coast or sighted at sea and subsequently destroyed by the naval service. Some, however, were carried by the prevailing tides and currents and drifted across the busy coastal shipping routes.

The hazard posed by these mines was a problem that Captain Keefe, in command of *Gertie*, was acutely aware. In the past week, *Gertie* had sighted mines adrift in the same vicinity and had been forced to open fire. Around 0100 hrs on 8 December, the keen-eyed lookouts once again spotted mines rising up on the swell ahead of the ship. Captain Keefe joined the Chief Mate on the bridge, looking out for additional mines and for three hours they managed to evade the partially submerged threat. Their luck ran out when just after 0400 hrs, a mine that had gone unnoticed made contact with the small coaster on the starboard quarter. The explosion was fatal for the vessel, but the crew of eleven managed to abandon ship in good order and fortunately there were no casualties. The survivors were taken on board the RNLI lifeboat and brought back to Rosslare.

After the rescue of the *Gertie* crew, fifteen months passed before another lifeboat from a sunk ship landed on the coast of Ireland. In 1942 the survivors from *Richmond Castle* and *Empire Breeze* were landed at Irish ports after being rescued by Irish ships in the Atlantic. For any lifeboat stranded in the expanse of mid-ocean, reaching Ireland was a gruelling undertaking fraught with danger and little chance of success. The lifeboat from *Richmond Castle* had been at sea for some time when its passengers were eventually rescued. The strain of such an undertaking is evident from the number of men who died before the rescuers arrived.

In January 1943 the German U-boats were experiencing a calamitous reversal of fortunes in the Battle of the Atlantic. Throughout the first month of the new year there were several convoy engagements with success rates far below those achieved the previous year. Large pack operations were being foiled by Western Approaches Command's ability to re-route convoys around known U-boat concentrations. This was only achievable through ULTRA and the decryption of German naval messages sent between the U-boats and BdU.[1]

In contrast to the disappointing January, was a notable encounter in early February against convoy SC-118 over a five-day period with the loss of eleven merchant ships. The ferocity of the fighting was not without loss to the attackers and three U-boats were sunk, with several others seriously damaged by air and depth-charge attack. The increasing effectiveness of Allied escort groups to detect and destroy U-boats was attributed to the great technological strides made by the Allies and a ruthless efficiency developed through continually developing tactics. Meanwhile, escort carriers produced in the shipyards of the USA were becoming the nucleus of deadly support groups able to reinforce the convoy escorts when they were hard pressed by shadowing U-boats. While the battle may have been fought far away from Ireland, the escort groups sailed from Londonderry and Belfast along the northern coasts from Donegal to Antrim to practise their tactics and hone their lethal skills.

As the Allies appeared to hold all the aces and their ascendancy against the U-boats seemed to be growing without any effective response, the Germans still enjoyed some successes with their own radio intelligence service. The information this provided was particularly important as there was a lack of consistently reliable air reconnaissance over the western Atlantic. As had been the case from the very beginning of the war, U-boat pack operations were only successful as long as they could locate and track convoys.

On 18 February 1943 the Luftwaffe radio intercept service in Paris was able to plot convoy ON-166 outward from the North Channel. Several DF cross-bearings taken from sources identified as convoy escorts enabled BdU to deduce the probable route to be followed and as a consequence two large patrol lines were disposed to act against the expected convoy. However, an Allied intelligence counter-stroke diverted the convoy further south when it became aware of the waiting U-boats. It appeared that ON-166 would be another in a long succession of convoys to frustrate German plans.

Since forming up after exiting the Irish Sea, ON-166 had run into the persistent Atlantic gales that were a constant bother to shipping at this time of year. The large convoy was composed of mainly Norwegian, American and British merchant steamers, which were protected by an international escort force of American, Canadian and British warships. As was usual in the outward convoys, many ships were sailing in ballast and returning to the USA to load cargo. Making up the large contingent of Norwegian ships was the tanker *Stigstad* under the command of Captain Odd Pettersen. In keeping with the international flavour of the convoy, the crew was a mix of Norwegian and British seamen, with one Canadian and one Irish crew member on board – in total thirty-seven men. Since the beginning of the war, *Stigstad* had sailed back and forth across the Atlantic without any interference. However, on this occasion, the unpredictable winter weather and bad luck conspired against the Norwegian tanker.

On the evening of 20 February ON-166 was struggling to maintain a south-westerly course against gale-force winds and a heavy swell. To compound the difficulties of the ships fighting to stay in position, driving rain and a depressed cloud base reduced the visibility. Once night was upon them, *Stigstad* lost sight of the dimmed navigation lights from the nearest merchant ships. Throughout the night Captain Pettersen sought to regain contact with any of the ships belonging to the convoy, but by daybreak on 21 February the conditions had moderated enough to reveal that *Stigstad* was quite alone. Although not overly concerned about having to steam independently until the convoy was regained, there was a lingering worry in Pettersen's mind that trailing behind a convoy without the reassuring presence of its escort was not the safest place to be. As the day progressed, the strong winds, constant for over a week, gradually eased, although the visibility remained poor. *Stigstad* was steaming at its best available speed so as to catch up with the lost convoy.

A pack of U-boats in pursuit of ON-166 was gathering in the surrounding area. The convoy was detected by U-604 on the morning of 20 February, south of the patrol lines the U-boat had originally intended to use to locate it. U-604 maintained contact for long enough to convince Dönitz that the sighting was the convoy that had been expected further north. All the nearest available U-boats were therefore ordered to proceed against ON-166.

Unknown to Captain Pettersen, by the morning of 21 February the pursuing U-boats were fast approaching from astern of the convoy and *Stigstad* was soon to be the first contact of the day. In the afternoon, two U-boats spotted the solitary tanker and were both preparing to attack. Unaware of enemy activity in the vicinity, Pettersen was pressing on, hoping to sight the convoy before dark. Then, in an instant, the thud of a torpedo impact crushed any hopes of reaching their companions. The torpedo, fired by U-332, hit on the starboard side. The ship took on a list, but the damage had only affected one cargo tank. With the engines still capable of propelling the ship and electrical power running, the ship remained under Pettersen's control.

As he assessed the damage and as lookouts scanned the misty horizon, another two torpedo explosions struck the starboard side. This time the attacker was U-603 and the end result was much more serious. Another large hole opened up additional empty cargo tanks to the sea while the second torpedo punctured the engine-room side plates and flooded that compartment. Without power and listing heavily to starboard, Pettersen was left with no alternative but to abandon ship. The successive explosions had destroyed both lifeboats on the starboard side, which left just the port lifeboats available for use. However, as the list became progressively steeper, it was only possible to launch one of these. The end came quickly after the second attack. The survivors, some of whom had jumped into the water, squeezed together in the solitary survival craft.

U-603, under the command of Oberleutnant zur See Bertelsmann, approached the lifeboat to question the survivors. The dialogue between the conning tower and the lifeboat was straightforward and workmanlike. Once the informal interrogation ended, Bertelsmann handed over a varied selection of supplies and made off to continue his pursuit of ON-166. For the thirty-four survivors left behind and isolated far out in the Atlantic, their situation did not look promising.

Captain Pettersen was faced with several critical problems that risked unhinging his crew's timely rescue and chances of survival. The quick sinking of *Stigstad* had prevented the transmission of a distress message, so nobody knew what had become of the ship since contact was lost with ON-166 the previous night. Another unpredictable element was the winter weather. Finally, there was the harsh realisation that they were adrift over 725 miles away from the nearest land. Nevertheless, it seemed that their only option was to attempt the journey east to Ireland. The lifeboat was well provisioned and, provided they enjoyed the favour of a good prevailing wind and the changeable Atlantic weather did not intervene, then the possibility did exist that the undertaking might succeed.

February passed and there had been no word from *Stigstad* since it was last seen with ON-166. The missing tanker was assumed to be another casualty of the great battle that had developed around ON-166, and the ship was presumed lost.[2] Then, on 8 March, the Milford Haven trawler *Thomas Booth* was fishing off the Kerry coast when its crew spotted a lifeboat under sail. At first there appeared to be no sign of life and it was assumed the empty vessel was an abandoned artefact from the bitter struggle being fought far out to sea. As the trawler approached, the occasional sight of a head appeared over the gunwale and an arm, awkwardly raised, waved at the fishermen. Once alongside, the fishermen were confronted with a pitiful sight. Most of the men looked more dead than alive: their limbs had become bloated and swollen, and their exposed skin was covered with grotesque boils inflamed by constant seawater abrasion. The thirty-four *Stigstad* survivors had completed their journey under the most difficult of circumstances with the odds firmly stacked against them. Despite the haggard condition in which they were found, Captain Pettersen (himself badly affected by the strenuous ordeal) had kept his men alive for sixteen days within the confines of the lifeboat, to be rescued just beyond the fringe of Ireland's coast.

The Milford Haven fishermen had to manhandle the survivors on board *Thomas Booth*. Then, with its unexpected catch on board, the rescue trawler proceeded to Valentia Island, where later that afternoon all the survivors were landed. The true extent of their remarkable journey was downplayed at the time as just another story from one of the countless ships sunk throughout the Second World War. However, this was an epic undertaking in a crowded lifeboat, forced into an extended voyage that seemed unlikely to succeed from the very outset. Defying those odds and sailing the treacherous seas over that distance without the loss of any lives was an achievement that cannot be underplayed.

On Valentia, the men were quickly transferred to the island's hospital. Exhausted and suffering from all the ailments that plague men forced through such an ordeal, it took some time convalescing before they were considered fit enough to travel. All thirty-four were cared for by an attending doctor, while the reliable representative from the Shipwrecked Mariners' Society was available to ensure that all their other needs were looked after. Despite the small size of the island and the limited resources to hand, especially with wartime restrictions imposing severe shortages of basics on the local community, the survivors were given the best treatment and care possible.

The crew of *Stigstad* left Valentia in groups over the coming weeks as their condition dictated. The first group of sixteen that left for Dublin on 16 March included the Irishman Kevin McClory.[3] For the young McClory the entire ordeal, beginning with the sinking of the ship, had proved a terrible strain and as a result of the trauma he endured McClory was left with a stammer for the rest of his life. While in the lifeboat he kept an unusual diary by scrawling words onto the sole of his shoe with a nail taken from the boat. In appreciation for the treatment he received at Valentia Island hospital, McClory left his unique diary with the matron.[4]

The group was met in Dublin by representatives from several bodies including the Norwegian Consulate, the Red Cross and of course the Shipwrecked Mariners' Society. The men were accommodated at the Seaman's Institute on Eden Quay, where they were treated to a hearty tea on arrival. It was not until 26 March that the last of the *Stigstad* crew left their island refuge on Valentia and travelled to Dublin. Among those last to go was Captain Odd Pettersen. Bureaucratic delays and diplomatic formalities were of little consequence to Pettersen and his men as they enjoyed the hospitality of Ireland's capital city. Considering what the men had struggled through to reach Ireland, they had earned the unplanned holiday and the reprieve it brought from the war at sea.

In the months that followed the attack on ON-166, the central Atlantic remained desperately contested. Towards the end of March the fierce convoy battles that developed around HX-229 and SC-122 marked the high-water mark for the U-boat campaign in the Atlantic. Over a period of five nights a total of forty-three U-boats pressed home determined attacks and sank twenty-three ships. This unprecedented success would never again be repeated, as the initiative was wrested back by the Allies and ruthlessly exploited for the remainder of the war. By the end of May 1943 the entire U-boat campaign in the Atlantic was on the verge of collapsing due to unsustainable losses. The irrepressible Allied pressure obliged Admiral Dönitz to move his remaining U-boats out of the murderous cauldron that the central Atlantic had become for the Germans.

In the meantime the solitary steamers of Irish Shipping continued their transatlantic trade, unflustered by the maelstrom surrounding their shipping lanes. The year 1942 was a significant one for the men on board *Irish Pine*, who rescued the shipwrecked men of *Richmond Castle*, and also for *Irish Willow*, which went to the aid of the merchant seamen of *Empire Breeze*, and 1943 was to be no less dramatic for the men of Irish Shipping.

In May 1943 the steamer *Irish Oak*, under the command of Captain Eric Jones, was returning to Dublin from Tampa, Florida, with a cargo of phosphates.[5] Since entering service with Irish Shipping in September 1941, *Irish Oak* had gone unmolested by the ravages of the war at sea that had affected so many of its Irish counterparts. Nevertheless, as the war continued, the crew could not let complacency put at risk the vital supply routes between Ireland and its trading partners. Captain Jones' own career had certainly had its share of danger and he was no stranger to the perils of war. When he was in command of *Luimneach* in September 1940, the ship was stopped and sunk by U-46, whose commander was unsure as to the true nationality of the steamer.[6] The crew took to the lifeboats, and Jones and his men eventually landed at the northern Spanish port of Pasejes.[7]

By 14 May *Irish Oak* had completed most of the journey home and Captain Jones expected to make landfall off Fastnet without much further delay. As the lone Irish ship travelled eastward it remained oblivious to a convoy battle that had been developing nearby over the previous three nights. Convoy SC-129 was also travelling east and was following a track to the north of *Irish Oak*. Since 11 May the convoy had been trailed by a large U-boat pack. As was their tactic, the U-boats formed an extended patrol line and swept eastward searching along the estimated route of SC-129.

Forming part of this patrol line was U-650, under the command of Oberleutnant zur See Ernst von Witzendorff. On the afternoon of 14 May, Witzendorff and his crew were searching for the convoy that had so far eluded them when they were attacked by an RAF Coastal Command Liberator. Owing to the good visibility, U-650 sighted the aircraft well in advance of the attack and managed to dive to a safe depth before the Liberator dropped its payload. Nevertheless, it had been a close encounter. After remaining submerged for two hours, Witzendorff surfaced to resume the search. It did not take the conning tower lookouts long to report the sighting of an unescorted ship to their stern. After an hour spent observing the unidentified ship Witzendorff ordered the U-boat to dive and prepare for a submerged attack. Without a single hit against any of the Atlantic convoys during this patrol, any ship that could be claimed by the crew of U-650 would be gladly taken.

The ship that Witzendorff viewed through his periscope was *Irish Oak* and, as he got nearer, the German commander was able to make out the neutral markings emblazoned along its sides. Although he was unable to read the ship's name, he was satisfied that it was indeed a neutral and did not attack. U-650 surfaced and left *Irish Oak* to continue on its voyage. The materialisation of the U-boat nearby did cause some concern initially, but the crew of *Irish Oak* were reassured as U-650 departed on a diverging course.[8]

The nearby SC-129 proved to be an unwelcome neighbour because of the U-boats that trailed in its wake, but by late afternoon on 14 May, BdU had called off operations against the convoy and the hunting U-boats were redirected elsewhere. U-607, under the command of Oberleutnant zur See Wolf Jeschonnek, was ordered to take up a new patrol station. Just as dawn was beginning to break on 15 May, the lookouts sighted a ship with thick black smoke billowing out from the funnel. The telltale trail of smoke and the ship's tall masts were an easy reference point for Jeschonnek and U-607 kept a respectable distance away as it slowly overtook the unknown steamer. Once more it was *Irish Oak* that had attracted a U-boat's unwanted attentions. For over three hours U-607 stalked the unwitting steamer until Jeschonnek positioned the U-boat ahead of *Irish Oak* for a submerged attack. As U-607 approached underwater, the apparently erratic movements of the unidentified steamer were a concern for Jeschonnek. It appeared that the ship was zigzagging through a course alteration of 40 degrees while adjusting the speed of the engines. This odd behaviour suggested to Jeschonnek that he might be facing an Allied Q-ship. By 0800 hrs, U-607 had closed the distance sufficiently for Jeschonnek to read the ship's name. With the ship properly identified as *Irish Oak* Jeschonnek wanted to verify that it was listed as a known neutral ship. When he consulted the latest standing war order, there was no mention of *Irish Oak*, which confirmed his doubts. With what appeared to be overwhelming evidence against *Irish Oak*, Jeschonnek decided to attack.

On board *Irish Oak*, the proximity of the U-boat had gone unnoticed and the first Captain Jones and his crew knew of its presence was the explosion of the first torpedo. This erupted through the side plating of No. 1 hold and brought the ship to a sudden stop. Stunned by the explosion, Jones and his crew were soon catapulted into activity, as preparations got under way to abandon ship. In the wireless room Radio Officer James Burke was able to transmit a partial distress message with only the latitude included before the aerial rigging collapsed.

Jeschonnek watched the crew prepare the lifeboats through his periscope. *Irish Oak* began to settle by the bow, but stubbornly remained afloat long enough for the crew to clear the lifeboats away from the ship. Jeschonnek watched the organised men rig sails and move away and then, just over an hour after the first torpedo was fired, he delivered the *coup de grâce*. The end came soon after the second explosion and *Irish Oak* slipped beneath the waves leaving two lifeboats and a mixture of floating wreckage and fuel oil as the only visible remains of this victim of mistaken identity.

As U-607 crept away from the scene underwater, Jones and his crew got used to their new circumstances. There had been enough time to load plenty of additional provisions into the lifeboats before abandoning ship and although only a partial distress message had been sent, the radio officer did bring along the emergency lifeboat set. Crew spirits were high from the very beginning. Donkeyman William Barry, who was on duty in the engine room at the time of the attack, did have one regret: in the rush to board the lifeboats he had left behind his pet cat. This animal, and two other cats kept on board, were the only casualties.

The weather was most agreeable, even marooned in the open ocean, and both lifeboats remained in the vicinity of the sinking. If they did not stray too far from the position transmitted in the distress message, an early rescue seemed certain as they had recently been in radio contact with another Irish ship known to be nearby. Good fortune was indeed shining on the crew of *Irish Oak*, for the partial distress message was received by *Irish Plane*. On receipt of the message, the astute Captain Henderson suspected that *Irish Oak* may have been its author. By extrapolating the position report received from *Irish Oak* that morning and comparing it with the fragmented coordinates from the transmission, Henderson correctly deduced the identity of the ship in distress. Later, another distress message, this time from the lifeboat of *Irish Oak*, confirmed Henderson's deductions and by late afternoon *Irish Plane* had located both lifeboats and all thirty-four occupants were once again standing on the decks of an Irish ship.[9]

Instructions were received from the ship managers and Captain Henderson was ordered to return to Ireland where the rescued crew would be landed. On the night of 19 May the survivors were landed at Cobh, bringing another rescue to a successful end. The crew travelled home while Captain Jones went to the Irish Shipping offices to make his report.

Over the following days, carefully censored stories without any real detail about the loss of *Irish Oak* were printed in the national newspapers. Over the weeks that followed, allegations that the ship may have transmitted a U-boat sighting report to the nearby British warships overshadowed the actual loss of the ship. Political machinations stepped up a gear as national elections were expected in the summer.[10] The first publicly voiced intimation that *Irish Oak* may have alerted the nearby convoy to the presence of the U-boat was raised on 26 May in the Dáil. The possibility of Irish involvement in actively reporting the position of a U-boat was denied.

The matter should have been laid to rest there; however, lingering doubts remained about this most serious matter and Irish Shipping issued a press statement on 28 May reiterating its stance that there had been no sighting report made by *Irish Oak*. The story was approached from the opposite viewpoint when the questions raised in the Dáil became known in England. In Westminster, Members of Parliament wanted to know why, if *Irish Oak* had indeed sighted a U-boat, the nearby SC-129 was not advised of its location. These baseless political ramblings, which only fed the appetites of public hearsay and rumour, did nothing to protect the good reputation of Captain Jones and his crew. They had acted in accordance with the strict rules being a neutral ship imposed upon them. Any report relating to the position of nearby U-boats passed on to the Allies would have been a flagrant dereliction of duty that would have put the safety of the entire crew at risk.

With the full facts of the situation surrounding *Irish Oak* and SC-129 known, it is a straightforward matter to debunk the question of Irish duplicity. On the afternoon of 14 May, the escorts of SC-129 were already aware of the location of U-650 when it was reported by the attacking Liberator aircraft. The supposition of Irish guilt for not reporting the sighting was immaterial. That evening, when *Irish Oak* spotted U-650, if any radio transmission was made it would have been in the form of the plain language signal code or in a coded message sent to the Admiralty. The plain-language message would simply have been an invitation for any U-boat to attack *Irish Oak*, while the second option would have required British merchant navy code books, which no Irish ship would have been allowed to carry.[11] Last, the Admiralty records for convoy SC-129 and Western Approaches Command make no mention of any sighting report ever being received from *Irish Oak*.

In any event, the convoy's experienced escort group proved to be too powerful for the attacking U-boats.[12] Only one managed to penetrate the escort screen and launch an attack against the convoy.[13] SC-129 was further reinforced on the afternoon of 14 May when the support group comprising the escort aircraft carrier HMS *Biter* arrived.[14] The presence of the carrier and the increased air threat it brought forced Admiral Dönitz to cancel any further operations against SC-129.

While the story of the great convoy battles of the Atlantic continues to be told, the footnotes, such as the story of *Irish Oak*, should not be forgotten. Caught up in events beyond their control, Captain Eric Jones and his crew were fortunate to survive the attack carried out by U-607 without any loss of life. The ill-judged decision by Oberleutnant zur See Wolf Jeschonnek to attack *Irish Oak* was made on the assumption that the ship was an Allied Q-ship. The frail foundation on which he based this decision was contradicted by the ship's clearly visible neutral markings.

Irish Oak still has great significance to Irish maritime history. It was the last large contingent of merchant-navy survivors to be landed in Ireland during the war. The coming winter months would bring the second-largest group of survivors to land in Ireland – and from a very unlikely source.

16

BAY OF BISCAY

The Atlantic convoy attacks were primarily carried out by U-boats, with only the occasional involvement by heavy surface units. From 1942 onwards, the larger Kriegsmarine ships were concentrated in the Norwegian and Baltic Sea theatres. The absence of the big guns did not preclude bitterly contested actions as the Royal Navy and Kriegsmarine fought for dominance of the English Channel. There were intense small-unit engagements on both sides of the channel, with attacks on coastal convoys and incursions into enemy waters conducted by both sides.

Extending out from the English Channel, the Royal Navy and RAF strengthened their operations against U-boats transiting the Bay of Biscay. In 1943 these operations were intensified, while the business of intercepting blockade runners based in occupied France was also given a higher priority. In response to the increased British activity in the Bay of Biscay, the Kriegsmarine deployed strong destroyer and torpedo boat flotillas along the west-coast ports. The use of the term 'torpedo boat' to describe this class of German warship can be misleading, as these ships were large multipurpose units comparable in size to the destroyer escort class of ships used by the Royal Navy and US Navy. With a main armament of four

10.5-centimetre guns and six torpedo tubes, these versatile ships could also carry fifty mines, which made them ideally suited to operations in the Channel and Bay of Biscay. With their mission being to escort coastal convoys and transiting U-boats and blockade runners, the German flotillas would also harry the Royal Navy and conduct mine-laying operations.

At the beginning of September 1943 the latest torpedo-boat reinforcements arrived at Brest to join the 4th Torpedo Boat Flotilla. Both T-26 and T-27 had only recently been commissioned, and this was their first active-service assignment. While the majority of their crews were young and untested under enemy fire, their commanders were vastly experienced officers and seasoned veterans of several engagements with the Royal Navy. In command of T-26 was Kapitänleutnant Joachim Quedenfeldt, who had seen service in torpedo boats since the beginning of the war and in several theatres of operations. One of his most notable operations occurred in February 1942, while in command of T-15 as part of the 3rd Torpedo Boat Flotilla based at Dunkirk. This force, along with several other escorting flotillas, screened the battleships *Gneisenau* and *Scharnhorst* and the heavy cruiser *Prinz Eugen* as they sailed from Brest back to Germany.[1] There were other escort missions in March and May when German heavy cruisers moved along the Norwegian coast.[2] Quedenfeldt was then called to the Mediterranean, where he took command of TA-11 before the Italian surrender and sailed the warship back from La Spezia to the French port of Toulon. His time in the Mediterranean was cut short when he was recalled to take command of T-26.

T-26 and T-27 took part in their first operation on 29 September as part of a mine-laying operation by the 5th Flotilla, to which they were temporarily attached, during which the German force remained undetected. Although the mine-laying mission was a success, it did not result in any shipping losses.

Over the coming weeks and months there was an escalation in naval activity in the Channel and Biscay areas. In October Kriegsmarine ships were busy providing protection for coastal convoys along the French coast. The Royal Navy had reliable intelligence regarding the movements of the 4th Flotilla ships and acted to intercept the German force.

During the night of 23 October Kapitänleutnant Quedenfeldt and T-26 sailed with the 4th Flotilla, which was protecting the German blockade runner *Münsterland*.[3] In command of the flotilla was the bold Korvettenkapitän Franz Kohlauf. A massive torpedo barrage launched by the Germans caught the Royal Navy ships completely unawares, sinking one light cruiser and badly damaging a destroyer escort.[4] The young crews who manned the ships of the 4th Flotilla had given a good account of themselves and had inflicted an embarrassing defeat on the Royal Navy. Quedenfeldt was reassured by the actions of his crew during their first naval engagement. They had displayed the fortitude and good character necessary to a disciplined and cohesive fighting ship. These strengths would be sorely tested in the final days of 1943.

As Christmas approached, the crew of T-26 were excited at the prospect of returning home on leave. Since joining their new ship they had been stationed in France with no travel back home allowed. However, hopes of Christmas at home soon dissipated when, with heavy hearts, the flotilla was ordered to sea on 24 December. Espionage and a less than cooperative local populace in Brest meant that the ships did not sail until the last moment and were only told of their mission once at sea. Quedenfeldt informed the crew of T-26 that they were proceeding across the Bay of Biscay to rendezvous with the German blockade runner *Osorno*, returning from Japan with a cargo of vital war materials. The 4th Torpedo Boat Flotilla was joined by the 8th Destroyer Flotilla from Bordeaux. This combined escort force was under the overall command of Kapitän zur See Hans Erdmenger of the 8th Destroyer Flotilla. Although less experienced than Kohlauf, Erdmenger was the senior officer and so took command for this operation. This concentration of Kriegsmarine surface units was a clear sign of the importance attached to the safe arrival of *Osorno*.

Shortly after noon on Christmas Day the escort group met *Osorno* and surrounded the blockade runner with an impressive defensive screen. Earlier that morning a Sunderland Coastal Command aircraft had spotted the elusive blockade runner and reported its position, while shadowing from a safe distance. Returning blockade runners were high priority targets for the British, and patrols were instituted by the Royal Navy and Coastal Command with the sole mission of enforcing the blockade. For the remainder of Christmas Day, successive air attacks on *Osorno* were repulsed by the concentrated defensive fire of the escorts. *Osorno* reached the entrance of the Gironde River as the first dim light of a winter dawn broke through the clouds and was taken upriver by a minesweeper escort.

Meanwhile, the warships of each flotilla returned to base to refuel. The 8th Flotilla proceeded to Bordeaux along with T-25 and T-27 of the 4th Flotilla, with the remainder of the torpedo boats returning to Brest. The crew of T-26 must have enjoyed a sense of fulfilment as they entered Brest with their mission accomplished, hoping for the opportunity to enjoy the remainder of the Christmas holidays on shore. Once alongside the naval pier in Brest the ships immediately started to refuel and load ammunition. No personnel were allowed ashore, however, and within hours of their arrival the ships were back at sea. This unexpected turn of events came as a great surprise. The crew's disappointment at the lack of leave was compounded by the feeling of injustice at missing Christmas. A growing mood of despondency fermented throughout the complement of T-26.[5] This highly contagious demoralised state was most unwelcome on board a warship travelling through hostile waters. Quedenfeldt informed his crew that they were to proceed across the Bay of Biscay once again to escort a second blockade runner. Sensing the mood of his crew, the commander informed the dispirited sailors that on their return from this latest escort mission they would be given a month's leave. This was an astute announcement by the commander, who guessed that his ship would be engaged once again by the enemy and who knew that an unhappy crew was a vulnerability he could ill afford. The announcement had the desired effect and the spirits of the crew rose once again. This resurgence in the morale of the inexperienced crew would be dearly tested over the coming days as events conspired against the ships of the 4th Flotilla.

The second German blockade runner attempting to cross the Bay of Biscay was *Alsterufer*, which had departed Kobe only two days after *Osorno*. The ship had left Bordeaux in March and, after the long return journey from Japan, the crew looked forward to celebrating their safe return and a belated Christmas in the French port. With Christmas celebrations postponed until they arrived in Bordeaux, the crew worked a normal day. *Alsterufer* was the smallest blockade runner used by the Germans and had enjoyed a charmed wartime career.

Aware that a blockade runner was returning home, Coastal Command began to search the seas south of Biscay on Christmas Day. With the poor Atlantic weather and the short winter days, *Alsterufer* evaded detection for two days until its luck finally ran out on the morning of 27 December. Several air attacks failed to stop the German merchant ship, but it was forced to break radio silence to report its position and situation. Captain Piatek was informed of the imminent arrival of the Luftwaffe and the escort ships, but the combined flotilla force was too far away to assist until early the next morning and the JU88 fighters failed to materialise in time. Attacked with rockets and bombs from a Coastal Command Liberator, the German merchant ship was set ablaze and sunk.

Kapitän zur See Hans Erdmenger and his escort force were unaware of the loss of *Alsterufer*, and ploughed on westward towards the expected rendezvous. The ships sailing from Brest made a more northerly approach to the rendezvous than those coming from Bordeaux, and the increased air activity had kept the men at action stations for most of the day, relying on Pervitin tablets to stay alert.[6] Dawn on 28 December brought no respite to Quedenfeldt and his crew, who had little sleep during the night. The flotilla came under air attack by a large force of US Navy Liberators who doggedly harassed the ships throughout the morning. By midday the warships from Bordeaux had been sighted, but it was not long before news of the loss of *Alsterufer* and a sighting report of Royal Navy ships approaching from the north-east convinced Erdmenger to return to base.

The pursuing Royal Navy force comprised the cruisers HMS

Glasgow and *Enterprise*, and although Erdmenger possessed superior firepower, he was unwilling to risk an engagement. The poor sea conditions that day would undoubtedly have affected the accuracy of the German gunfire. Both the German destroyers and torpedo boats were less able gun platforms under these conditions when compared to the larger, more stable Royal Navy cruisers.

FW200 aircraft attacked the Royal Navy force with radio-controlled glider bombs, but without any success. The faster British cruisers continued to close on the fleeing German ships and battle commenced when *Glasgow* fired the opening salvoes. During the next three hours a confused engagement developed with the German force dividing into two groups. This controversial manoeuvre by Erdmenger was to prove costly. The British cruiser force maintained its cohesion and concentrated its firepower. In the ensuing melee Z-27, T-25 and T-26 were disabled and left drifting helplessly while the British cruisers closed to finish them off.

On board the three German ships, men had already begun to abandon ship. Rafts were flung into the sea and stunned sailors jumped into the inhospitable waters. Many of the survivors in the water remained close by the battered remains of their ships when *Enterprise* and *Glasgow* closed to within point-blank range and opened fire. This deadly *coup de grâce* of shellfire and torpedoes sank T-25, T-26 and Erdmenger's flagship destroyer Z-27. There were numerous indirect casualties amongst the sailors who were clinging to rafts nearby. The British cruisers steamed away from the area, leaving the German survivors angry at what they considered to be the callous nature in which they had been left adrift.[7]

Those German warships that were undamaged continued at

high speed towards the French coast leaving hundreds of German sailors, many of whom were badly wounded, on their own. There was a heavy sea running, which made conditions difficult for the many men seeking shelter on the crowded rafts. Some had to sit submerged in seawater up to their chests. The dwindling light from the short winter day gradually faded and the insecurity of night descended upon the survivors. In the impenetrable darkness conditions degenerated into bitter personal struggles for survival. A biting cold wind whipped up the sea which lashed against the flanks of the exposed rafts, a succession of large waves breaking over them and testing everyone's endurance. Those who had been wounded during the battle were the first to falter and were silently committed to the deep. But the greatest number of men were lost when they were no longer able to hold on to the rafts and were washed off by the unrelenting waves.

When morning came, it was found that between half and two-thirds of their number had been lost during the night. On one raft, which originally had eleven men, only four had survived. On another, three out of seven had made it, while on another only two out of ten. More lives were lost overnight than in the combat the previous afternoon. For the remaining young sailors, the belief that rescue would doubtless come and a determination to return home to their waiting loved ones fortified their will to continue. However, rescue would need to come soon, before another unholy night consigned more weary souls to a Biscay grave.

In the early half-light of 29 December, FW200 aircraft took off from their bases in France to search for the survivors from the sea battle. In addition, U-boats in transit across the Bay of Biscay were diverted to assist with the rescue operation. The first aircraft to reach the area found the sea scattered with rafts, and their arrival gave an immediate boost to the sailors, with the hope of an imminent rescue revitalising their spirits. The FW200 dropped a rubber dinghy containing rescue stores and provisions and then headed north in search of a ship that could participate in the rescue mission. As the FW200 flew low under the thick blanket of cloud cover, a small vessel appeared in the distance. The aircraft turned to approach the unidentified coaster and, spotting the neutral markings emblazoned across the sides and hatches, began to signal using the daylight signal lamp in English: 'SOS LIFEBOATS.'

Captain Tom Donoghue had travelled to Cork to take command of the Wexford Steamship Company's humble coaster *Kerlogue*. Donoghue had survived the sinking of *Irish Oak* in May 1943 and was returning to the short sea trade with which he had grown familiar over the years. *Kerlogue* had been attacked by RAF aircraft in October 1943 and had undergone repairs. It then resumed trading between Ireland and the Iberian Peninsula and was returning to Dublin with a full cargo of fresh oranges loaded at Lisbon. The weather had been dismal since leaving port and the small Irish trader laboured through the heavy swell running into the Bay of Biscay.

The morning of 29 December was as uneventful as any other day until the captain sighted the familiar outline of a German FW200 approaching from astern. Afraid that the ship was about to suffer an unjustified aerial attack, Donoghue called out all hands as a precautionary measure.[8] His concerns were soon allayed when the German started to circle the ship. Once the blink of the signalling lamp was interpreted, the requested rescue effort was set in motion.[9] Flag signals from the aircraft gave Donoghue the direction in which the lifeboats could be found and *Kerlogue* altered course and headed south-east. Straying too far east towards the French coast was inadvisable, as they risked entering the danger zone the British had declared around the French west coast. (It was a transgression into the declared danger zone that had resulted in the attack on *Kerlogue* the previous October.) After following this new heading for a while, the circling FW200 began to mark the location of the survivors by dropping flares. As the rescue ship grew closer, the men hanging onto the rafts greeted the appearance of the mastheads on the horizon with a barrage of distress rockets.

The crew of *Kerlogue* prepared to receive the survivors, unaware of the full extent of the terrible scene that awaited them. Captain Donoghue remained on the bridge with his helmsman and altered course towards the first rafts that came into view. Soon a flurry of sighting reports were shouted back to the bridge as momentary glimpses were caught of rafts, tossed on the peaks of the rolling swell waves. As realisation of the enormity of the situation dawned on them, the crew of *Kerlogue* remained undeterred and pressed on. The rescue work continued throughout the afternoon with the weather refusing to improve and allow the mercy mission to be conducted under more benign conditions.

At first the nationality of the men in the water was unknown, but as they were hauled on board their uniforms identified them as being German sailors of the Kriegsmarine. The crew's living quarters and alleyways on *Kerlogue* began to fill with the bedraggled figures of exhausted German sailors. For Donoghue there appeared to be no end to the sprawl of rafts and as the last light of an indistinct sunset faded, the deck floodlights were switched on to allow the rescue work to continue. It was hard, back-breaking work for the crew of the Irish ship who toiled ceaselessly under the most difficult circumstances.

Not long after coming on board, Kapitänleutnant Quedenfeldt made his way through the packed alleyways towards the bridge, where he found Captain Donoghue. The German commander had a natural desire to return to any port that was under German control or even neutral Spain and requested that *Kerlogue* return them to any of these destinations once the rescue work was completed. Donoghue must surely have known that to acquiesce to such a request would have serious repercussions with the British authorities who could, at the very least, revoke the ship's Navicert.[10] Placed in this difficult position Donoghue deferred final judgement on the request until they had finished pulling the survivors out of the sea.

After nearly ten hours of unceasing manoeuvring through uncooperative seas, Captain Donoghue took the unpleasant decision to halt the rescue work. *Kerlogue* had become so packed with German sailors that there was no free space anywhere on board the ship. Unable to support any more survivors, the Irish ship sailed away from many men still stranded in the water.[11] In total, 168 German sailors had been rescued, which was quite an achievement.[12]

There was now the matter of deciding at which port *Kerlogue* should land the German sailors. Donoghue was mindful that in addition to caring for the many survivors he also had an obligation to ensure the safety of his own crew. Another factor was the terms imposed by the Navicert system, which required *Kerlogue* to proceed directly to Milford Haven for inspection by the naval authorities.

However, in view of the serious condition of many of the rescued men, the overcrowding on board and the limited supply of fresh water and food, Donoghue decided to proceed directly to Cork on the grounds that it was the nearest port that could be reached without endangering the ship. Quedenfeldt was advised of this decision and, despite his earlier request to be repatriated to France, the German commander accepted the judgement without protest.

The voyage north was cramped and uncomfortable for everyone on board, but the grateful Germans never complained and made do with what could be provided. The limited food supply was soon exhausted and the four-ton capacity freshwater tank was emptying rapidly. Many of the resourceful survivors had taken the rations from the rafts, which went some way towards supplementing the provisions on board. Another source of food was the cargo of fresh oranges which Donoghue ordered to be opened.

Rather than the shortages, it was the critical medical condition of some of the Germans that posed the greatest immediate dilemma for Donoghue. The injured were cared for and made as comfortable as possible, but some were already in a critical condition when they were hauled on board. Unfortunately, two German sailors were declared dead on 30 December. Later that same afternoon *Kerlogue* stopped to bury both men at sea. With several others in declining health Donoghue knew it was imperative to reach Cork as soon as possible.

There was another death in the early hours of 31 December when Oberleutnant (Ing.) Adolf Braatz succumbed to his injuries.[13] Braatz was the engineering officer on board T-26 and had been horribly scalded by high-pressure steam during the battle. Joachim Quedenfeldt and Adolf Braatz were close personal friends, and his death had a profound emotional effect on the battle-hardened commander. Unlike the previous two casualties, Quedenfeldt would not allow the remains of his friend to be buried at sea and the body of Braatz remained on board to be interred on arrival in Ireland.

Kerlogue was unable to alert the authorities on shore by radio until they had almost made landfall off the Fastnet Rock. The radio telephony set on board had been originally intended for use on board trawlers and had a limited effective range. So it was that at 2136 hrs on 31 December that *Kerlogue* sent a message to Valentia radio station giving a brief account of the events of the past two days.[14] Donoghue requested that medical assistance be ready at Cork for the ship's arrival, which was expected to be about 0200 hrs on 1 January. *Kerlogue* continued towards Fastnet and then turned right to follow the coast towards Cork Harbour.

The radio transmission had been received not only by Valentia but also by the radio intercept station at Land's End. The British naval authorities were duly informed of the content of the message sent by *Kerlogue*, and at 0030 hrs, Land's End transmitted a message instructing *Kerlogue* to proceed to Milford Haven in accordance with the terms of its Navicert. The airwaves were silent, with no response forthcoming. Another message was sent again an hour later, which was met with the same static.

Much has been said about this apparent act of defiance shown by Captain Donoghue in not acknowledging the radio calls from Land's End. It is a straightforward matter, however: *Kerlogue* never heard the transmitted messages. At the time of the transmissions, between 0030 hrs and 0130 hrs, the ship would have been steaming between Seven Heads and Roberts Head on the west coast of

Cork. At this juncture, Captain Donoghue would have been with his watch officer on a bridge full to capacity with German sailors. There was no dedicated radio officer to maintain a watch and with all the deck officers busy, the Marconi radio set would have been unattended when Land's End broadcast its two messages. In any event, when the second call was transmitted, *Kerlogue* was busy transferring personnel to a naval patrol boat, which took precedence over all other considerations.

The expected arrival of *Kerlogue* at Cork had set in motion plans by several organisations for dealing with large numbers of survivors coming ashore. As it was known that there was a considerable number of injured sailors on board, the Irish Naval Service MTB (Motor Torpedo Boat) M1 was ordered from Haulbowline with an advance party of medical staff that included two doctors. M1 departed the naval basin at Haulbowline at 2345 hrs on 31 December and rendezvoused with *Kerlogue* just off Flat Head at 0110 hrs. The medical team boarded, while twelve German sailors were transferred to M1 to ease the congestion on the rescue ship.

With the transferred German sailors on board, the Irish patrol boat proceeded back to Cork Harbour. Waiting at Cobh was a strong Irish army presence, not with the intention of presenting a military force to subdue the expected rescued combatants, but simply to provide the logistics required to transfer so many men to Collins Barracks. In Dublin, government officials were telephoned and apprised of the situation. The discretionary nature of Irish politics during the war would have to be carefully negotiated to ensure that this episode did not generate any undue discord in the sometimes difficult relationship between Dublin and London.

As M1 neared Cork Harbour, it passed the patrol ship *Muirchu*, sent out to rendezvous with *Kerlogue* and escort the Irish trader into Cobh. At 0248 hrs, *Kerlogue* was finally alongside at Cobh, bringing an end to a voyage that was the crowning achievement of its career and those of its crew. Seven injured men were taken off to waiting ambulances while the remainder boarded army transports and were taken to Collins Barracks.[15] It took several hours to transport all the men into the city.

Although the Germans knew that they were being driven off into internment for the remainder of the war, they remained very appreciative of Captain Tom Donoghue, unwitting saviour of so many. In Cork the tired and hungry sailors were treated to their first Irish meal, which made such an impression on them that they described the quantity and quality of the food with great admiration when writing home to their families in Germany.

The German sailors remained in Cork until late January while suitable accommodation was prepared at the Curragh internment camp. The status of the recently arrived Kriegsmarine crews had been discussed at great length, with the British and German legations each requesting differing terms of the Irish government for their treatment. The British position was that if the Germans were to remain in Ireland they should be interned with no possibility of repatriation until after the war was over. The German legation, led by Edouard Hempel, naturally took the polar view. Hempel rightly knew that under international law the shipwrecked crew of a belligerent warship picked up by a neutral merchant ship and landed in a neutral port should be allowed to leave that country.

It was decided that all the German sailors would be interned on the grounds that precedence had already been shown by the internment of all other belligerent persons in Ireland since the beginning of the war and, more importantly, by the Department of Defence Internment Order issued in 1941 following the DEMS gunners incidents. The sailors quietly accepted internment, with some even expressing a small degree of anticipation for their new adventure. At the Curragh the living quarters provided for the Kriegsmarine personnel were far from ideal. Damp and overcrowded barrack huts did not impress Quedenfeldt, who protested about the conditions. However, despite the bad first impression and some problems regarding the issue of parole from the camp, the sailors settled down into a routine.

The final word on this captivating story must surely belong to Captain Tom Donoghue and the crew of *Kerlogue*. Their exploits during those last days of 1943 showed an adherence to the best traditions of seamanship and an uncompromising attitude to assist any fellow seafarer in peril. *Kerlogue* finally sailed from Cobh and continued towards Milford Haven, where the waiting naval authorities interrogated the Irish captain for several hours. The brusque manner in which Donoghue was questioned was an unjustified assault on the unblemished reputation of this extraordinary ship's master. *Kerlogue* was allowed to proceed to Dublin where Donoghue received a letter from Edouard Hempel expressing his gratitude for the rescue of so many German sailors. This letter of thanks was followed up some weeks later when Hempel met Donoghue to present him with a silver cup engraved with the words 'Bay of Biscay'.

17

U-260

In March 1944 Admiral Dönitz decided that, due to the heavy losses of U-boats, there would be no more wolf-pack operations against convoys. The abandonment of large-scale attacks followed a period when U-boats operated closer to the Irish coast and the approaches to the North Channel than at any other time in the preceding two years. The Allied surface escort and air protection had proved to be too strong, and Dönitz needed to conserve his remaining fleet. It was hoped that U-boats fitted with the latest improved weapons and electronic detection equipment would revive the potency of the U-boat force, and indeed there was good reason to do so as Allied plans for an invasion of France were known to be well under way.

Towards the end of March 1944, large groups of U-boats were gathered at their French bases, ready to operate against the anticipated invasion fleet. Among those waiting inside the great U-boat pens at Saint-Nazaire was U-260, which had completed its last patrol at the end of February and was in need of lengthy mechanical repairs. Not the most successful of U-boats, it had only managed to sink one ship since becoming operational in September 1942. Nevertheless, U-260 had come through some difficult situations and had thus far survived where many others had been lost. While at Saint-Nazaire, command of U-260 was handed over to Oberleutnant zur See Klaus Becker. The young commander was familiar with U-260 and its crew, having served as first watch officer before going ashore to complete his commander's training course.

At about this time it was decided that as many as possible of the U-boats entering French bases after completion of a war patrol would be fitted with the latest technological enhancements being produced in Germany. For detection of aircraft and ships while the U-boat was running on the surface, the Hohentwiel radar set provided a much-needed early warning. Being able to run their diesel engines while submerged to recharge their batteries was an imperative need and the snorkel system was introduced from 1944. Air was supplied and exhaust gases removed via an extended mast whose top rose above the sea surface. New tactics and procedures accompanied both these new developments, and many crews had to learn on the job. Despite the urgent demand for this new equipment, the constraints of wartime production and delays caused by Allied bombing raids prevented many U-boats from receiving theirs. U-260 was one of the many boats compelled to return to sea without the modifications.

When the Allies invaded Normandy on 6 June 1944, Admiral Dönitz ordered all available U-boats against the invasion fleet. The snorkel-equipped boats proceeded towards the Allied armada, and those without maintained a patrol line in the Bay of Biscay to thwart any attempted landing by Allied forces on the west coast.

On the afternoon of 6 June, U-260 sailed out into waters swarming with Allied air patrols. For the next eleven days it remained submerged, surfacing only to recharge its batteries. Whenever an Allied aircraft radar transmission was detected by the radar warning receiver, U-260 would dive and remain submerged until the danger was thought to have passed. This endless cycle of surfacing to recharge the batteries then diving at the first sign of trouble, as well as the uncertainty of not knowing if they had been detected and were in danger of imminent attack, put an enormous strain on the crew.

It had been rightly assessed by BdU that the omnipresent Allied air patrols over the Bay of Biscay would take a heavy toll on the boats not equipped with snorkels and, accordingly, on 12 June the boats were recalled to the safety of the U-boat pens. U-260 returned to Lorient on 16 June, where the dockyard workers were fitting snorkels to as many boats as possible. On 22 July U-260 was commanded to attack Allied shipping outside the port, but the operation was cancelled shortly afterwards and Becker returned to Lorient where he waited for his U-boat to have the important snorkel device fitted.

By the first week in August, the situation on land had become dire and the northern French U-boat bases were being threatened by the advancing US Army. On 7 August U-260, along with U-608 and U-981, departed Lorient in an attempt to reach the southern port of La Pallice, where it was hoped they could be fitted with a snorkel. The Bay of Biscay was by now completely controlled by the Allies. The constant air patrols were backed up by AS surface patrols covering the approaches to the U-boat bases.

Despite intense enemy activity, U-260 managed to evade the deadly patrols, largely due to the recent installation of its Hohentwiel radar set. Travelling submerged during the daytime,

Becker surfaced only at night to recharge his batteries. Once a radar contact was received, the boat dived. The transit south was slow, but the judicious use of time on the surface and the crew's speedy response to reported radar contacts undoubtedly saved U-260. The other two boats that had left Lorient at the same time were not so lucky and both were sunk near the approaches to La Pallice.[1]

La Pallice port was a hive of activity as work continued at a frantic pace on the waiting U-boats. Fortunately there was a snorkel unit available and installation work immediately began on U-260. By the end of the month the system was ready for testing, and soon after U-260 was back at sea, ready to make the circuitous journey to Bergen. The chosen route kept the U-boat well to the west of the British Isles where roving Allied patrols meticulously combed the North and South-West Approaches. The extended voyage lasted just over six weeks and was a gruelling ordeal for the crew. However, it also provided vital experience of sailing with the new snorkel device, which would be needed when the boat returned to continue the inshore campaign.

U-260 remained submerged for almost the entire voyage to Bergen, running on its diesel engines. Oberleutnant Becker surfaced only every three or four days for a couple of hours – always at night – to dispose of accumulated waste and to ventilate the boat. In theory it should have been as possible to ventilate the boat while it was submerged by using the snorkel, but a defect in the system redirected diesel exhaust gases into the boat, causing carbon-monoxide poisoning. Despite these complications, U-260 arrived at Bergen, from where, after a brief stopover, it continued on to Flensburg in Germany for repair work on the diesel engines and the snorkel.

While U-260 was making the voyage from La Pallice to Bergen, the first snorkel-equipped U-boats were sent to patrol the coastal waters of the North Channel and the sea area covering the entrance to St George's Channel and the Bristol Channel. Initial reports seemed to suggest that good results could be gained by a U-boat in which the crew was sufficiently experienced in snorkel operations. Capable of remaining submerged and undetected by Coastal Command aircraft, the boats also enjoyed the added advantage of the complex hydrographic conditions experienced in shallow water that drastically reduced the detection of U-boats by AS warships. In coastal waters there was interference from underwater background noises that reduced the effectiveness of Allied warship underwater listening equipment. Moreover underwater objects such as wrecks, rocks and fish shoals also reduced the effectiveness of sonar. This in turn made it difficult to detect submerged U-boats.

In late November 1944, U-boat operations in the Irish Sea and Bristol Channel were implemented in earnest. Outbound U-boats from Norway made the transit north of Scotland and then followed the Irish coastline. Once south of Fastnet lighthouse, they could proceed towards their assigned patrol area.

The presence of U-boats in these waters did not go unnoticed by the British and measures were undertaken to prevent any further intrusions into the busy coastal shipping waterways. Experience from the summer campaign in the English Channel had shown that defensive minefields laid deep underwater in known U-boat transit areas or near Allied convoy routes were an effective deterrent against the snorkel boats. It was therefore decided that a series of deep minefields would be laid off the south coast of Ireland. The fast cruiser-minelayer HMS *Apollo* was assigned the task and was to conduct operations out of Milford Haven. In the early morning of 26 October 1944, *Apollo* arrived in position just 9 miles south of Galley Head and began to lay the first of several minefields off the Cork coast. By the end of November the minefields were in place, sufficiently deep to pose no danger to passing surface ships, but ready for any unsuspecting U-boats.

The winter months at the beginning of 1945 saw the continued worsening of the German situation on the Continent. At sea, however, optimism had remained high since the inshore campaign had commenced. The introduction of snorkel-equipped boats against coastal shipping and the fleet's greatly reduced losses meant that the campaign would continue into the New Year.[2]

The crew of U-260 had spent the winter waiting for repairs to their boat to be completed. The disruptions of Allied air attacks caused exasperating delays while shortages in materials and stores added to the difficulties that plagued the battered German infrastructure. Eventually, on 18 February, Becker and his crew left the U-boat base at Horten with orders to proceed to a waiting position west of Ireland. The sea lanes north of Scotland were heavily patrolled, but the route followed ensured the best possible chance for making a successful breakout from the North Sea. By staying well north of the Shetland Islands, the U-boat could then turn south, keeping west of the Hebrides until it reached the Irish coast.

It was a stressful three weeks for Becker and his crew, but their previous extended voyage with the snorkel had provided invaluable experience. While en route to the waiting area, engagements with enemy patrols were to be avoided so as not to betray their location. Nevertheless, the strong enemy presence was a persistent feature of their daily lives. On 12 March U-260 had reached a position just west of Fastnet Rock. Once to the south of the landmark the boat could continue east along the coast towards its operational area.

Since the German departure from France, the South-West Approaches were open once more to convoy traffic and, consequently, patrols in the area were increased to deter the unyielding U-boats. Enemy activity along the south coast was particularly heavy on 12 March, with the 19th Escort Group conducting AS sweeps along the Irish coast, complemented by RAF Coastal Command patrols from above. In the afternoon, the incessant overhead flying and the detection of destroyer noises ahead did not bode well, and Becker decided to suspend snorkel operations for fear the mast would be sighted. The U-boat dived to a depth of 80 metres and continued east on electric motors, all the time listening for the sounds of an approaching destroyer. The distant noises gradually faded as the two destroyers responsible for the alarm continued east away from U-260. Becker thought it prudent to remain deep until nightfall, when they could resume operating the snorkel.

Suddenly a violent explosion rocked the U-boat, which tilted down alarmingly and began to dive. Initial damage reports coming back to the control room told of some flooding in the forward compartments. The U-boat's descent was abruptly halted by the seabed, providing a pause for Becker and his crew to assess their situation. It was apparent that the boat had suffered considerable damage and, with no contacts in the vicinity immediately prior to the explosion, it was most probable that it had collided with a mine. The full extent of the damage was unknown, but the outer hull had almost certainly been irreparably damaged, causing the forward diving tanks to flood.

It was imperative that the boat regain the surface as remaining on the seabed might further weaken the structurally compromised pressure hull. Escape would only be guaranteed if they could reach the surface. High-pressure air was blasted into the forward tanks while the electric motors were run astern to help raise the critically wounded boat from the seabed. As it reached the surface, the high-pressure air introduced into the compromised tanks escaped, allowing seawater to fill the tanks once again and sending the boat into another dive. Their predicament seemed dire. As a means of maintaining sufficient pressure in the tanks to prevent recurring flooding, the diesel engines would have to be run via the snorkel, with the exhaust gases redirected through the flooded tanks.[3]

The damaged U-boat finally broke the surface with its diesel engines running. Becker was acutely aware of the importance of reporting what had happened and that there was a minefield to the south of Ireland. This vital intelligence would save many boats from sharing their fate. With the urgent radio message transmitted back to headquarters, there remained the question of what was to happen to the boat. The damage was so severe that no thoughts of it reaching a safe port could be entertained and Becker gave the order to abandon ship and to scuttle the boat. With the neutral coast of Ireland just to the north, he ordered the crew to close the distance to the shore before abandoning ship. Men prepared to leave and gathered together the few personal belongings they had on board. On deck the forward emergency rafts were taken from their stowage compartments and inflated. Elsewhere, the confidential books, decipher books and the rotors from the Enigma machine were placed in a cylindrical container and thrown overboard.[4] Lights along the shore were soon discernible and Becker gave the order to abandon ship. Before leaving the engine room, crewmembers opened the sea valves to ensure the demise of the boat. The young commander was last to leave and joined the rest of his crew in the water.

Under the command of Klaus Becker, U-260 had survived incredible odds to escape from the French ports in the summer of 1944. Together the crew had endured the lengthy voyage back to Germany. Yet, in spite of all these obstacles, U-260 had returned to the fray undetected and unchallenged by the omnipresent Allied patrols. It was only the unquantifiable factor of a minefield that had undone the hardy U-boat. U-260 was finally consumed by the cold seas and disappeared from the surface for the last time.

A strong easterly-flowing tidal stream caught the rafts and they soon became separated in the darkness. The close proximity of the shore lights and the reassuring beacon of Galley Head lighthouse meant that safety was close at hand. At 0405 hrs the volunteers manning the Coast Watching Service lookout post on Galley Head spotted flares coming from the sea. Evidently there was someone in distress, but although the sighting was reported, no rescue craft was launched. At 0450 hrs the lookouts sighted a single raft crowded with men approaching the headland and the volunteers guided it into a safe landing site using an Aldis lamp. The eleven German sailors were taken up to the lighthouse and were questioned by the local police superintendent there. By conversing in French it was ascertained that another thirty-seven sailors remained at sea.

News of the distressed seamen was forwarded to the Courtmacsherry lifeboat, which put out to sea to search for the rafts. At Haulbowline the Naval Service patrol boat M1 was also dispatched to the area to assist. It did not take the lifeboat long to locate and pick up all the remaining survivors who were drifting south of the entrance to Glandore Harbour. With thirty-seven soaked sailors on board, the overcrowded lifeboat headed back to Courtmacsherry, where the army and the Shipwrecked Mariners' Society were waiting.

After searching the area for several hours, the crew of M1 recovered some items from the water, mainly discarded escape apparatus and items from the rafts. A large stain spreading out over the sea marked the final resting place of U-260.

The German sailors disembarked at the small Courtmacsherry pier and were provided with welcome refreshment – courtesy of the quick organisation of the Shipwrecked Mariners' Society's honorary agent. Then army transport took all forty-eight men to Collins Barracks, Cork, where they stayed for several days. Two sailors were taken to the barracks infirmary, but their condition was not serious and they were treated for minor colds.

Becker and his officers were interviewed at Collins Barracks, but were not forthcoming about the circumstances that had led to the loss of their boat. The conversations were benign and the Irish authorities did not learn much about the boat's movements. A casual mention of mines by a sailor who landed at Galley Head lighthouse was the only indication of what may have happened to the boat.

On 16 March the crew of U-260 were transferred to the Curragh camp, where they were greeted by Kapitänleutnant Quedenfeldt. The crew from U-260 enjoyed the same privileges of parole from the camp as the other internees. The final payment of wages from the German legation was received in March and many of the U-boat men joined the others in working outside the camp. With the war drawing to an end, the time spent in Ireland by the crew of U-260 was short. In August 1945 arrangements were made for the Germans internees in Ireland to be repatriated.

* * *

On 24 April the British coaster *Monmouth Coast* departed Sligo with a cargo of barite destined for Liverpool. The Coast Watching Service lookout posts lost sight of the ship at around midday as it headed across Donegal Bay. Unfortunately it was spotted by U-1305 under the command of Oberleutnant zur See Helmut Christiansen, who had taken up a patrol line south of Tory Island. A single torpedo wrecked the small ship. In the aftermath of the attack, only three men managed to make it off. Two were unable to reach the only raft and for two days mess boy Derek Cragg drifted off the Donegal coast before he was picked up by local fishermen and brought to Arran Island. The long shadow that had hung over the Irish coast for six long years had seen its last survivor ashore. Within two weeks the war in Europe was over and with its conclusion the cost in human suffering could finally be counted. From the long list of casualties at sea, just a fraction saved from the final reckoning found solace along a hospitable Irish coast.

CONCLUSION

Between the winter months of November 1945 and January 1946, the calm that had been restored to the seas off the coast of Donegal was interrupted once again. The sound of explosions resonated across the scene of recent convoy battles with Operation Deadlight: the Allied plan to dispose of 116 surrendered German U-boats by scuttling them 130 miles north-west of Donegal. With the sinking of these weapons which had once wreaked havoc across the Atlantic, the Royal Navy closed the final chapter on that bitter struggle known as the Battle of the Atlantic. Their final resting place lies across the shipping lanes of the North-West Approaches, where they had attempted to strangle the vital flow of supplies destined for Britain. In turn the vast numbers of wartime convoy escorts and other ancillary warships were decommissioned and scrapped as the Royal Navy returned to a peacetime footing. The machinery of war was dismantled and the war-ravaged nations of Europe looked towards a new future.

Ireland briefly remained outside the new world order that was being drawn up, excluded by the victors for remaining steadfastly neutral and apparently indifferent to the fate of those nations that had suffered through the darkest days of the war. The contentious issue of the former Treaty ports was amongst the arguments vehemently directed against Ireland in the post-war period of reflection and analysis. Those who thought that the use of Ireland's ports by the Allies may have helped save lives at sea during the Battle of the Atlantic, or helped bring about a quicker victory in the war against Germany, did not dwell on the positive attitude that the Irish government had adopted towards the British or the assistance provided despite Ireland's neutrality. In addition, the assistance afforded to the men and women who came to Ireland as victims of the countless engagements off its coasts was quickly forgotten. Indeed, many other instances of unobtrusive Irish involvement in the war were ignored until recently, when significantly more works have been published on the subject of Ireland's history during this period.

It was not Ireland's neutrality that was the contributing factor in determining the fate of the survivors from the ships covered in this book. Irrespective of the national boundaries that demarcated friend from foe, the strategically important position of Ireland in the Western Approaches, combined with the prevailing winds and ocean currents of the north Atlantic, made it inevitable that casualties from the war at sea would arrive on its shores. What was important for the men who landed from the lifeboats and rescue ships was that they were treated with compassion and kindness, regardless of nationality or personal loyalties to the different belligerent nations. As the war progressed and economic hardships gripped the isolated island, the survivors did not want for anything to ease their circumstances.

For the survivors themselves, the memories of their time in Ireland were always filled with the relief of having found safety from the deadly Atlantic battleground and glowing praise for the people who cared for them while they were fleeting guests across the four provinces. There was no better tribute paid to the effort made by the countless volunteers, civilians and service personnel who helped in every survivor landing, than that of Captain Klemp from the ill-fated steamer *Petrel*. Summing up his time in Clifden, where he and many other survivors were treated, Klemp said that Ireland was, 'That one little haven of peace in this storm-tossed world.' With so many nations enveloped in a war of unimaginable suffering, it was humbling to be described in such a dignifying manner by a ship's captain who had first-hand experience of the desperate struggle at sea.

As the years progressed and the memories of the war faded, occasional visitors would return to Ireland to thank the locals who had helped them in their hour of need. Passengers from *Athenia*, who landed unexpectedly in Galway in September 1939, were frequent visitors to that city, but their subsequent visits were intentional and their glowing praise for the people of Galway even more forthcoming than it had been back in 1939.

Official ceremonies were held to commemorate the rescue of survivors who reached Ireland. One such was in 1994, when German survivors from the battle of Biscay who were rescued by *Kerlogue* returned to Ireland for a series of events and meetings, including a special remembrance ceremony held at the Abbeyside Church in Dungarvan in honour of Captain Tom Donoghue. Dieter Kluber, who was one of the former German sailors attending the ceremony, described their Irish rescuers who 'ignored the dangers, the storm and the high seas to save our lives. God bless Ireland and her people.'

The commander of U-35, Werner Lott, returned to Ventry in 1984 to see the location where he landed the rescued Greek crew from *Diamantis*. This incident was commemorated by a memorial, which was unveiled in 2009. But there were many more events like the one that occurred in Ventry. Most went unheralded and their exploits were consigned to obscurity or were vaguely remembered by a few residents who told stories about men from the sea. We should not forget the deeds of these survivors or the effort made by the men and women of Ireland who helped them in their hour of need.

Appendix I

SHIPS SUNK THROUGH BELLIGERENT ACTION THAT LANDED SURVIVORS IN IRELAND

Date sunk	Ship name	Notes on landing	Number of Survivors
3 September 1939	*Athenia* (British)	*Knute Nelson* landed survivors at Galway on 5 September.	449
7 September 1939	*Olivegrove* (British)	Picked up by the liner *Washington* and landed at Cobh.	33
14 September 1939	*British Influence* (British)	*Ida Bakke* picked up survivors and transferred them to Courtmacsherry lifeboat on 15 September. Landed at Courtmacsherry.	42
15 September 1939	*Cheyenne* (British)	*Ida Bakke* picked up survivors and transferred them to Courtmacsherry lifeboat on 16 September. Landed at Baltimore.	37

16 September 1939	*Rudyard Kipling* (British)	Crew lifeboat taken in tow by U-boat to Irish coast. Lifeboat landed at Malin Bay on 16 September.	13
24 September 1939	*Hazelside* (British)	Crew rescued by *St Ultan* and landed at Schull on 24 September.	23
3 October 1939	*Diamantis* (Greek)	Crew taken on board the U-boat and landed at Ventry on 5 October.	28
16 November 1939	*Arlington Court* (British)	*Algenib* (Dutch) picked up survivors and landed them at Cork Harbour on 21 November.	22
20 November 1939	*Thomas Hankins* (British)	Picked up by trawler *Esher* and landed at Moville on 21 November.	12
20 November 1939	*Delphine* (British)	Landed at Malin Head on 21 November.	13
22 January 1940	*Songa* (Norwegian)	Eleven crew members were picked up by the British trawler *Lodden* and landed at Kinsale on 27 January. Remaining ten landed in a lifeboat at Crookhaven on 26 January.	21
28 January 1940	*Eleni Stathatos* (Greek)	Landed at Portmagee on 1 February.	20
11 February 1940	*Togimo* (British)	Survivors landed at Cobh by Spanish ship *Monte Nevajo*.	11

12 February 1940	*Dalarö* (Swedish)	Rescued by the Belgian trawler *Jan De Waele* Landed at Buncrana on 14 February.	29
14 February 1940	*Langleeford* (British)	Fifteen survivors landed at Fodry on 16 February 1940. Remaining fifteen survivors landed at Glenderry on 17 February.	30
15 February 1940	*Steinstad* (Norwegian)	Survivors landed in Co. Donegal on 20 February.	11
27 May 1940	*Sheaf Mead* (British)	Survivors picked up by *Frangoula B. Goulandris*, landed at Cobh on 31 May.	5
19 June 1940	*Labud* (Yugoslavian)	Landed at Dirk Bay, near Galley Head, on 20 June.	34
25 June 1940	*Saranac* (British)	Landed at Berehaven.	16
30 June 1940	*Georgios Kyriakides* (Greek)	Landed at Valentia Island on 2 July.	30
2 July 1940	*Athellaird* (British)	Picked up by *Moyalla*, landed at Fenit on 12 July.	20
5 July 1940	*Magog* (Canadian)	Landed at Cobh.	23
10 July 1940	*Petsamo* (Finnish)	Landed at Baltimore on 10 July.	34
18 July 1940	*Woodbury* (British)	One lifeboat landed at Castletown, one lifeboat landed at Ballinskellig.	35
19 July 1940	*Pearlmoor* (British)	Landed at Gola Island.	26

28 July 1940	*Auckland Star* (British)	Nineteen landed at Dingle on 30 July and fifty-five landed at Clifden on 31 July.	74
30 July 1940	*Clan Menzies* (British)	One lifeboat landed at Enniscrone on 1 August and one lifeboat landed at Belmullet.	88
5 August 1940	*Pindos* (Greek)	Landed at Downings on 7 August.	29
9 August 1940	*Canton* (Swedish)	Landed at Killala Bay on 11 August.	16
16 August 1940	*Clan MacPhee* (British)	*Kelet* picked up survivors. Landed at Galway on 26 August.	12
19 August 1940	*Ville De Gand* (Belgian)	Landed at Belmullet on 21 August.	12
19 August 1940	*Kelet* (Hungarian)	Survivors from *Clan MacPhee* and *Kelet* were picked up by *Varegg* and landed at Galway on 26 August.	13
24 August 1940	*Cumberland* (British)	Landed at Moville.	22
24 August 1940	*Havildar* (British)	Landed on Inishtrahull Island.	27
25 August 1940	*Goatland* (British)	Eighteen survivors picked up by *Lanahrone*, remaining eighteen landed at Dursey.	36
29 August 1940	*Empire Moose* (British)	Landed at Killybegs, Co. Donegal, on 31 August.	21

28 August 1940	*Dalblair* (British)	Picked up by tug *Englishman* and landed at Buncrana on 31 August, along with thirteen survivors from *Alida Gorthon.*	4
28 August 1940	*Alida Gorthon* (Swedish)	Landed at Buncrana on 31 August. The ship had earlier picked up survivors from *Dalblair.*	13
26 September 1940	*Siljan* (Swedish)	Landed at Ballydavid on 29 September.	9
27 September 1940	*Vestvard* (Norwegian)	Landed at Clifden on 1 October.	28
2 October 1940	*Latymer* (British)	Survivors picked up by the trawler *Kilgerran Castle* and landed at Valentia.	22
7 October 1940	*Touraine* (British)	Landed at Arranmore Island and Tory Island, Co. Donegal, on 9–10 October.	16
12 October 1940	*Davanger* (British)	Landed at Broadhaven on 18 October 1940.	12
12 October 1940	*Pacific Ranger* (British)	Landed at Killybegs, Co. Donegal, on 18 October.	23
18 November 1940	*Nestlea* (British)	Landed at Ballycotton, Co. Cork.	22
2 December 1940	*Cetvrti* (Yugoslav)	Landed at Cahirciveen, Co. Kerry, on 2 December.	22
18 December 1940	*Osage* (British)	Crew picked up by *Crewhill* and landed at Rosslare, Co. Wexford.	21

19 December 1940	*Isolda* (Irish)	Crew landed at Kilmore Quay, Co. Wexford.	31
26 January 1941	*Beemsterdijk* (Dutch)	Landed at Dunmore East on 30 January.	3
28 January 1941	*Pandion* (British)	Landed at Doagh Beg, Co. Donegal, on 29 January.	26
30 January 1941	*Austvard* (Norwegian)	Landed at Dingle peninsula on 4 February.	5
31 January 1941	*Olympier* (Belgian)	Landed at Downings, Co. Donegal, on 2 February.	15
16 February 1941	*Naniwa* (British)	Picked up by trawler *Iwate* and landed at Cobh on 17 February.	8
24 February 1941	*Nailsea Lass* (British)	Landed at Caherdaniel, Co. Kerry, on 27 February.	31
1 March 1941	*Castlehill* (British)	Picked up by Belgian trawler *Roi Leopold* and landed at Passage East.	1
8 June 1941	*Baron Nairn* (British)	Landed at Galway on 27 June.	21
17 June 1941	*Cathrine* (British)	Picked up by trawler *Boreas*, landed at Valentia on 19 July.	3
4 August 1941	*Tunisia* (British)	Landed at Roundstone, Co. Galway, on 12 August 1941. Taken to Clifden.	5
20 August 1941	*Juliet* (British)	Survivors picked up by another trawler and landed at Kinsale.	11
8 September 1941	*Abbas Combe* (British)	Survivors picked up by *Clapham* and landed in Dublin.	7

26 September 1941	*Lapwing* (British)	Landed at Clifden on 10 October.	9
26 September 1941	*Petrel* (British)	Landed at Clifden on 10 October.	9
26 September 1941	*Cortes* (British)	Landed at Clifden on 10 October.	1
19 October 1941	*Rask* (Norwegian)	Landed at Rosslare and Wexford on 20 October.	10
2 November 1941	*Caliph* (British)	Survivors picked up by trawler *Thomas Booth* and landed at Kinsale.	4
7 December 1941	*Gertie* (British)	Rescued by Rosslare lifeboat and landed at Rosslare Harbour on 8 December.	11
4 August 1942	*Richmond Castle* (British)	Picked up by *Irish Pine* and landed at Kilrush on 17 August.	19
24 August 1942	*Empire Breeze* (British)	Picked up by *Irish Willow* and landed at Dunmore East on 1 September.	47
21 February 1943	*Stigstad* (Swedish)	Picked up by trawler *Thomas Booth*, landed at Valentia on 8 March.	34
15 May 1943	*Irish Oak* (Irish)	Rescued by *Irish Plane* and landed at Cobh on 19 May.	34
28 December 1943	T-25 (German)	Rescued by *Kerlogue*. Landed in Cobh on 1 January 1944.	8
28 December 1943	T-26 (German)	Rescued by *Kerlogue*. Landed in Cobh on 1 January 1944.	88

28 December 1943	Z-27 (German)	Rescued by *Kerlogue*. Landed in Cobh on 1 January 1944.	68*
12 March 1945	U-260 (German)	Landed between Galley Head and Baltimore.	48
24 April 1945	*Monmouth Coast* (British)	Rescued by local fishing boat and landed at Arranmore Island on 26 April.	1

* Three died en route, and one died in hospital.

Appendix II

EXPLANATION OF THE ALLIED CONVOY CODE

HG CONVOYS

The HG convoys were a series of Atlantic convoys that ran during the Battle of the Atlantic from September 1939 until September 1942. They were the reverse homeward convoys of the OG convoys that sailed from Gibraltar.

HX CONVOYS

The HX convoys were a series of north Atlantic convoys that ran during the Battle of the Atlantic. They were eastbound convoys and originated in Halifax, Nova Scotia, from where they sailed to ports in the UK. When the USA entered the war, the HX convoys sailed from New York.

OA CONVOYS

The OA convoys were a series of north Atlantic convoys that ran during the Battle of the Atlantic from September 1939 until October

1940. They were westbound convoys that originated from the Thames and sailed through the English Channel until July 1940, when the series originated from Methil and travelled north of Scotland. The OA series ran concurrently with the OB series. These convoys dispersed west of the UK when outside the U-boat danger area.

OB CONVOYS

The OB convoys were a series of north Atlantic convoys that ran during the Battle of the Atlantic from September 1939 until July 1941. They were westbound convoys originating in the UK and comprised sections that sailed from ports in the Bristol Channel, Liverpool and the Clyde. Initially the OB convoys sailed through St George's Channel, but from July 1940 they were diverted north through the North Channel. These convoys dispersed west of the UK when outside the U-boat danger area.

OG CONVOYS

The OG convoys were a series of Atlantic convoys that ran during the Battle of the Atlantic. They were southbound convoys originating in the UK and comprised sections that sailed from ports in the Bristol Channel, Liverpool and the Clyde. The convoys sailed north of Ireland and from there they sailed to Gibraltar.

ON CONVOYS

The ON convoys were a series of north Atlantic convoys that ran during the Battle of the Atlantic from July 1941 until May 1945 and were the successor to the OB series. They were westbound convoys originating in the UK and comprised sections that sailed from ports in the Bristol Channel, Liverpool and the Clyde. Ships sailing in ON convoys were destined for ports in North America and the Caribbean. For slower ships unable to sail with these convoys there was the ONS series, the S denoting that it was a slow convoy.

SC CONVOYS

The SC convoys were a series of north Atlantic convoys that ran during the Battle of the Atlantic. They were eastbound slow convoys originating in Sydney, Cape Breton, Canada, from where they sailed to ports in the UK.

SL CONVOYS

The SL convoys were a series of Atlantic convoys that ran during the Battle of the Atlantic from September 1939 until December 1944. They were for vessels returning to the UK from the South Atlantic and sailed from Freetown, Sierra Leone.

GLOSSARY OF NAUTICAL TERMS

adrift   Afloat but not under way. The term implies that a vessel is not under control and will go where the wind and current takes her.

ahead   Forward of the bow.

amidships (or midships) In the middle portion of ship.

ASDIC   Detection device used by Allied ships to locate submerged submarines. ASDIC was the forerunner of modern-day sonar.

astern   Towards the stern (rear) of a vessel, behind a vessel.

athwart, athwartships At right angles to the fore and aft or centreline of a ship.

bridge   An elevated platform running athwartships that is designed to afford a full view of shipboard activities and permit safe navigation and lookout.

bow   The front of a ship.

DEMS   Defensively Equipped Merchant Ships.

dodger   A hood forward of a hatch or cockpit to protect the crew from wind and spray.

draught   The depth of a ship's keel below the waterline.

fetch   The distance across water which wind or waves have travelled.

flotsam   Debris or cargo that remains afloat after a shipwreck.

forecastle (fo'c'sle) The extreme forward compartment of the vessel.

forward (fore) Towards the bow.

freeboard   The height of a ship's hull above the waterline.

hatch   A covered opening in a ship's deck through which cargo can be loaded or access made to a lower deck.

headway   The forward motion of a vessel.

heave to	To bring the bow of the vessel up into the sea and use sufficient propulsion to hold position.
helmsman	A person who steers a ship.
in way of	In the vicinity/area of.
Jacobs' ladder	A portable ladder made of rope with wood or metal rungs.
knot	A unit of speed: 1 nautical mile (1.8520 km/ 1.1508 miles) per hour.
lee side	The side of a ship sheltered from the wind.
leeway	The amount that a ship is blown leeward by the wind.
list	A vessel's angle of lean or tilt to one side.
making way	When a vessel is moving under its own power.
monkey island	Ship's upper bridge or deck above bridge on modern vessels.
pintal	The pin or bolt on which a ship's rudder pivots.
pitch	A vessel's motion, rotating about the beam/transverse axis, causing the fore and aft ends to rise and fall repetitively.
poop deck	A high deck on the aft superstructure of a ship.
port	Towards the left-hand side of the ship facing forward.
rudder	A steering device that is placed aft.
S-boat	A small, fast surface craft armed with torpedoes.
sea anchor	A stabiliser deployed in the water for heaving to in heavy weather. It acts as a brake and keeps the hull in line with the wind and perpendicular to waves. Often in the form of a large bag made of heavy canvas.
starboard	Towards the right-hand side of a vessel facing forward.
stern	The rear part of a ship.
tiller	A lever used for steering, attached to the top of the rudder post.
under way	A vessel that is moving under control.
weather side	The side of a ship exposed to the wind.
wheelhouse	Location on a vessel where the steering wheel is located. Also called the bridge.

NOTES

INTRODUCTION

1   *Britannic* was scheduled to stop at Cobh, while *Scythia* was due to call at Galway. Both Atlantic crossings were cancelled. At the end of 1939 both ships were requisitioned by the Admiralty and converted for carrying troops.

2   *Dáil Debates*, vol. 77, 29 September 1939.

3   These Royal Navy personnel were usually retired or reservist rating from the Royal Navy or Royal Marines.

4   Department of Foreign Affairs, *Shipwrecked Crews Landed in Ireland*.

5   *Ibid.*

6   The society is known today as the Shipwrecked Mariners' Society.

7   While the majority of the crew from *Athenia* were landed at Greenock, Scotland, they did not require the high degree of assistance that was provided at Galway. This was due to the fact that they were almost exclusively living in Glasgow and so were able to provide for themselves through their own means.

8   *Southern Star*, 6 April 1940.

9   Shipwrecked Mariners' Society Annual Reports, 1940.

10 *Ibid.*

11 *Southern Star*, 8 March 1941.

12 *Ibid.*

13 *Ibid.*

1   *ATHENIA*

1   The timely closing of the watertight doors was probably the most important factor in determining how long *Athenia* remained afloat.

2   After the arrival of the large yacht *Southern Cross*, the British

destroyers HMS *Electra* and *Escort* arrived on the scene, joined later by HMS *Fame*. The American steamer *City of Flint* was the last ship to participate in the rescue effort. Later the survivors picked up by *Southern Cross* were transferred to *City of Flint* and the destroyers on the basis of their nationality. The American and Canadian survivors were transferred to the American steamer as it was continuing across the Atlantic, while the British destroyers took their survivors to Greenock.

3   *Connacht Tribune*, 9 September 1939.

4   *Knute Nelson* had on board 449 survivors, the largest number of personnel rescued from the lifeboats of *Athenia*.

5   Of the 112 casualties, ninety-three were passengers and nineteen were crew. From the passenger casualties, sixty-nine were women and sixteen were children.

6   The speed of *Athenia* at the time was just over 15 knots. In all the archival material and witness reports reviewed there is no record found of anyone belonging to the crew or from the Admiralty mentioning that *Athenia* was actually zigzagging at the time of the attack. This is not to say that the ship was not engaged in evasive steering, but merely that it is not recorded anywhere.

7   Armed Merchant Cruisers were converted merchant passenger ships used by the Royal Navy as ocean patrol ships.

8   It is believed that the crew and passengers from *Athenia* who claimed that they saw gunfire coming from a submarine, actually saw the exploding faulty torpedo. The flash from the explosion and subsequent smell of cordite could be misidentified given the duress that the witnesses would undergo in the coming hours.

9   Befehlshaber der Unterseeboote was the Commander-in-Chief for U-boats in the Kriegsmarine. The term also referred to the Command HQ of the U-boat division.

10 Lemp reported the sinking of the British steamer *Blairlogie* on 11 September. He would not report the sinking of *Athenia* until he returned to Wilhelmshaven on 27 September and discussed the matter in private with his superior, Admiral Karl Dönitz.

2   A TALE OF TWO TANKERS

1   The Admiralty was very quick to implement the convoy system and the first outbound convoy from the UK sailed on 7 September 1939.

2   The London Naval Treaty of 1936 contained Article 22, which stated:

> The following are accepted as established rules of International Law:
> 1   In their action with regard to merchant ships, submarines must conform to the rules of International Law to which surface vessels are subject.
> 2   In particular, except in the case of persistent refusal to stop on being duly summoned, or of active resistance to visit or search, a warship, whether surface vessel or submarine, may not sink or render incapable of navigation a merchant vessel without having first placed passengers, crew and ship's papers in a place of safety. For this purpose the ship's boats are not regarded as a place of safety unless the safety of the passengers and crew is assured, in the existing sea and weather conditions, by the proximity of land, or the presence of another vessel which is in a position to take them on board.

3   The German Prize Regulations were based on the London Naval Treaty and so German U-boat commanders were duty bound to comply with Article 22 at the beginning of the war.

4   The first HG series convoy departed Gibraltar for the UK on 26 September 1939.

5   The crew of *Neptunia* wisely declined to offer the information that they were proceeding toward an RN destroyer that was drifting in the Atlantic. This would have been a target that Schuhart could not have passed up the opportunity to attack.

6   Schuhart also considered using one of the tanker's lifeboats to transfer the prize crew from the U-boat to the tanker. However, he suspected that the men of *British Influence* would not have been enthusiastic about assisting the Germans and the operation would have taken too long.

7   *Cork Examiner*, 16 September 1939.

8   *Ibid.*

9   Captain Kerr did take with him the ship's official logbook and other paperwork which he kept in a bag while in the lifeboat.

10 *Cheyenne* Survivors' report ADM 199/2130.

11 *Ibid.*

12 *Rothesay Castle* was a sister ship to *Richmond Castle*.

13 Heinicke noted in the war diary for U-53 that the unseen ship was travelling at high speed as indicated by the rapid change in bearing. This ship was almost certainly *Mackay*, who we know was already searching too far south for *Cheyenne*.

3   DESTINATION VENTRY

1   U-27 was sunk by repeated depth-charge attacks from the Royal Navy destroyers HMS *Fortune* and *Forester*. The German crew were in the water for almost an hour and a half before they were picked up by HMS *Faulknor*. All thirty-eight crew survived and were taken prisoner. A boarding party from *Fortune* was sent over to the stricken U-boat which remained afloat and one officer did board, but the U-boat sank shortly afterwards.

2   U-39 was sunk on 14 September 1939 and the crew was captured by the Royal Navy. In the interrogation report was a list detailing all the types of cigarettes carried by the German sailors. One of the brands was an American cigarette called North State. Somehow, the word 'state' was misconstrued as referring to the 'Irish Free State'. This incident of the 'Irish' cigarettes was reported by Churchill at a war cabinet meeting on 16 September 1939. It was hoped that this information could be used to persuade the Irish government to allow the British forces to use Berehaven.

3   Later accounts of the story relating to the landing of the crew from *Diamantis* alleged that, when departing Ventry, Werner Lott shouted from the conning tower, 'Give my best wishes to Mickey Long.' Years later, after the publishing of Robert Fisk's book *In Time of War*, Lott wrote to the author explaining that he had never known any such person.

4 *ARLINGTON COURT*

1   Due to the lack of facilities and the extended delays at Freetown, ships' hulls became fouled. Coal for bunkers was delayed and, when it did arrive, was generally of poor quality, which caused problems for ships maintaining speed in a convoy. Fresh water was always in short supply as were stores and there were very limited medical facilities for anyone ill.

2   One interesting addition to the harbour authority's inventory of tugs was the small tug taken from the German ship *Uhenfels*, which had been captured by the Royal Navy ships of Force K.

3   While some of the earlier SL convoys did proceed at a slower speed, the need to maintain a speed dictated by the convoy commodore was usually to ensure that the convoy arrived at the rendezvous in the approaches on time to meet the local escort force. Additionally, SL convoys would sometimes merge with HG convoys sailing from Gibraltar. It was imperative, therefore, that the convoy adhered to the rigid timetable which had been imposed. Ships that failed to maintain the required speed might be told by the ocean escort to proceed independently or to return to Freetown.

4   The other two U-boats to sail with U-43 were U-41 and U-49. Originally the intention had been that they would also be joined by two other U-boats, but U-38 was diverted to operate against shipping along Norway's north-west coast and U-47 was still undergoing repairs and was not ready for the operation.

5   A third boat was launched from *Arlington Court* which contained the Chief Officer, Third Officer and one Able Seaman. This had been the last boat to leave the sinking ship and neither lifeboat had any contact with it once they were waterborne. None of the three occupants were rescued.

6   The survivors in the port lifeboat were later rescued and taken to Dover.

5 A BAD WINTER FOR NEUTRALS

1   U-46 returned to Germany on 2 January due to the failure of one of its main engines. U-30 was en route to the Irish Sea to conduct

a mine-laying operation off Liverpool. This was a very successful operation that resulted in the port of Liverpool being temporarily closed, with four ships sunk and one damaged. U-32 was en route to the North Channel to conduct a mine-laying operation off the Clyde. Due to the strong naval presence there, the U-boat was unable to lay its mines at the designated area and had to complete the mine-laying operation at an alternative location. There were no recorded losses from these mines.

2   From 6 January 1940 the Germans began to impose a series of defined unrestricted areas around the UK, where all shipping except friendly neutrals (and, from 11 January, American shipping) would be attacked on sight.

3   In the two prior patrols, U-34 had sunk five ships totalling 22,586 gross register tonnage. Another ship was so badly damaged that it had to be sunk by its escorting destroyers. In addition, Rollmann had also taken two ships as prizes.

4   *Lorentz W. Hansen* was sunk on 14 October 1939 while on a voyage from Canada to the UK. The survivors were transferred to *Kongsdal* after the Germans had ascertained that the ship was bound for a neutral port, and it was allowed to proceed on its passage. *Kongsdal* was subsequently stopped by the Royal Navy and ordered to proceed to Kirkwall for an inspection. The survivors remained there for another twelve days before finally boarding a vessel sailing for Norway. *Deutschland* returned to Germany and was renamed *Lutzow*.

5   *Southern Star*, 3 February 1940.

6   *Irish Independent*, 27 January 1940.

7   Germany issued the following order on 29 November 1939: 'Unconditional contraband carried in neutral ships about to pass through the English Channel is to be regarded as bound for an enemy destination, as these ships are obliged to call at English controlled ports.' Ministry of Defence, *German Naval History: The U-boat War in the Atlantic, 1939–1945.*

8   *Loddon* was to have further wartime experiences. On 18 July 1940 it was attacked and damaged by an FW200. Then, on 27 January 1941, it struck a submerged object near the Saltee Islands and began

taking on water quickly. It managed to reach Rosslare where it was beached.

9   The people of Buncrana felt aggrieved at this slight from Londonderry. Thinking only of the best interests of the survivors, one Buncrana resident would later say, 'One would think that we can do nothing without Derry's help.' *Donegal Democrat*, 24 February 1940.

10 The inquest into the death of Captain Neilson held at Buncrana found that he had sustained a fractured hip and bruising about the head during the torpedo explosion. The coroner gave the cause of death as shock following the injuries and exposure.

11 U–53 was sunk on 23 February 1940 with all hands lost.

12 On 23 September 1939 German High Command issued an order stating that 'All merchant ships making use of radio on being stopped are to be either sunk or taken in prize.' *BdU War Diary*, September 1939.

13 Q ships were decoy ships designed to lure U-boats into a surface attack and then engage the unsuspecting U-boat with concealed guns. They were only used in limited numbers during the Second World War. Although they enjoyed limited success in the First World War, Q Ships did not account for any U-boat losses during the Second World War.

14 The motor boat from *Steinstad* was put to good use later when it was used as a work boat by the Moy River Fishery Company.

15 The funeral was very well attended by fellow seafarers who were in Dublin at the time and by representatives from the Norwegian consulate, Dublin Port, the Shipping Federation and the Irish Red Cross. A guard of honour was formed by the Sea Scouts of Dublin. Wreaths from several shipping companies were laid at the grave.

6   THE HAPPY TIME

1   On 29 June the lifeboat containing the captain and six other crew members was picked up by *Caliph*. Then, on 1 July, nine more crew from *Saranac* were picked up by *Caliph*; both rescued parties were landed at Castletownbere.

2   Kretschmer was mindful of the expenditure of torpedoes at all times and tried to adhere to the ethos of 'one torpedo, one ship'.

3   Other victories for U-34 at the beginning of July were *Vapper*, *Lucrecia* and *Tiiu*.

4   The lifeboats were spotted by a Sunderland aircraft sent out to investigate the distress message from *Auckland Star*. The sea conditions were so good that the pilot landed to enquire as to whether there were any injured personnel who required immediate evacuation. As all the crew were unharmed, the Sunderland took off again, leaving the men with the news that assistance was on its way from Londonderry. HMS *Highlander* and *Viscount* were refuelling there and were ordered to proceed and pick up the survivors.

7   *CLAN MACPHEE* AND *KELET*

1   The Downings rescuers were Anastrasis Dosantos from Brazil and Emanuel Lismas and Viterino Ramos from Portugal. *Pindos* was originally part of convoy SL-40, but was unable to maintain speed and was soon straggling behind. It was sunk by U-58 when 24 miles north-west of Tory Island.

2   *Kelet* arrived at Port Talbot on 2 August 1940. The port had been opened at 1628 hrs after the channel had been swept, and permission was granted for degaussed ships only to enter the docks. *Kelet* was fortunate to pass through the breakwaters safely before a mine was exploded in the channel at 1848 hrs and the approach channel was closed once again.

3   The Queen's Channel and approaches were swept during the day but no mines were found. The danger from these mines was not over, however, as after OB-197 had sailed on 13 August a mine was detonated by a minesweeper.

4   David Murray had been serving as Captain's Steward on board *Athenia* in September 1939. After the loss of the ship and the outbreak of war, he trained as a wireless operator.

5   At 1700 hrs on 14 August, Kapitänleutnant Schnee, in command of U-60, sighted OB-197 and the patrolling Coastal Command aircraft. Approaching the convoy submerged, Schnee successfully

evaded HMS *Heartease* and manoeuvred between the first and second columns of the convoy. He fired two torpedoes but failed to hit any ships within the convoy.

6   Following the brief meeting between U-30 and *Kelet*, the rescue attempt of the six men in the partially flooded lifeboat ended in tragedy. Before *Kelet* could reach the lifeboat two of the occupants died, while another two were lost overboard and drowned as they attempted to climb on board.

7   With the fall of France, Germany extended its declared area further west to impede Britain's supplies. It just so happened that this occurred on 17 August, the day following the attack on OB-197.

8   There was only one exception to this order and that was the ships registered in Ireland.

9   The Kriegsmarine took control of several foreign submarines during the war, including some being built in Germany for other nations. These submarines were given an alphabetical designation rather than a numerical one. U-A, which was built in Germany for the Turkish navy, became the first of these foreign U-boats to be commissioned into the Kriegsmarine.

10   When the crew abandoned *Kelet* they also launched two smaller boats which were discarded once the provisions had been distributed and they were ready to set course for Ireland.

8   DISASTER OFF DONEGAL

1   Many of the aircraft types used by Coastal Command at this time were short-range models unsuitable for extended patrols over the sea. While a version of the standard naval depth charge adjusted for use by aircraft existed, the majority of attacks were carried out using bombs. Later analysis would show that up to September 1940 around 80 per cent of all attacks conducted against sighted U-boats resulted in the enemy escaping without any material damage.

2   The conference was held on 8 August 1940 in the Custom's House, Belfast. This meeting between the Royal Navy and RAF was the first where close cooperation for hunting U-boats was discussed. Detailed exploratory work concluded that a well-organised and equipped

striking force operating out of Londonderry could impose serious difficulties on the enemy active in the North-West Approaches.

3   These three Norwegian ships *Bur*, *Veni* and *Brask*, would continue to straggle astern of the convoy whenever the speed was increased above 8 knots, until it finally dispersed.

4   It was necessary to retire the older type IIA and IIB from active service because they were needed as training boats at the U-boat schools in the Baltic.

5   After U-57 had fired the three torpedoes, the boat submerged; however, a failure with the engine exhaust valves caused seawater to leak into the boat and it went into a steep dive, hitting the seabed and lying there while the leaks were brought under control. After repairs had been affected, Topp ordered the boat up to periscope depth, but it continued to rise and broke the surface ahead of *Winchelsea*, which released depth charges. Topp ordered the boat to remain on the bottom for the remainder of the day as he could hear the destroyers involved in the follow-up rescue operations.

6   The master of *Gyda* had reported to *Witch* that he suspected he had hit an unknown object. *Witch* accordingly instructed him to return to Gourock with forty-six crew of *Havildar*. There was one other crew member of *Havildar* who made it ashore by other means: an injured rating who had been transferred to *Witch* was later landed at Belfast.

7   *Gyda* arrived at Gourock on the evening of 24 August carrying forty-seven crew from *Havildar*; the remaining twenty-seven crew landed at Inishtrahull. The last survivors to come ashore on that day were on the lifeboat from *Cumberland*.

8   *Wanderer* eventually sailed into Belfast on 28 August; it had on board fourteen survivors from *St Dunstan*, two survivors from *Cumberland* and fourteen survivors from *Jamaica Pioneer*. *Witch* had on board thirty-one survivors from *Cumberland* and thirty-eight survivors from *St Dunstan*.

9   Überwasserzieloptik (UZO): literally 'above water target optics'. These consisted of special heavy, pressure-proof binoculars mounted on a pedestal on the U-boat's bridge which in turn was connected to the Torpedo Data Computer (TDC) usually mounted in the

conning tower. The operator (usually the XO) lined up the cross hairs with the target ship and the bearing to the target would be transmitted to the TDC.

10   On reaching the scene, *Gleaner* found the merchant ships *Svint* and *Lom* picking up survivors from *Astra II*.

11   *Hartismere* would eventually make its way back to the Clyde while being escorted by *Gleaner.*

12   The port lifeboat contained twenty-eight persons when it was lowered, twenty of these from *Dalblair* and the remainder from *Alida Gorthon.* The only survivor was an Indian fireman from *Dalblair.*

13   In just over four hours attacking convoy OA-204, U-100 had sunk four ships and severely damaged another.

14   Before leaving the bridge of *Empire Moose*, the second officer took the navigation chart with him to the lifeboat. This allowed Captain Richardson to give a very precise course for each lifeboat to steer.

15   HMS *Clematis* left OA-204 shortly before midday on 29 August to rendezvous with HG-42. *Clematis* would finally arrive at Methil on 4 September, where the fourteen survivors picked up from the second lifeboat of *Dalblair* were landed.

9   *ISOLDA*

1   The British-registered ferry *Munster*, en route from Belfast, struck a mine early on the morning of 7 February 1940 while manoeuvring to enter the entrance channel for Liverpool. There were no casualties from the 235 crew and passengers on board, although Captain Paisley was badly injured as a result of the concussive force of the explosion.

2   In addition to the lightship personnel, *Isolda* was carrying marker buoys on the foredeck that were to be used to mark sandbanks off Dungarvan after the lightship reliefs had been completed.

3   The CIL ships would continue to be registered as British ships and fly the blue ensign until 1969.

10   NO SAFETY FOR STRAGGLERS

1   Von Stockhausen sank eight ships and damaged another during this successful patrol.

2 The ocean escorts for the SL convoys continued to be AMCs. While providing some protection to the convoy against a German surface raider or air attack, the unwieldy AMCs were of no use against submarine attack.

3 Convoy SL-61 lost *Heemskerk* and *Templemead*, while convoy SLS-61 lost *Langleegorse* and *Lurigethan*. Both convoys had sailed from Freetown on 1 January 1941.

4 The two vessels engaged in laying the boom defences were *Barcastle* and *Barbrook*. Both ships and their crews worked continuously from first light until dark, seven days a week until the work was completed. Completion was a significant achievement given the primitive working facilities available at Freetown and the severe climatic conditions with which the Europeans had to contend.

11 *TUNISIA*

1 The materials shipped from Sweden in Operation Rubble had been ordered by British firms, but with the fall of Norway they could no longer get through to Britain. The availability of the Norwegian ships and the British seamen interned in northern Sweden were fortuitous factors that made the operation possible. The five ships were *Elisabeth Bakke, John Bakke, Ranja, Tai Shan* and *Tauras*. The other necessary requirement for the operation to be successful was approval from the Swedish authorities, which was forthcoming.

2 In an unfortunate twist of fate, SL-81 had been detected on the same day Shute received his message from the Admiralty. German radio intercept signals advised BdU of the approximate course and speed of the convoy. SL-81 was soon located by shadowing U-boats, and during an intense night of action on 5 August five merchant ships were sunk.

3 Flying a kite was similar to flying barrage balloons over cities: if an aircraft flew low it might get tangled up with the kite and be forced to crash. The idea was fairly useless on a merchant ship, but with the lack of armament to go around, ad-hoc devices such as kites gave some reassurance of protection to the crew.

4 This was a common FW200 tactic. It would approach from the

direction of the wind, making it difficult to see, and switch off the engines so it was silent on approach. As the aircraft passed overhead on the first attack the engines were restarted.

5   The PAC rocket had a steel cable which was fired upwards and then suspended under a parachute that opened once it reached its working height. This was supposed to act as an obstacle to deter low-flying aircraft from flying over the ship.

6   The distress message from *Tunisia* had indeed been picked up, and a rescue operation was organised. However, bad weather hampered RAF Coastal Command aircraft who failed to find the life rafts from *Tunisia*. The weather and low cloud cover were so bad at the time that they were also unable to locate SL-81.

12   ENGLISH NAVVIES IN IRELAND

1   Kampfgeschwader (KG) was the German bomber wing. KG40 was primarily involved in flying maritime reconnaissance patrols and used the FW200 Condor in this role.

2   *Pegasus* had been fitted with a catapult and carried two Fulmar fighters. The ship normally operated out of Belfast and would escort an OG convoy out, then leave to join an HG convoy returning home through the FW200 danger zone. The first convoy to be escorted by *Pegasus* was OG-47, from 9 to 15 December 1940. This convoy was later attacked by the Italian submarine *Mocenigo* which sunk the Swedish ship *Mangen*.

3   OG-71 comprised four different sections: the Milford section sailed on 12 August, followed by the Liverpool section the next day and the Clyde and Oban sections on 14 August.

4   The U-boats initially ordered against OG-71 were U-201, U-204, U-106 and U-564. U-201 made first contact and shadowed the convoy while the others converged on its position.

5   This is clear from the description of events given by Klemp and Woodhouse in Admiralty survivors' reports, from the history of GSN company book *Semper Fidelis* and from an account by passenger Roy Wearne.

6   At the time, *Zwarte Zee* was at Milford Haven waiting orders.

7 Leonard Lambert was only eighteen years old when he joined *Lapwing*. This was his first ship and he was the only member of the engine-room staff to survive the sinking. Lambert was killed when his next ship, *Gloucester Castle*, was attacked by the German raider *Michel*.

8 Wave-quelling oil was used to dampen the effect of waves around a lifeboat. A canvas bag filled with this oil was attached to the sea anchor. When in the water the oil would leak out through a hole in the bag's cork top and float around the lifeboat. This had the effect of reducing the wave height and sea spray.

9 *Galway Observer*, 18 October 1941.

10 *Connacht Sentinel*, 14 October 1941.

13 *RICHMOND CASTLE*

1 Lourenço Marques is the former name of Maputo, the capital city of Mozambique.

2 *City of Bangalore* was sunk by using the 4-inch gun mounted on the stern of *Richmond Castle*.

3 The term 'plastic armour' did not describe synthetic plastic as it is known today. Instead, this added protection was a composite mixture of asphalt and stone chippings.

4 This was a version of the SOS signal indicating that the transmitting ship was under attack by A for Aircraft, R for Raider or S for Submarine. Normally this message would be accompanied by the name or call sign of the ship and their position. Later in the war it was changed from three to four letters.

5 German auxiliary cruisers were still operating in the south Atlantic at this time. On 21 June 1942 the German auxiliary cruiser *Michel* attacked and sank *Gloucester Castle* off Ascension Island.

6 Amendment No. 31 to MARI dated 24 June 1942: 'Ships on passage in either direction between UK and South American ports south of Cape St. Roque are to be routed Northbound between 200' and 300' east of Abrolhos Rocks and to pass between positions 05 degrees South 030 degrees West and 07 degrees North 025 degrees West.'

7 According to survivor John Lester.

8 The lifeboat davits in use at the time were radial davits. Under normal circumstances the lifeboat would be stowed under the radial davits resting on chocks on deck. To swing the lifeboat out ready for embarkation and lowering could be a laborious and time-consuming task. Most ships would already have their lifeboats hoisted on the davits and swung outboard. The lifeboats would then be secured to the davits by resting against a griping spar spread across both davit arms, with gripes holding the lifeboat and preventing it from swinging freely.

9 Although all three lifeboats lost contact with each other, they were all rescued over the following days. On 10 August, the lifeboat under the command of Second Officer Pye was rescued by the merchant ship *Hororata* and on 13 August the lifeboat under the command of Chief Officer Gibb was rescued by HMS *Snowflake*.

14 *EMPIRE BREEZE*

1 In the Admiralty survivors' report from Captain Thomson, he states, 'All my crew behaved very well and I was very pleased with them, as previously I had little confidence in them.'

2 The shipyard of J. L. Thompson & Sons of Sunderland had a remarkable output capacity during the war, which included twenty-three Empire-class ships. Another less well-known legacy occurred in America. One of their chief designers, Cyril Thomson, was among the British Shipbuilding Mission sent to America in September 1940 with instructions to purchase sixty ships. As events progressed, the mission ended up building two new shipyards where a Thompson ship design based on *Dorrington Court* was produced. The American government would later use this concept as a basis for the *Liberty* ship programme in 1941.

3 The two ships that were causing so much smoke were *Amberton* and *Jan*. Both ships were sent several messages by the commodore in relation to the smoke. However, they were unable to remedy the problem. They reported that they had bad coal and that this was causing the smoke problem. In his report, Commodore Martin stated that he held the supplier of the coal to these two ships directly

responsible for the loss of the four ships in the convoy and the resulting deaths.

4   The German Beobachtungsdienst had managed to decipher a noon position report from a convoy on 13 August. Admiral Dönitz had then displaced the patrol accordingly to intercept this expected convoy.

5   Dönitz had received routing positions for SC and ON series convoys earlier in the month from the Beobachtungsdienst.

6   In addition to depth-charge attacks, *Viscount* used a new AS weapon for the first time in the war. This was the Hedgehog forward-firing mortar system. The first operational use of the system by *Viscount* was not a success.

7   The first U-boat to attack was U-605, which managed to sink *Sheaf Mount* and *Katvaldis* before counter attacks from HNoMS *Montbretia* and *Eglantine* forced it to submerge.

8   Following the receipt of the distress message by Belle Isle radio station, on 27 August the rescue tug HMS *Frisky*, escorted by the corvette HMCS *Rosthern*, was sent to locate *Empire Breeze*. Neither the ship nor the lifeboats were found. The ship had finally sunk.

9   *Munster Express*, 4 September 1942.

15   BEGINNING OF THE END

1   ULTRA was the name used by the British for intelligence resulting from the decryption of German radio communications.

2   There would be another thirteen merchant-shipping losses from ON-166 before the U-boat attacks finally ended.

3   This young Irish radio officer would later go on to be a highly successful Hollywood writer and director. Among the films he directed was the James Bond film *Thunderball*.

4   Kevin McClory presented the 'sole' diary to Sr Mary O'Sullivan prior to leaving Valentia in March 1943. On a return trip to Ireland in 1990, McClory revisited Valentia, where he was reunited with Sr O'Sullivan and presented with his leather sole.

5   There was one passenger on board *Irish Oak* who joined in Tampa. Michael Minihan was a seventy-year-old immigrant who was

returning to Limerick for the first time in forty-seven years. He signed on *Irish Oak* and worked his passage back to Ireland.

6   Oberleutnant zur See Endrass suspected *Luimneach* of being a British merchant ship, despite the neutral markings on display.

7   Jones and his lifeboat crew were initially picked up by a French fisherman, who later transferred them onto a Spanish steam trawler. The second lifeboat was picked up by French fishermen and landed at Lorient. The Irish crewmembers were allowed to travel to Lisbon, while the British crew members were sent to a prisoner-of-war camp.

8   On the same day that *Irish Oak* was shadowed by U-650, another Irish ship found itself in a similar situation. Further north, *Irish Ash* also found itself being observed by a U-boat. The identity of this U-boat is not known to the author. *Irish Ash* passed HMS *Biter* and its support group when they were en route to rendezvous with SC-129.

9   Another Irish ship was involved in the rescue operation. *Irish Rose* also searched for the lifeboats and was in radio communication with *Irish Plane* throughout the day. *Irish Ash*, which had sighted a U-boat the day before, was too far away to take immediate action but did listen to the radio conversations between both searching ships.

10   In addition to the claims that *Irish Oak* had reported a sighted U-boat, the opposition Labour party in Ireland attempted to gain political leverage over the government by claiming that Irish unemployment and economic immigration to England during the war were a result of the policies of the Fianna Fáil government. Amazingly Captain Eric Jones, who was a British national, was dragged into this argument, one of the less memorable moments to come out of the *Irish Oak* incident.

11   Many of the plain-language letter series coded messages were known to the Germans. The signal SSSS indicated that a ship was under attack by a submarine. The German radio operators monitored the distress frequency for any Allied transmissions.

12   The B2 Escort Group under the command of Commander Donald Macintyre on board HMS *Hesperus* was a very experienced and successful AS force. Under the command of Commander Macintyre,

Hesperus was responsible for sinking three U-boats. This included U-186, which was sunk on 12 May 1943 while operating against SC-129.

13 On the night of 11 May 1943, U-402 sank two merchant ships. These were the only ships lost from SC-129.

14 It has been suggested that the arrival of *Biter* may have been in response to a sighting report of a U-boat by either *Irish Oak* or *Irish Plane*. However, *Biter* had received orders to join SC-129 on the morning of 13 May, which was well before the events involving the Irish ships.

16   BAY OF BISCAY

1 The movement of these capital ships through the English Channel was given the codename Operation Cerebus by the Germans, but it is more commonly referred to as the 'Channel Dash'.

2 From 19 to 21 March 1942, T-15 was part of the escorting force for the heavy cruiser *Admiral Hipper* when it moved from Germany to Trondheim. Then, from 18 to 20 May, T-15 was again involved in escort duty from Kristiansand to Trondheim for the heavy cruiser *Lutzow*.

3 *Münsterland* was returning to Germany to be used in the Baltic Sea trade.

4 HMS *Charybdis* was sunk when hit by two torpedoes, while HMS *Limbourne* was hit by one torpedo and was later sunk by the surviving Royal Navy ships.

5 Letters from German crew written in the Curragh camp were read by Irish censors. Missing Christmas and the lack of home leave were the most common themes in the early letters home.

6 Pervitin was used by the German armed forces during the Second World War to help stave off the effects of tiredness. It was a mixture of benzedrine and l-amphetamine issued in tablet form. It was noted by the Irish army that the survivors landed at Cobh all carried an individual supply of what they described as vitamins and 'pep pills'.

7 Although the battle of Biscay is only briefly described here, a full in-depth description of the battle along with the subsequent German

inquest into the events of the battle can be found in Whitely, *German Destroyers of World War Two*.

8   Captain Tom Donoghue had first-hand experience of air attacks when he was serving on board the Irish steamer *Lady Belle*. Although the ship was badly damaged in the attack, Donoghue and his crew escaped unharmed.

9   After the initial sighting of the first FW200, a second aircraft also began to circle *Kerlogue*. Both FW200s flew off together in the direction of the survivors.

10   The Navicert system was introduced by the British in November 1939 as a means of regulating the trade with mainland Europe and of ensuring that vital war materials were not shipped into one country and trans-shipped to Germany. It applied to all merchant shipping and not just British and Irish ships. From 1941 it remained in operation for ships still trading to Spain and Portugal. Ships trading to these countries without a Navicert would be detained by the British.

11   The rescue operation did not end when *Kerlogue* left the scene to return to Ireland. Six survivors were rescued by a Spanish destroyer while U-505 and U-618 rescued another fifty-five.

12   The survivors picked up by *Kerlogue* belonged to all three of the sunk German ships. Of those who landed in Cobh, ninety came from T-26, sixty-eight from Z-27 and the remainder from T-25.

13   (Ing.) signifies in German rank that this officer was an engineer.

14   When Captain Donoghue told Valentia radio station that he had picked up survivors from a sea battle in the Bay of Biscay, he simply told them how many he had on board and not their nationality. This is a significant insight into the character of the man, who was only concerned with the saving of lives.

15   Helmut Weiss was admitted into hospital at 0415 hrs on 1 January and died later that afternoon. He is buried along with Adolf Braatz in the German war cemetery in Glencree.

17   U-260

1   U-608 was sunk on 10 August by depth-charge attacks from a Royal

Navy sloop and RAF Coastal Command aircraft, while U-981 was sunk by a combination of contact with a mine and a depth-charge attack from an RAF Coastal Command aircraft.

2   Although U-boat losses did fall at the beginning of the inshore campaign, they soon increased again as the British adapted. For the final months of the war there was a sharp increase in losses.

3   The only eyewitness report from the survivors of U-260 described how the crew managed to bring the boat to the surface. See Patterson, *Dönitz's Last Gamble: The Inshore U-boat Campaign, 1944–45*.

4   This container was later picked up by an Irish fishing boat and handed over to the army for evaluation of its contents.

BIBLIOGRAPHY

PRIMARY SOURCES

The National Archives, Dublin

Department of Foreign Affairs, *Shipwrecked Crews Landed in Ireland*
Department of Foreign Affairs, *Articles Washed Ashore on the Coast*
Department of Foreign Affairs, *Rescue of German Naval Personnel by Kerlogue*
Individual Irish-Registered Ships' Official Logbooks

Irish Military Archives, Dublin

G2 File *Shipwrecked Survivors in Ireland*
G2 File *Loss of Irish Oak*
G2 File *German Naval Internees*
U-260 File 10 and 11

The National Archives, London

ADM 1 *Sinking of Athenia*
ADM 1 *Interrogation of Captured Crews*
ADM 1 *Experience in Dealing with the Schnorchel U-boat*
ADM 1 *Sighting Schnorchel, Provisional Admiralty Instructions*
ADM 1 *German Offences Against Merchant Shipping*
ADM 116 *Issue of Navicerts*
ADM 116 *Protection of Convoys*
ADM 116 *Details of Minefields in British Waters*
ADM 199 *Neutral Ships Sailing in British Convoys*
ADM 199 *Losses of Neutral Shipping Due to Enemy Action*
ADM 199 *Survivors' Reports*
ADM 199 *Individual Convoy Reports*

ADM 199 *Analysis of Attacks on Convoys*
ADM 199 *Enemy Submarine Attacks on Merchant Shipping*
ADM 199 *Western Approaches Command War Diary*
ADM 199 *South Atlantic Command War Diary*
ADM 219 *Independent Routing of Merchant Ships*
FO 837 *Contraband Control*
MT 9 *Preliminary Inquiry into Loss of Athenia*
MT 59 *Chartering and Purchasing of Neutral Shipping*
Individual British-Registered Ships' Official Logbooks
Individual British Warships' Logbooks
British Cabinet Papers, 1939–41

German Sources

BdU War Diary, 1939–45
Individual U-Boat War Diaries, 1939–45

NEWSPAPERS

Connacht Sentinel
Connacht Telegraph
Connacht Tribune
Cork Examiner
Derry Standard
Donegal Democrat
Donegal Vindicator
Dungarvan Observer
Galway East Democrat
Galway Observer
Guardian

Irish Independent
Irish Press
Irish Times
Kerryman
Leitrim Observer
Mayo News
Munster Express
Nenagh Guardian
Scotsman
Southern Star
Western People

SELECTED BOOKS

Bennet, G. H. and Bennet, R., *Survivors: British Merchant Seamen in the Second World War* (London: Hambledon Continuum, 1999)
Blair, Clay, *Hitler's U-boat War: The Hunters, 1939–1942* (New York: Random House, 1996)

Brice, Martin, *Axis Blockade Runners of World War II* (London: Batsford, 1982)

Caulfield, Max, *A Night of Terror: The Story of the Athenia Affair* (London: Frederick Muller, 1958)

Dwyer, Ryle T., *Guests of the State* (Dingle: Brandon, 1994)

Fisk, Robert, *In Time of War: Ireland, Ulster and the Price of Neutrality, 1939–45* (Dublin: Gill & Macmillan, 1983)

Forde, Frank, *The Long Watch: World War Two and the Irish Mercantile Marine* (Dublin: New Island, 2000)

Hancock, H. E., *Semper Fidelis: The Saga of the Navvie* (London: The General Steam Navigation Co., 1949)

Hurley, Michael, *Home from the Sea: The Story of the Courtmacsherry Lifeboat, 1825–1995* (Dublin: Colour Books, 1995)

Hurst, Alex A., *A Succession of Days* (Worcester: Square One Publications, 1992)

Jordan, Roger, *The World's Merchant Fleets 1939* (Annapolis, Md: Naval Institute Press, 1999)

Kennedy, Michael, *Guarding Neutral Ireland: The Coast Watching Service and Military Intelligence, 1939–1945* (Dublin: Four Courts Press, 2008)

Leach, Nicholas, *The Lifeboats of Rosslare Harbour and Wexford* (Dublin: Nonsuch Publishing, 2007)

McCue, Brian, *U-Boats in the Bay of Biscay* (Newport, RI: Alidade Press, 2008)

Ministry of Defence, *German Naval History: The U-boat War in the Atlantic* (London: HMSO, 1989)

Mitchell, W. H. and Sawyer, L. A., *The Empire Ships* (London: Lloyds of London Press, 1990)

O'Hara, Vincent P., *The German Fleet at War, 1939–1945* (Annapolis, Md: Naval Institute Press, 2004)

Patterson, Lawrence, *Dönitz's Last Gamble: The Inshore U-boat Campaign, 1944–45* (Barnsley: Seaforth Publishing, 2008)

Poolman, Kenneth, *Scourge of the Atlantic* (London: MacDonald and Jane's, 1978)

Rohwer, Jürgen, *Axis Submarine Successes of World War Two* (Annapolis, Md: Naval Institute Press, 1999)

—— *Chronology of the War at Sea 1939–1945* (London: Chatham Publishing, 2005)

Roskill, S. W., *The War at Sea 1939–1945,* vol. I (Uckfield: Naval & Military Press, 2004)

Showell, Jak P. Mallmann, *U-Boat Commanders and Crews 1935–45* (Ramsbury: The Crowood Press, 1998)

Smith, Peter C., *Hold The Narrow Sea: Naval Warfare in the English Channel, 1939–1945* (Annapolis, Md: Naval Institute Press, 1984)

Taprell, D., *Blue Star Line: A Record of Service 1939–1945* (Liverpool: John Gardner, 1948)

Whitely, M. J., *German Destroyers of World War Two* (London: Arms & Armour, 1991)

Wills, Clair, *That Neutral Island* (London: Faber & Faber, 2007)

Woodman, Richard, *The Real Cruel Sea: The Merchant Navy in the Battle of the Atlantic, 1939–1943* (London: John Murray, 2004)

Wynn, Kenneth, *U-Boat Operations of The Second World War,* 2 vols (London: Chatham Publishing, 1998)

WEBSITES

www.uboatarchive.net

www.uboat.net

www.uboatwaffe.net

www.warsailors.com

www.mercantilemarine.org

www.convoyweb.org.uk

www.naval-history.net

www.u-35.com

www.forum.12oclockhigh.net

www.shipnostalgia.com

www.bluestarline.org

www.secondworldwar.org.uk

www.german-navy.de

www.milfordtrawlers.org.uk

INDEX